CARL A. RUDISILL LIBRARY
LENOIR RHYNE COLLEGE

658.91 97618
C61e

DATE DUE			
Apr18 77			
May16'77 L			
Dec13 77			
Nov 8 '82			

Educational Theatre Management

John E. Clifford

BRADLEY UNIVERSITY

Educational Theatre Management

CARL A. RUDISILL LIBRARY
LENOIR RHYNE COLLEGE

NATIONAL TEXTBOOK COMPANY • Skokie, Illinois 60076

658.91
C61e
97618
July 1976

1973 Printing

Copyright © 1972 by National Textbook Co.
8259 Niles Center Road, Skokie, Illinois 60076
Library of Congress Catalog Number: 77-190376
All rights reserved, including those to reproduce this book or parts thereof in any form.
Manufactured in the United States of America

For their personal sacrifices—my wife and daughters for hundreds of hours of peace and quiet; and my parents for years of education.

Contents

Acknowledgments

For their help in making this book possible, I thank my many Educational Theatre Management students at Bradley University who, during the past six years, contributed ideas, read chapters, made numerous suggestions, and helped put into practice most of the theories found within these pages. Space will not permit me to list all of their names, but I wish each one of them to know that I appreciate and remember his or her work and help.

I am also specially grateful to my student and friend Mr. Steven Dresdner, Director of Drama at Yates City High School, Yates City, Illinois from whom I learned so much during and after his student days at Bradley.

I also wish to thank my colleagues at Bradley for carrying on the business of education and theatre production while I spent hours away from the office working on this manuscript.

More indirectly, I wish to remember my teachers. During seven years as a student at John Carroll University, St. Louis University, and Michigan State University, each faculty member who attempted to direct me toward a meaningful career in theatre and education left his imprint on my life as an educator and theatre director. As a result, I am convinced that any worthwhile theories to be found in this book can be attributed to those who taught me: Mr. Leone J. Marinello, Rev. Robert A. Johnston, Dr. C. B. Gilford, Dr. John E. Dietrich, Dr. E. C. Reynolds, and Dr. Robert Lee Smith.

Finally, I am grateful to Professor William Buys for his helpful comments and suggestions, and to a patient, knowledgeable editor at National Textbook Company.

Preface

EVERYONE WHO is familiar with play production procedures and practices is aware of the various activities involved: the "role" of the director in interpreting the script and in casting, blocking, and rehearsing the actors; the "role" of the actor as he learns his lines, interprets the characters, creates his own special role, and brings the words of the playwright to life on the stage; the activities of the designers in interpreting the script in terms of light, color, costumes, mass, and the arrangement of three-dimensional forms and shapes; and tasks of the scene painters, property masters, makeup artists, and stage manager.

Indeed, when one thinks of theatre and play production it is usually in terms of the director, actors, designers, and technicians. It is *their* work with which audiences come into contact when they attend the theatre, and it is normally *their* work which receives the plaudits or rebukes of audience and critics. And it is *their* names which are given greatest prominence in programs, on posters, and sometimes even on the tickets.

In the education of prospective theatre workers great attention is paid to the skills and techniques of script interpretation, directing, acting, designing, lighting, makeup, and costuming. Each of these areas of play production is fully covered in courses in college and university programs; general play production curricula include courses on directing, acting, stagecraft, designing, and costuming. Books on play production cover each of these areas chapter by chapter. In addition, dozens of special books are devoted to directing, designing, acting, stagecraft, lighting and costuming. The artistic aspects of play production have not been slighted in the training of educational, community, or professional theatre staffs.

However, numerous other tasks are also involved in both seasonal and repertories and individual play production in the school, community, and professional theatre which do not fall within the broad category of "artistic functions." Plays must be selected, budgets prepared and adhered to, tickets printed, programs designed, publicity and promotion arranged and executed, box offices operated, and money spent and received—among many other menial, often unrecognized, and sometimes "dull" activities. These "non-artistic" or "commercial" functions of play production receive little glory or recognition from audiences, critics, or in headlines. And yet they are as essential to a successful theatre program as the artistic activities of directors, actors, and designers.

There are only a few colleges and universities where one can study these non-artistic functions of play production, and there are fewer still where such in-depth study and training are available. The latest figures compiled by the American Educational Theatre Association's Theatre Management Committee indicate that 120 colleges or universities offer courses in theatre management, but the vast majority does not provide this type of theatre management course on the undergraduate level for prospective secondary-education teachers of drama and theatre. Play production books, on the whole, also neglect these most important management areas of budget, advertising, ticket, and box office operations. Finally, no book has yet been written from the theatre management point of view for prospective educational theatre directors in either secondary or higher education.

This book, therefore, was written to fill that void. Its purpose is threefold: (1) to formulate a sound theory of the overall aims, specific objectives, and values of educational theatre; (2) to present, consistent with the aims and objectives of educational theatre, both a theory of theatre management and programs for the practical application of that theory (that is, specific educational theatre management problems in theatre organization, play selection, preparation of a budget, advertising and publicity, ticket sales and box office procedures, purchasing, and house management; and (3) to provide sufficient theoretical and practical information about these areas to enable the student to establish and administer a successful theatre program in an educational institution.

This book is written in the belief that educational theatre will have a better chance of success when devotion, creative effort, and co-operative energies are applied to the various areas of theatre management with the same intensity with which they are applied to the "artistic" activities of play production.

1 The Nature of Educational Theatre

EVERY HIGH school, college, and university theatre director or teacher who is engaged in a theatre production program will one day be placed in a position of having to justify this activity to his principal, dean, academic vice president, or president. Most often these sessions occur as a result of requests for larger budgets, additional staff or facilities, course additions, or curriculum changes. In defense of his play production program the theatre director must answer such questions as "What is the purpose of theatre in a school?" "What is the relationship between your play production program and your instructional, classroom program?" "What does 'educational' mean in the concept 'educational theatre'?" "How does educational theatre educate?" "What are the values of educational theatre, and to whom are they directed?"

Even though the answers to such questions might seem too basic, simple, or elementary to be considered important to those who are deeply involved in theatre production and education, they will be asked by school administrators. Moreover, they form the basis and the groundwork upon which judgments and appraisals of existing and future theatre programs are made. In every school in which this author has taught, administrators have asked all of the above questions—and a great many more.

Not only is it important that school administrators have sound knowledge and understanding of the philosophy behind educational theatre to be able to assess its programs and needs, but educational theatre administrators themselves must be constantly aware of the aims, objectives, purposes, and values of their activity. *A sound program of educational theatre management must be based upon sound principles pertaining to the nature of educational theatre.*

The solution to many managerial and administrative problems can be easily found if the problems are seen in light of an overall, guiding administrative philosophy. In addition, overall consistency in theatre policy, which is always advisable in management, will be easier to obtain if all policy decisions reflect a basic philosophical point of view toward educational theatre and theatre in general.

The purpose of this chapter, therefore, is to present a broad, philosophical basis for the nature of educational theatre—one, moreover, that can serve as a guideline for answering the types of questions posed above and can facilitate the solving of managerial and theatre policy problems. Specifically, this chapter will deal with the overall aims, specific objectives, and values of educational theatre.

Finally, the discussion which follows contains controversial subject matter because the very nature of the material, the aesthetics of the theatre, has been debated by critics and theorists in great depth ever since Aristotle wrote his *Poetics* in the fourth century B.C. The various theories propounded over the ensuing centuries have led to many controversies and interpretations; however, the outline of theatre-as-art, which follows, is not presented as a definitive discussion of theatre aesthetics, nor does it seek to resolve the various controversies and interpretations, nor does it argue aesthetic positions. Rather, it is intended only as a summary of the nature of art and the artistic process from a practical point of view so as to impart a better understanding of the nature of educational theatre.

"THEATRE IS THEATRE": AN ART IN THE TRUEST SENSE

Educational theatre, children's theatre, community theatre, professional theatre, commercial theatre, amateur theatre—how many kinds of theatre are there? How many types or kinds of theatre can be defined and classified? Is it possible that because there appear to be several kinds of theatres, there are also, then, several different purposes and objectives of theatre depending upon the kind of theatre?

The answer to all these questions is simple: Theatre is theatre regardless of what adjectives are used to describe it—regardless of where and under what circumstances it exists; regardless of who directs it, or acts in it, or writes it, or sees it. The basic nature of theatre as a fine art remains unchanged and constant despite all qualifying adjectives which appear, on the surface, to emphasize distinctions that do not and should not exist.

The basic aims, objectives, and values of theatre transcend all types of theatre activities. The same objectives are valid for community theatre, children's theatre, educational theatre, and professional theatre simply because they are all *theatre*. Each of these activities is primarily *theatre*, and only secondarily educational, community, children's, or professional. Thus, to discover the nature of educational theatre—its objectives and values—it is necessary to discover the nature of theatre itself, its general objectives and values.

Theatre, in its broadest aspects, is art. As an activity of man, which is as old as man, theatre, like the other fine arts—music, dance, literature, architecture, painting, sculpture—provides man with new, exciting, stimulating, emotional and aesthetic experiences. While it is true that, historically and traditionally, theatre has not always been considered one of the fine arts, in the same company as music, dance, literature, painting, and the others, few will doubt that the theatre has become, as it were, a meeting place for most of the other arts and a vibrant and vital source of aesthetic pleasure.

THE NATURE OF ART

An empirical and historical study of the human activity called art reveals the involvement of the following elements: an inspirational idea, an artist, the creation or construction of an art object, the display or promulgation of that object, an audience, or "public," that comes into contact with the art object, and an emotional and pleasurable reaction by this public. When we put all these elements together, art can be seen as the process in which an artist, after experiencing inspiration, attempts to share that experience with others by creating an object which, when experienced by others, will provoke a pleasurable and emotional experience similar to the original inspiration.

The Idea

The activity of art, viewed as a process, originates with an artist who, contemplating nature, life, or the world around him, receives an idea as an intuitive vision of some hitherto hidden verity or beauty. To the artist, nature is composed of an objective, observable surface reality and a hidden or less objective reality. By opening his mind and making it receptive to suggestion, the artist is able, with the help of contemplation and intuition, to "see through" the surface or objective nature of everyday objects, events, and human actions and to experience the inner truth and beauty of nature. It is this pleasurable experience and communion with hidden truths that give birth to the artistic idea. It is in nature, which in its broadest sense includes all reality and human phenomena, that the poet or painter experiences hidden truth in the beauty of a sunset, a daffodil, or a face. It is in nature that the dramatist or sculptor experiences a certain beauty and truth in birth, life, death, or love. It is in nature that the composer hears the song of birds, the hush of the wind, the breath of a forest, or the movements of the sea and unites them to his aesthetic vision.

The idea or prime subject of art is seldom limited to the surface, objective reality of objects and events but goes beyond them to the more obscure and often difficult to observe inner realities of nature. In this sense, beauty is the subject and idea of all art.

The Artist and the Art Object

The aesthetic vision of the artist, as we have noted, comes from a great emotional and highly pleasurable experience as he discovers various hitherto hidden truths of life and nature and, through his special medium, tries to objectify that vision and thereby share that pleasurable experience with others—through music, literature, sculpture, painting, drama, etc. If he is a dramatist, he will write a play, using conflict, suitable characters, appropriate language, significant action, and the like. The artist takes these materials, which he finds in objective reality, and selects, arranges, emphasizes, and "distorts" them in order to reshape nature into a new object that best reflects his vision.

The Audience

The audience (or viewer, reader, whatever) is both the ultimate end of the creative process and a link with the beginning of what is essentially a circular process. As a person contemplates an art object, he intuitively experiences its reflection of the beauty and truth in nature, similar to that which the artist originally experienced. This emotional, aesthetic experience is one of pleasure and a special kind of heightened satisfaction.

Art Is a Process

Art, then, can be viewed as a circular process in which nature, the artist, the art object, and the audience share more or less equally (see figure 1-1). Generally speaking, an artist does not exist inde-

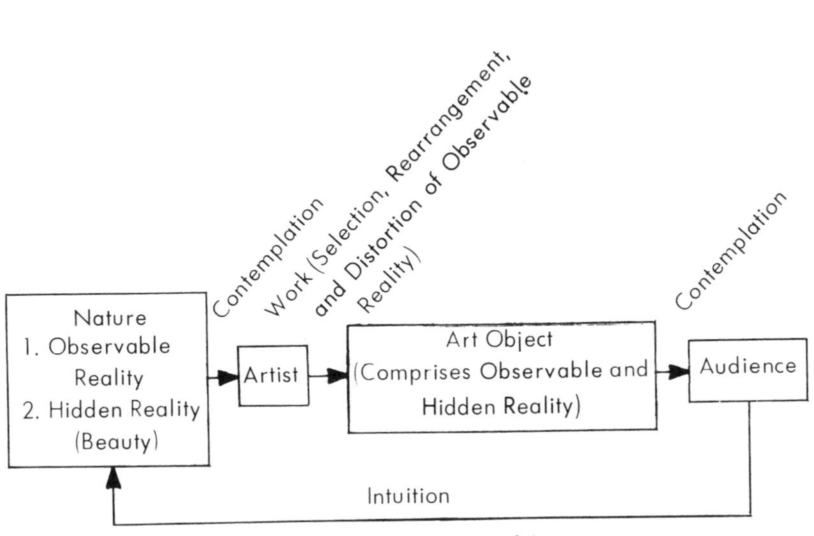

Figure 1-1. The Process of Art

pendently of these other factors, nor does an art object exist solely for the sake of the artist or for its own sake. Without all of these various elements, the process cannot exist. If this were not so, authors would not publish, actors and directors would produce plays without audiences, painters would not display their works, and composers and musicians would not be heard.

Art, then, does not exist for itself in any rational scheme. It does not exist solely in the creation of an art object. It does not exist in the emotional experience and reaction of the artist or the audience. As an activity of man, it is a process in which an artist and his public mutually share an intuitive emotional experience (aesthetic vision) through the creation and contemplation of an art object.

THE NATURE OF THEATRE AS ART

If figure 1-1 in a general way represents the process called art, and if drama is art, the figure—with a few substitutions—can also be applied to drama, as in figure 1-2. Here the inspiration which motivates the dramatic artist is human action; the artist is a dramatist, the art object is a drama, and the audience is all those who either read the script or witness the performance of the drama.

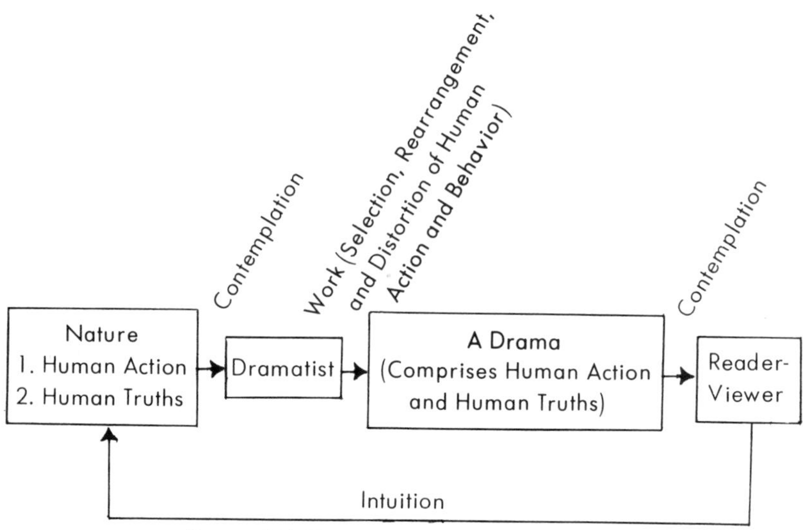

Figure 1-2. The Process of Dramatic Art

Like other artists, a dramatist has a significant vision of human beings in conflict; he perceives a certain truth about humans and human behavior, a peculiar kind of inner order and beauty. Then, because he wishes to share that vision with others, he works according to the principles and techniques of dramatic construction to create an object of art: a drama.

Upon reading that drama in script form and contemplating its content and thematic ideas, a reader vicariously experiences the dramatist's emotions and visions vis-à-vis human behavior. This, briefly, is the nature of the art of reading drama; but what of the theatre?

Those who constitute the reading audience for dramas might be called the "theatre people"—actors, directors, designers, and so on. Upon reading a drama, they receive a vision or form an image of the drama not so much in terms of plot, conflict, or theme in the dramatic or literary sense but in terms of action, movement, color, tempo, and pictorial composition. Then, wishing to share this experience with others (or whatever other reasons they might also have), as did the dramatist before he created the drama, they set about to create another art object.

The materials of their art are far different from those of the dramatist. Instead of using plot, theme, characters, etc., the directors, actors, and designers use movement, sound, pace, tempo, space, color, composition, and pantomime (among other devices) to create their work of art. The result, an art object, or play, is totally different in its material composition from a drama created by a dramatist, and yet in many respects they are similar. Just as a written drama is different from and yet somewhat similar to those phenomena of nature which inspired it—that is, before the dramatist set to work—so the corresponding play, in its existence in performance, is different from and yet similar to the drama which inspired it.

Continuing the process, an audience contemplates the new art object, the play in performance, and in pleasurable attention or entertainment undergoes the emotional experience of the theatre people-artists when they contemplated the drama as well as that of the dramatist-artist as he contemplated nature. Thus the process is complete; the activity of art exists.

As was previously indicated, each element in the process of art does not exist for itself; it exists and functions for the completion of the whole. The artist functions for the sake of the object, which in turn functions for the sake of the audience, and all of these elements function for the sake of the process as a whole—for the sake of art itself and the sharing of an aesthetic experience and vision.

In terms of the art of the theatre, which includes the art of the drama (see figure 1-3), each element functions for the existence of the whole. In theatre as such (see figure 1-4), in which the creation of a play to be performed for an audience is based upon the inspiration received from a drama, theatre functions as art through the entertainment of an audience. Theatre activity completes the process of art through the entertainment of an audience.

What then, is the purpose and nature of the art of the theatre? It

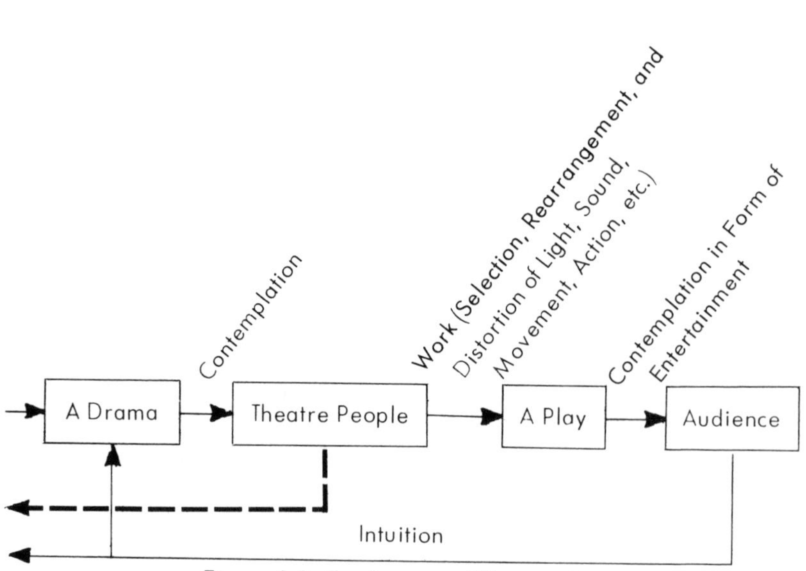

Figure 1-3. The Process of Theatre Art

is no different from the purpose and nature of art—to exist as art; to comment on nature, life, man, the world, creation, human actions; to see into the world and to share that vision with the world in the form of entertainment. The major principle of the nature of theatre activity must therefore be to exist and function for the sake of the completion of the process of art. To use it exclusively for other purposes and at the expense of its nature as art is to destroy its essential reason for existence.

This is not to imply, however, that legitimate theatre has no other reasons for existence, no other values. Historically, the theatre has performed a multitude of diverse, and legitimate, functions. Theatre contributes not only to the aesthetic needs of man but also to his intellectual, social, moral, and recreational needs.

Theatre, because it reflects nature and human behavior, has at times led the way in promoting new and revolutionary philosophies, economic theories, and social reform. It has shown man moral evils in human attitudes and behavior. It has chastized human conduct, moral degeneration, religious hypocrisy, and political injustice and has helped in isolating personal mental disorders and in teaching psychological theories. It has interpreted historical trends and attempted to clarify future trends and conditions. It has appeared as teacher, communicator, philosopher, historian, social worker, literary critic, and moralist.

But above all these functions the theatre, at its greatest moments,

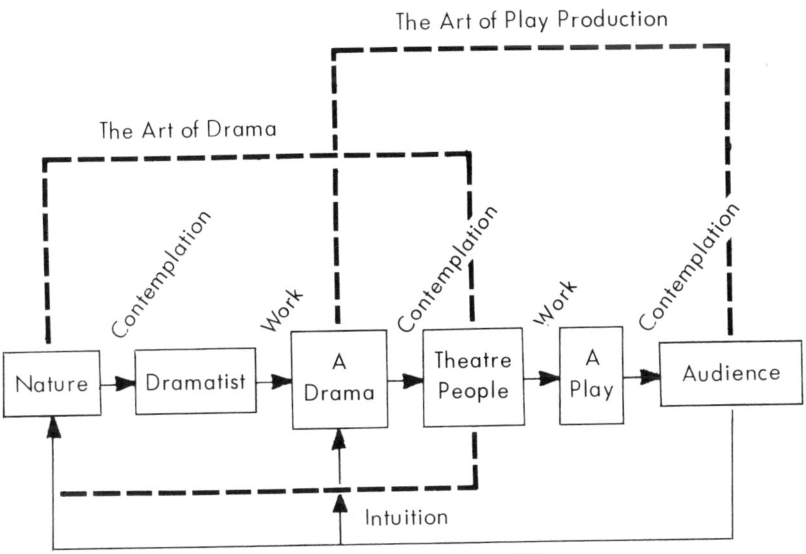

Figure 1-4. The Art Process of Theatre

can almost universally be seen as *great art*—as a medium that interprets and shares with all mankind the emotional experiences and visions of the diverse worlds of nature. In this context, it functions for the benefit—the enjoyment and entertainment—of an audience.

THE NATURE OF EDUCATIONAL THEATRE

Now that the idea of theatre activity (directing, acting, designing, etc.) has been established as aesthetic in nature, as existing in order to complete the process of art by which emotional and aesthetic experiences and visions are shared between artist and public, what happens to this principal function of theatre when the adjective "educational" precedes it?

Empirically, the term "educational theatre" originated, and still refers to, theatres which exist as part of formal educational institutions—most often high schools, colleges, and universities. But "educational theatre" does not refer to, or necessarily imply by any formal definition, specific purposes, uses, or functions but merely a production and an instructional, classroom program within an institution of learning. When applied to theatre, "educational" is helpful only in designating the locale or environment of a particular theatre. It is a generic term which is not as helpful in identifying a particular theatre as the more specific terms "high school theatre" or "college theatre" or "university theatre." Thus the adjective "educational" does not, by tradition or use, change the basic nature of "theatre."

Even grammatically, an adjective cannot totally change the noun it modifies. It can change a noun *somewhat*; it can limit, partially alter, or make a concept more exact by adding nuances to another word. In the case of educational theatre, the adjective adds specificity to the environment in which a theatre exists and thereby indicates its additional nuances, functions, and values because it is in an educational environment. All these, however, are *in addition* to its values and functions as *theatre*.

Here again, discussion may tend to become controversial. The nature of theatre, with the qualifying "educational" preceding it, is strange and paradoxical, and the views of educational theatre directors and managers often reflect that paradox. The essence of the argument revolves around the question Is educational theatre primarily *theatre* or is it primarily *educational* in nature?

If one views it as primarily theatre (the position taken in this book), the director, theatre manager, and administrator must adopt the policies and procedures which will best ensure the success of the theatre productions from the point of view of the audience. As a result, the criterion for a successful production and theatre program becomes "Has the audience been entertained?" Pleasing the public is therefore the major goal of educational theatre production for one who considers it primarily theatre.

The opposing view is that educational theatre, because it is produced in an educational institution, is primarily educational in nature. In this case, its major goal is to educate—both the student participants and the audience. It can best educate the students by using theatre productions as one might use a classroom—as a learning tool, a sort of three-dimensional audio-visual teaching device. And the audience, in this case, sits in on the "classroom final exam" to watch the students demonstrate what (if anything) they have learned. The perfection of the product for the benefit of the audience is not the major criterion for evaluating the success of the theatre program; instead, the "quantity and quality" of teaching and learning play production techniques become the criteria for evaluation. According to those who take this position, the educational goals of the theatre in terms of the audience can be accomplished by offering "classic" pieces of dramatic literature.

Extremists who believe that pleasing the public is the most important goal of educational theatre can convince themselves that this is the *only* goal. Similarly, extremists who believe that the education of the student participants is the major goal of educational theatre can convince themselves that *this* is the only goal. In the first instance, the student is *always* a tool, only a means to an end. In the second instance, the public is little more than a guinea pig—an excuse and/or tool for learning. The paradox, however, is that the human institution of the theatre has important aesthetic values, and when it is part of an educational institution it loses many or most of its aesthetic values and takes on the educational values and functions of the school. Educational theatre, to be true to both terms, must be two things at once: theatre *and* educational.

It is the author's opinion, and a rationale of this book, that the paradox can be resolved by taking a reasonable position on a middle ground. Educational theatre must be managed and administered so that the aesthetic values of theatre as an activity directed toward the entertainment of an audience are preserved and so that the educational values of a school, directed toward the education and learning of students, also are preserved. Simply put, the educational theatre manager must always aim to please and serve the public, while not forgetting his role as an educator.

This, admittedly, is more easily said than done. By admitting a pair of sometimes opposing goals, the theatre manager, in forming theatre policy, must always be aware of the conflicting values of the two hats he is wearing: that of a theatre director and that of an educator. His dilemma can be eased considerably if he devotes the major portion of his energies as a theatre artist to perfecting the theatre as a human institution, thereby teaching good theatre. A successful theatre is, of course, successful at the box office, but this need not mean that it is unsuccessful as an educational experience for the student participants.

On the contrary, if, as an educator, the educational theatre manager wishes to teach good theatre practice, high production standards, and appreciation of the art of the theatre while at the same time impressing upon his community the important cultural and aesthetic values of the theatre, he can best do this by managing an artistically successful theatre. One can hardly teach good theatre practice by doing bad theatre. Producing plays which do not please the public, which do not draw large audiences, can hardly satisfy any criteria of good theatre education. It is fallacious (and most often a poor attempt at rationalizing failure) for an educational theatre manager or director to say that he cares little for public success so long as he is educating theatre students. In most cases, he is doing neither. The conclusion, then, is simple: The audience must always come first. When the audience has been entertained and satisfied (not sacrificed), the education of the students must naturally follow.

The basic requirement of educational theatre, then, is that it *be* theatre; and, being theatre, its purposes, objectives, and values are those of the art of the theatre, or pleasing and entertaining an audience. In addition to these values, educational theatre also partakes of those functions and purposes which are part of the nature of the institution of learning of which it is a part.

PURPOSES AND VALUES OF EDUCATIONAL THEATRE

Based upon the preceding assumptions—namely, that (1) the basic nature of educational theatre is the same as that of the art of the theatre and (2) because an educational theatre exists as part of an educational institution it thereby shares that institution's purposes and values—the following purposes and values of educational theatre can be cited.

1. The Main Purpose of Educational Theatre Is to Entertain an Audience

Referring to figure 1-3, we see that theatre production leads to the creation of an art object, a play, which in turn, through entertainment, leads the audience back to the emotional vision of the dramatist. The creation of a work of art is normally motivated by a desire to share an aesthetic and emotional experience and vision with an audience. Thus play production, the activity of theatre, has for its purpose the entertainment of that audience in order to fulfill the dramatist's desire, and in its highest form, theatre is first and always a fine art. The audience is the ultimate goal for which all other elements in the process exist, as is also true in painting, music, sculpture, fiction, and poetry.

It is therefore mandatory that in play production the audience be always of the utmost importance. None of the many secondary purposes of educational theatre can be accomplished if all energies are not devoted primarily to giving the audience the best-quality entertainment and theatrical and aesthetic experience possible. Theatre activity and production exist first for the audience, not for themselves or their practitioners.

2. A Secondary Purpose of Educational Theatre Is to Preserve, in Living Form, the Great Heritage of the Dramatic Literature of the Past

One of the functions of education is to preserve and pass on the heritage of man—to make meaningful to the present generation the wealth of thought, accomplishments, and culture which civilized man has accumulated in his tenure on earth and to explain man to himself in the realms of thought, feeling, and action.

In an educational institution, the theatre can preserve part of that cultural heritage by bringing to contemporary audiences the great pieces of dramatic art from the past. By "reviving" the great works of Aeschylus, Sophocles, Racine, Shakespeare, Goethe, Shaw, Ibsen, and dozens of other major dramatists of the classical ages of drama, educational theatre can serve, in part, the aims and objectives of education in preserving and passing on man's cultural heritage.

3. Another Secondary Purpose of Educational Theatre Is to Raise the General Public's Level of Taste, Appreciation, and Standards for Theatre Art

Walt Whitman once said: "To have great poets there must be a great audience." This could be reworded as: To have a great theatre there must be audiences with great souls, with great capacities of critical judgment and discernment to appreciate it.

The development of such appreciation is a difficult task. Artists work with highly sensitive or complex feelings and highly developed intuitions. In order to share the experiences arrived at with those feelings and intuitions, the audiences for which an artist creates must also have a highly developed sensitivity. The best way in which to develop this sensitivity, this capacity for aesthetic discernment and appreciation, is by frequently coming into contact with the very best in works of art. A steady diet of pablum yields no taste for caviar; frequent contact with poor-quality drama and theatre production yields no taste for Shakespeare and other excellent productions. Educational institutions have, as one of their obligations, the teaching and development of cultural and artistic discernment as well as the teaching of facts.

Educational theatre can contribute to the development of high standards of public appreciation of the performing arts through a regular, planned, and conscious program of improvement in the level and quality of the dramas selected for production.

4. Another Secondary Purpose of Educational Theatre Is to Provide Quality Theatrical Entertainment for the Academic and the Local Communities

Theatre would have value for man even if, as its only purpose, it provided relaxation, recreation, and diversion from the daily cares and concerns of life. Going to the theatre as a "night out," to get away from "the kids," study, and worry, has its value and place. Indeed, this is the primary motivation of the vast majority of theatregoers: to relax, be "entertained," and enjoy themselves. But the theatre can provide more than just amusement and relaxation. It can do more for man than divert him in the same way as a circus, a baseball game, or a variety show. Along with diversion and relaxation it can give him special insights and perceptions of himself, the world around him, and the human condition. A man can be a more complete man because of a meaningful theatrical experience, which includes diversion, amusement, and artistic entertainment.

The term "quality theatrical entertainment" means (1) the best possible production work in acting, directing, design, and technical execution and (2) the production of the best possible dramatic scripts. The fulfillment of both these criteria leads to quality theatre and hence to meaningful experiences for audiences, as well as educational experiences for students.

5. Another Secondary Purpose of Educational Theatre Is to Provide Opportunities for Interested Persons to Participate in an Artistic Endeavor

The values derived by everyone who engages in an artistic activity are innumerable, as everyone who has painted, played a musical instrument, acted, directed, or designed is aware. Great personal values inhere in active participation in these activities.

Artistic creativity, moreover, breeds sensitivity. The creative person is one who is especially sensitive to the world around him. He is flexible in thinking, judging, and relating to problems; he is original in his development of ideas and in problem solving; he has rich but well-controlled emotional experiences. In the theatre, he learns social cooperation, poise, and the craft and art of one of the fine arts.

Indeed, every educational institution owes its students the opportunity to "taste" creativity by participating in the fine arts. Furthermore, inasmuch as educational institutions have special obligations to the communities in which they exist, it is imperative that they also provide the entire community the opportunity to participate in creative, artistic activities.

Traditionally, schools have always been considered the centers of culture, learning, and intellectual stimulation for the surrounding communities. From the Middle Ages until the present time, schools have been the gathering place for intellectual, cultural, social, and artistic stimulation. Most academic institutions have acknowledged this fact and the attendant obligation to extend their activities and benefits to the community, and most have acted upon it. Thus educational theatre is in a unique position to help extend the cultural influence and benefits of a high school, college, or university into the community. It can do this through its public performance program, by offering quality theatre to the entire public and by making opportunities available for all persons to engage in the creative activity of theatre production.

Interested persons, then, ought to include students and all members of the educational institution, as well as members of the community of which the educational institution is a part. The majority of these opportunities should go to the registered members of the schools, but a portion should go to the community at large. A responsible educational theatre director can distribute these opportunities fairly and equitably, depending upon local situations and circumstances.

6. Another Secondary Purpose of Educational Theatre Is to Provide an Opportunity to Learn the Arts and Crafts of Quality Theatre to Students Interested in Pursuing Theatre as a Profession.

"Educational" in the term "educational theatre" does not mean that the theatre teaches, that one learns from the theatre, or that theatre is primarily a training ground for future professionals. To use it as this kind of "visual aid" or tool of education is to destroy its essential nature. "Educational" means that the theatre exists as a part of an educational institution and as such has an opportunity to serve the practical educational functions of that institution. One of these functions is to furnish students the means of living useful lives and to prepare them to participate in a profession of their choice. The theatre is *one* of these professions.

Educational theatre can serve as a training ground for students interested in pursuing careers in the theatre at the high school, college or university, community or professional levels in two ways. First, it can provide experiences in theatre productions before audiences under the guidance of highly trained directors. In this manner, participation serves as both a creatively rewarding and meaningful learning experience. Second, theatre can educate by offering formal classes in the arts and crafts of directing, acting, designing, stagecraft, and management. Students can thereby learn theory and technique which they can apply to their subsequent performance and production situations.

This second area of theatrical activity in a school might better be called "academic theatre," in contrast to "educational theatre." The distinction between the two is that in the former the major emphasis is upon learning in the academic (or classroom) situation, whereas the emphasis is on the audience in the educational theatre. This does not mean that educational theatre cannot contribute to the learning process of theatre students; it can, and certainly does. But it does this best by strongly emphasizing the production of quality theatre for the purpose of sharing an aesthetic experience with an audience through entertainment.

This is the art of theatre—and how better to learn good, quality, artistic theatre production than by participating in it?

SUMMARY

The first principle in thinking of the aims and values of educational theatre must be that theatre is first and foremost an art. As such, its greatest commitment is to the audience, for it is the audience for whom the dramatist wrote and it is the audience to whom the object of the sharing is directed.

Educational theatre means, simply, theatre that is part of an educational institution. As such, it also has secondary goals and purposes, derived from the institution of which it is a part. These include the preservation of the great dramas of the past, raising the level of taste and discernment within the public, providing a high level of culture to the campus and the community, providing opportunities for interested persons to participate in theatre activity, and serving as a training ground for students who wish to engage in theatre as their life's work.

Of all these secondary aims, the most important one is entertaining the audience, for it is through this aim that all of the other goals are reached.

2 Aims and Objectives of Educational Theatre Management

EDUCATIONAL theatre management can be defined as the control, direction, and handling of all commercial (non-artistic) aspects of an educational theatre production program in order to accomplish all the purposes and achieve all the values of educational theatre. In this sense, the non-artistic aspects of a theatre production program share a common aim with the artistic aspects. Management policies and decisions, then, should not be considered as separate from the artistic policies of a theatre but should be developed in concert with them. Both should work together for the success of the "educational" and "theatrical" values of the organization.

The commercial or non-artistic aspects of play production in the educational theatre include the activities of play selection, budget preparation and control, purchasing, advertising and publicity, ticket sales, and house management.

More specifically, the aims and objectives of educational theatre management are (1) to facilitate the operation of all commercial aspects of play production and handle these operations in an efficient, responsible manner; (2) to coordinate, under a central director, all of the theatre's business, purchasing, sales, and publicity activities; (3) to facilitate the jobs of the directors, designers, and technicians in the performance of their artistic production duties when those duties have commercial aspects; (4) to carry out theatre policy as it relates to the public performance program; (5) to act as a liaison between the theatre staff and the business officers of the school; and (6) to contribute as best as possible to the overall aesthetic impression of each production.

Facilitation of all commercial aspects of play production in educational theatre is one of the practical objectives of efficient theatre management. Much of the history of educational theatre in this country shows that its management has traditionally lacked competence, organization, and professionalism. Educational theatre directors and teachers have shown much more interest, imagination, capability, and professionalism in directing, acting, designing, and stagecraft than in bookkeeping and financial management. Few educational theatre directors have looked upon themselves as business managers, financial managers, or public relations directors. They have been, first and foremost, play directors, acting coaches, and designers.

School administrators, as a result, faced with such a situation and the reality of operating theatre programs, generally subsidized production expenses and took over many commercial aspects of theatre production. Within the past twenty years, as theatre operations in schools increased due to greater interest among students in the theatre arts, the production of a greater number of plays each year, and more trained directors, teachers, and designers entering the teaching profession, the problem of educational theatre management has increased and become more complex and sophisticated. More and more, theatre production programs in schools, both high schools and colleges, have fallen into the untrained hands of theatre staffs. For the most part, these theatre teachers have not been equal to the task of meeting the increasing sophistication of educational theatre management. As a result, the general reputation of educational theatre directors and designers as theatre and business managers has not been good.

Because of the growing complexities in the management of the nonartistic aspects of educational theatre production and the customary lack of interest and talent which theatre directors have shown in this important area of play production, a new specialization has developed in the training of educational theatre directors and teachers. Educational theatre management, as an area of specialization in theatre training, has emerged to facilitate the commercial aspects of theatre production in the school theatre. It also seeks to ensure that the commercial and fiscal affairs of school theatres will be operated in an efficient, responsible manner under one central manager whose concern and training is in this area of theatre.

Often, directors and other members of a production staff who are directly engaged in the artistic activities of play production must order and purchase materials, rent equipment, or hire personnel. The function of the theatre's management staff should be to assist the artistic staff in the performance of the latter's production duties wherever possible—whenever they come into contact with the commercial areas of theatre production.

The management staff is concerned not only with the internal operations of the theatre as they affect the theatre personnel but also with the external operations as they affect the general public. It is the management staff which puts into operation literally all of the policies of the theatre that are related to the convenience and comfort of the theatregoer. Those responsible for management are not charged, and should not be charged, with arbitrarily making or establishing general theatre policy; rather, this policy should be arrived at by all members of the staff—artistic and commercial—in consultation with the producer. The management area of theatre is charged with seeing that the established policy is implemented in a successful, economic, and reasonable manner. This will include the policy areas pertaining to tickets, reservations, sales, promotion, purchasing, and house management.

It should be the function of the trained theatre staff member who is responsible for the management of the commercial areas of the theatre to act as the liaison between the theatre staff and the school's administrative officers. This is especially true in financial matters, but it also applies in academic, curriculum, and educational theatre policy matters. The business manager, treasurer, or comptroller of the school needs to know which theatre staff member will be in charge of and responsible for the commercial affairs of the theatre. The treasurer of the school needs to know whom he is to contact about sales, purchases, invoices, etc., who will be authorized to sign purchase requisitions, and from whom to expect financial reports and records.

The position of theatre manager as described thus far in this book is sometimes combined with that of administrative head of the theatre department. In those cases (usually in small-school situations with only two or three staff members), the duties of the administrator are far greater, and indeed all encompassing; he is responsible to the academic officers of the school for matters which are not included in the theatre production program, such as curriculum, staff, space allocation, educational policy, etc. Overall administration of an entire educational theatre program, including the curriculum, is not within the jurisdiction of this book. (Later, in the appendix, the student will find a number of questions which theatre department administrators have to cope with.) Our only concern here is with the commercial aspects of a theatre production program as they relate to the aims and objectives of educational theatre.

Finally, to summarize—or to put educational theatre management in its proper perspective—the management staff must keep in mind that the most important element of educational theatre is the production. All elements of production, artistic and non-artistic, exist only to serve the artistic effect of the production. All commercial and management decisions should be made with the good of the productions uppermost in mind.

Certain managerial, procedural, or sales and purchasing matters may occasionally be quite difficult or involved if decisions are made for the good of the productions, but purchasing doesn't exist for its own end—nor do managerial procedures and policies, or sales, or any other management areas. They exist only to serve the production, the end of *all* theatre activity. If a management decision or procedure is in any way detrimental to the audience's overall aesthetic impression of a production but eases the internal problems of the management personnel, or is "good education," it is a poor management decision.

Theatre management exists for the good of the product: the production or performance before an audience. However, it is sometimes easy for management to forget that it must serve the production. Management personnel can get very involved in managerial procedures, policies, and plain "red tape," but such procedures are valuable or good only if they contribute to the artistic success of the theatre. Educational theatre management, and indeed any theatre management, should contribute—in all its activities, decisions, and procedures—toward the artistic as well as the commercial success of the theatre and the theatre's productions in the greatest possible manner.

The Management Staff

In chapter 3, "Theatre Organization," the student will find a detailed outline of the duties and responsibilities of all members of an educational theatre organization. At this point, therefore, we will merely list the management staff positions—those whose responsibilities most directly include the implementation of the functions of educational theatre management.

The management staff of an educational theatre is normally headed by a member of the faculty called the *managing director*, *business manager* or *theatre manager*. He is directly responsible to the administrative head of the theatre (or speech) department, and ultimately to the producer. His duties include the administration and supervision of all commercial aspects of theatre production and all commercial, non-artistic personnel.

Normally, the managing director will hire or appoint a *business manager*, to whom he will entrust most of the day-to-day duties of the financial business of the theatre. Whether the business manager is a student or a member of the staff, he is directly responsible to the managing director, and his central area of responsibility is control of the budget, purchasing, and the design and printing of programs. Normally, he is also the direct supervisor of the box office manager, the publicity director, and the house manager.

A third member of the management staff is the *box office manager*. Working under the supervision of the business manager and the managing director, he operates and is responsible for ticket sales and the organization and supervision of the box office personnel. In small theatres, the box office manager and the business manager may be the same person.

The *publicity director* is also under the direct jurisdiction of the business manager and the managing director. His duties include handling all the publicity and advertising relating to the theatre and each production.

The final member of the management staff is the *house manager*. Directly responsible to the business manager and the managing director, he supervises all front-of-the-house operations, including ushers or usherettes and ticket takers.

Thus the management staff includes the managing director, the business manager, the box office manager, the publicity director, and the house manager. Depending upon the size of the theatre operation and the size of the entire theatre staff (both student and faculty), some of the above positions may be combined. In any case, their functions must be performed under the jurisdiction of the head of the management area.

SUMMARY

Educational theatre management is the control, direction and handling of all commercial aspects of an educational theatre production program, including play selection, budget preparation and control, purchasing, advertising and publicity, ticket sales, and house management.

The major objective of management should be to facilitate the jobs of the entire theatre staff as they seek to accomplish the purposes and achieve all of the values of educational theatre. It is the function of management to serve the production staff, crews, and audience, not to exist and operate for its own sake. The aim of the managing director, business manager, and box office managers must be to provide audiences with meaningful entertainment and to do everything possible to ensure that the artistic quality of each production is as high as possible. With that principle in mind, the nuts and bolts of theatre management will fit.

3 Educational Theatre Organization

THE PRODUCTION of a play or a series of plays is anything but a one-man effort. In no other art form do the talents, abilities, and cooperative efforts of so many people from so many arts, crafts, and professions blend together in the creation of an art work. Among these people are the director, actors, and designers; property men and light, sound, costume, and makeup technicians; musicians, singers, and dancers; business agents and box office and house personnel; and many more.

In any such cooperative endeavor, where the success of the product depends upon the successful coordination of many diverse talents and crafts, the overall organizational structure looms as a most important element in that endeavor. The proper organization of a theatre, be it for the production of one play or a season of plays, can make the complex task of play production smoother and easier. In general, a theatre organizational structure should be divided into the broadest possible areas of responsibility, such as (1) the artistic area and (2) the commercial area.

The artistic functions and the commercial functions of play production are, strictly speaking, headed by a producer. In educational and community theatres, the producer (or producers) usually concerns himself primarily with the commercial functions of the theatre, and so it can be said that—practically speaking—the artistic functions of play production come under the play director. It is the director who, during the rehearsal period, has complete control of all decisions and activities which bear on the artistic interpretation and creation of the play for an audience.

Figure 3-1 shows the typical organizational structure of the artistic functions of play production during the rehearsal period, or prior to the opening of a play. Immediately under the director are the stage manager, the assistant director, the artistic director, the musical director, and the choreographer (the last two if the play is a musical). The stage manager, who is in charge of the assistant stage manager, heads the production of the play after it opens. The assistant director heads the actors during rehearsal. The artistic director is in charge of all of the design activities of the production, including the setting, lights, costumes, sound, and properties (in some theatres he is called the scene designer). Under him, other designers and craftsmen construct sets and props, prepare costumes, etc. The musical director works with the director, and is in charge of the conductor, who in turn supervises the musicians. The choreographer works directly under the director and handles the dancers.

After a production opens, the director's functions usually cease. In his place, the stage manager has complete control of all those who are still involved in a play's production. Figure 3-2 diagrams the normal organization of a theatre's personnel after a play has opened.

The commercial functions of the theatre are headed by the producer. In educational theatre, he is typified in the school itself, in the person of the principal, but delegates the specific operation of the theatre to a managing director, who directly operates all of the commercial or non-artistic functions of the theatre production program. The managing director usually has a business manager under him who handles the day-to-day operations of the business of the theatre. In smaller schools, these two positions are usually combined. Under the business manager are the publicity director, the house manager, the ushers or usherettes, and the box office manager. Figure 3-3 outlines the structure of the commercial organization of an educational theatre.

The remainder of this chapter outlines in specific detail the duties and responsibilities of all educational theatre personnel (all of which

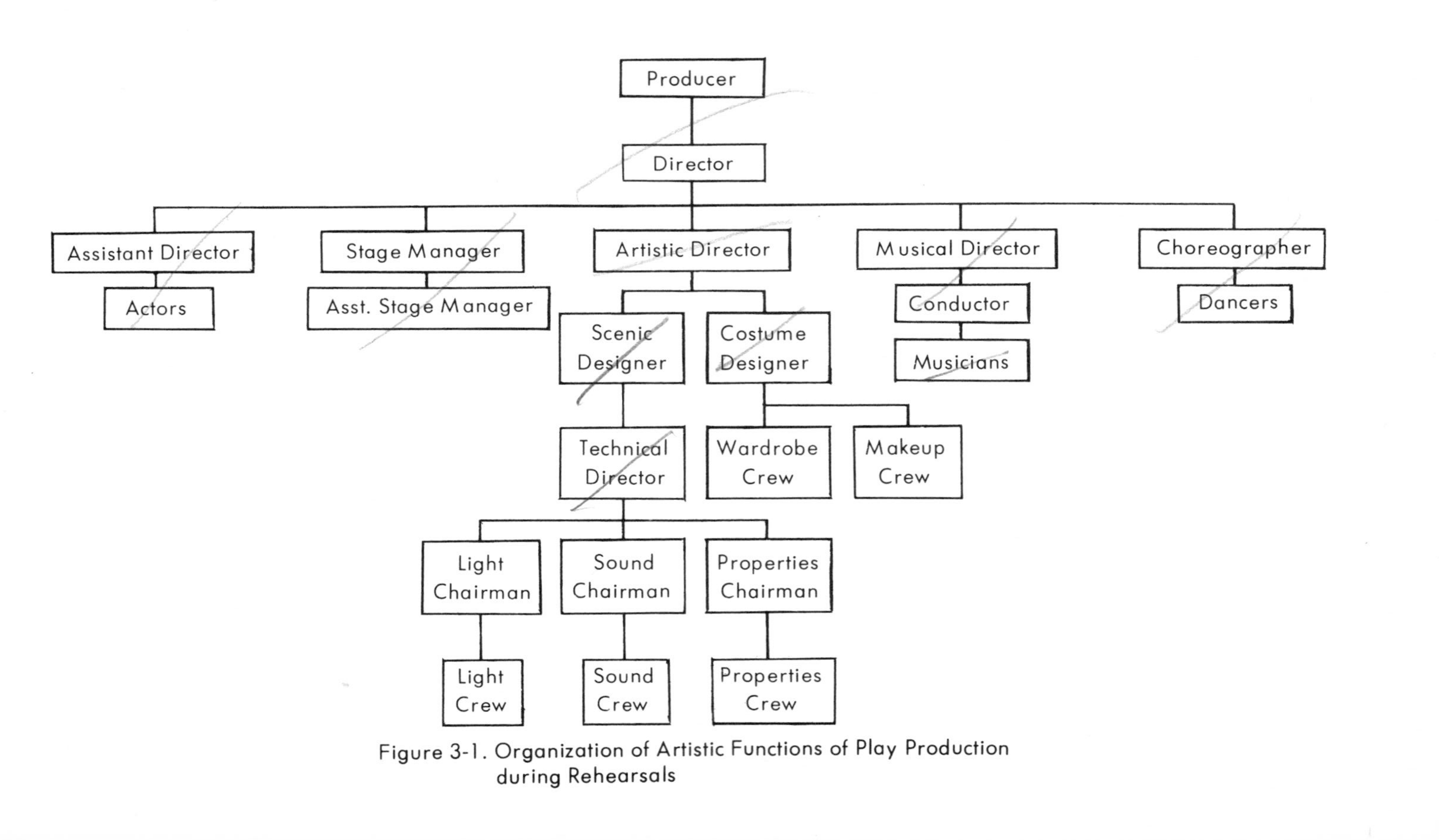

Figure 3-1. Organization of Artistic Functions of Play Production during Rehearsals

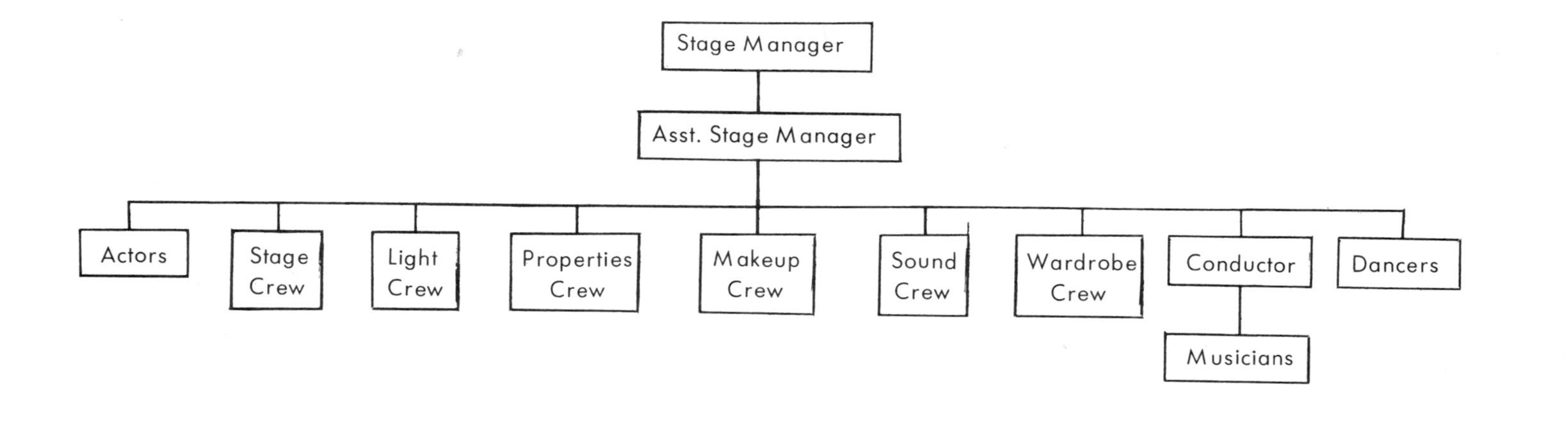

Figure 3-2. Organization of Artistic Functions of Play Production during Performance

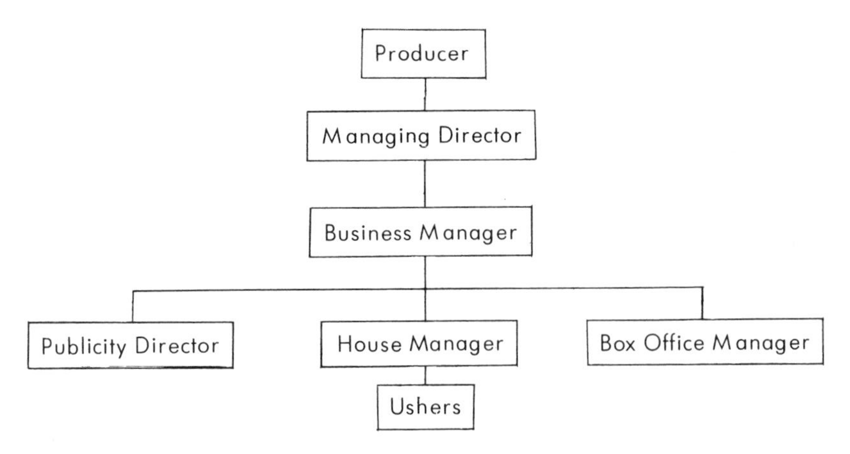

Figure 3-3. Organization of Commercial Functions of Play Production

must be fulfilled). In smaller schools there may be fewer personnel, but the workload is correspondingly greater. These outlines should serve as guides in establishing educational theatre organizations.

THE DIRECTOR

The director of a play is that person who has the ultimate control and responsibility for all the artistic aspects of play production. He supervises and controls the activities of the actors, artistic director, stage manager, musical director, choreographer, assistant director, and costume designer (see figure 3-1). His relationship to these people varies greatly; however, all of them are responsible to him in the production of a play.

The director assumes a great deal of responsibility in producing a play for he is directly responsible to the producer. It is up to him, the director, to see that the play comes to life in keeping with its unique vitality. After he selects the play, he interprets its thematic values, holds tryouts, conducts rehearsals, works with the scene designer, costume designer, business staff, musical director and choreographer, and finally presents the play in an entertaining form for viewing by an audience. The director is usually the key character in the production of any play.

The following are suggestions that a director may want to make use of during the different stages of the play production process.

1. Pre-Season
   A. Become familiar with many plays
   B. Study and analyze the scripts
   C. Discover the dramatists' purposes
   D. Test the plot structures to see that there are well-defined situations and characters that progress through a series of crises to a final climax
   E. Analyze the characters
   F. Evaluate the costs of production and any particular production problems a play might present in his particular theatre
   G. Consider the timeliness of the various plays
   H. Along with the rest of the theatre staff, choose a season of plays which meets all the criteria for feasibility of production (see chapter 4)

2. Pre-Tryout
   A. Select an assistant director
   B. Interpret the particular play
   C. Revise and adapt the play, if this is necessary
   D. Plan the action of the play so as to help the actors
   E. Hold series of production meetings with all designers and technical crew heads for the purpose of outlining and discussing a production's theme and style
   F. Begin work with the scenic director so that the stage will be ready when needed
   G. Decide how many characters and what types will be needed

3. Tryouts and Casting
   A. Decide upon tryout dates and give this information to the publicity director for dissemination
   B. Have those trying out read the play and the parts they hope to play
   C. Consider the theatre experience of those trying out
   D. Consider their willingness to work
   E. Consider the playing tonality for this type of play
   F. Provide for other than reading tests if they are found to be non indicative or inadequate

G. Work out different combinations of tests
H. Cast the play and post it
I. Approve all designs, scenic and costume

4. Early Rehearsals
A. Set up a rehearsal schedule that is adequate yet flexible
B. "Block" the play
C. Have the actors read through their parts while walking through the blocking
D. Have the actors memorize their lines
E. Have the actors go through the action of the play without reading their scripts
F. Step up the action of the play with the memorized lines
G. Consider each act of the play and rehearse accordingly
H. Give the names of the actors and crews to the business staff so that it can begin the layout of the program and write publicity articles
I. Become familiar with all aspects of the stage
J. Have the technical crews on hand so that they can learn the details of their jobs
K. Make sure the stage manager learns his duties and when and where they are to be performed
L. Continue to hold production meetings with the designer, costumer, lighting chairman, sound chairman, property chairman, technical director, and stage manager in order to coordinate their activites

5. Dress and Technical Rehearsals
A. Hold a costume review and rehearse with costumes so that the actors get the "feel" of them
B. Have the technical crews perform their duties during the rehearsals so that they respond to the proper cues, etc.
C. Rehearse according to the rate of progress
D. Polish the acts and scenes
E. Check with the business manager to make sure all house activities are taken care of and that the programs are prepared for opening night

6. Performances

   A. See that the play is creating the intended mood and emotional response
   B. View the play objectively and make necessary changes
   C. Make pertinent suggestions to the stage manager

7. Post-Production
   A. Thank all who took part in the production
   B. Be courteous to those who have questions about the play
   C. Assist crews with the "strike"
   D. Evaluate the production with a view toward self-improvement

THE SCENE DESIGNER (ARTISTIC DIRECTOR)

The scene designer, or artistic director, has the job of designing or supervising all visual aspects of a production except the actors' stage movements. He will go beyond mere scene design—as the artistic director—and will consider the visual aspects of costumes, makeup, and lighting. He designs the setting for the play, but he does this in close cooperation with the director and the technical director. (Scenery should provide a beautiful, meaningful, and harmonious background or environment for the action of the play, and in a simple or subtle manner suggest the spirit of the play.) The artistic director is responsible to the director for all visual elements of a production (see figure 3-1).

Briefly, the artistic director's tasks are (1) to make himself familiar with the material upon which the settings are based; (2) to plan each setting with respect to all essential requirements (as stated in the script or prescribed by the director) and the limitations of stage space, equipment, budget, etc.; (3) to make complete and clear representations of each setting, in sketches rendered in color, as well as ground plans and/or scale models from which all workers on a production may ascertain, when necessary, the nature of the scenery; (4) to make detailed drawings and specifications for the builders and stage carpenters, who are to construct and install the scenery on the stage; (5) to evolve a workable scheme of handling the scenery in shifts of allowable time duration; (6) to oversee costume and makeup plans so as to obtain visual harmony;

and (7) to supervise, with the technical director, the entire execution process of all parts of the scenic scheme.

The following are suggestions that the artistic director-scenic designer may want to use during the different stages of the play production process.

1. Pre-Season
   A. Assist the director in the selection of the script, keeping the following in mind:
      1. Artistic quality of the play (Will a script provide a setting which will be artistically effective and interesting to the audience?)
      2. Budget for the production (How much will the setting cost? What equipment does the theatre possess which can be utilized in the production?)
      3. Size of the playing area (Can this set be produced effectively on this stage? How much backstage area is needed?)
      4. Amount of time (How long will it take to build a set of this type? How much time is available for the production?)
   B. Make an analysis of the script for interpretation
      1. Study the script for the meaning of the author concerning the setting
      2. Collaborate with the director so that the interpretation is consistent

2. Pre-Tryout
   A. Meet with the director
      1. Discuss the director's interpretation
      2. Discuss the budget for the production
      3. Agree upon the style of the production
   B. Conduct research
      1. Read books on architecture, interior decoration, and perhaps social and cultural history if the play is set in a specific period of history
      2. Make a complete inventory of the scene shop to discover what is available for use in the production

C. Design floor plans
   1. Draw a representation of the position of all scenic units
   2. Decide if the plan is practical (Is it possible to build the set within the budget, the time allowed, and available space?)
   3. Determine the suitability of the set (Will the play "work" in the set? Is the set suitable for the action?)
   4. Determine the artistic quality of the setting (Is the set a simple box or does it have variety? Will it appear interesting to the audience?)
   5. Draw the designs to scale

D. Make either sketches or a scale model of the setting
   1. Make sketches
      a. Represent the setting from a front view
      b. Use one or more of four types of sketches:
         1) The perspective scene, which is a three dimensional sketch in linear perspective
         2) The isometric sketch, in which all lines have the actual dimensions of the objects
         3) Elevations, which are sketches of the elements of the set to accurate scale
         4) The perspective plan, which is a projection of the floor plan
   2. Make a scale model
      a. Build a miniature stage set representing each detail as the designer sees it
      b. Construct the model to exact scale (½″=1′)
   3. It is not always necessary for the designer to make both sketches and a model; he should decide which will be the most helpful to him and to the director

E. Prepare a list of scenery
   1. Name and classify all pieces of scenery which are necessary
   2. Note each piece as being in stock or to be constructed
   3. Summarize the scenic units to be constructed and make notes for painting: the color of base coat, painting technique, trim, and lining details

F. Prepare working drawings
   1. Make drawings for all scenic units showing all essential details of construction
   2. Draw them to scale

3. Tryouts and Casting
   A. Meet with the technical director
      1. Discuss the style of settings
      2. Formulate plans for shifting the sets
      3. Discuss and present to the technical director the following:
         a. Floor plans
         b. Sketches and/or models
         c. List of scenery
         d. Working drawings
      4. Decide upon a schedule for the completion of each piece of scenery
   B. Meet with the costume chairman
      1. Discuss the style of the play
      2. Formulate a harmonious color scheme
      3. Coordinate the costume designs with the set designs
   C. Meet with the makeup chairman and costume designer
      1. Discuss the style of the play
      2. Decide upon a makeup scheme which will best represent each character

4. Early Rehearsals
   A. Supervise, with the technical director, the execution of all parts of the scenic scheme
   B. Direct the scenic construction so that each aspect of the design is carried out in compliance with the style of the production
   C. Be available for further consultations with the technical director, the director, and the costumer

5. Dress and Technical Rehearsals
   A. Evaluate all visual aspects of the production
   B. Make suggestions for improvement to the technical director, costumer, and all other chairmen and responsible persons

ACTORS

The actor is an artist who creates, for an audience, a character in a play. He is under the jurisdiction of the assistant director and the director of the production during casting and rehearsals, and is responsible to the stage manager and the assistant stage manager between and during performances (see figures 3-1 and 3-2). The actor is the artist who takes the plot, theme, character, setting, action, and dialogue of the playwright, and the blocking of the director, and correlates his ideas of characterization with those of the playwright and the director to make the play happen for an audience. The actor is the "doer" of the characterization and staging of the play. His characterization and actions serve as the human vehicle for the ideas of the director and the playwright. The latter give him the words, the movement, and the feel of the script, but without the actor's creative characterization, living and breathing on the stage, theatre cannot happen.

The following are suggestions that actors may want to follow during the different stages of the play production process.

1. Pre-Season
   - A. Read the season's plays
   - B. Check their academic schedules against the schedules of rehearsals and performances to decide in which plays they can participate responsibly
   - C. Speak to the directors to learn how they wish to do the plays, and at the same time bring themselves to the attention of the directors
   - D. Form a rough idea of the characters they are interested in portraying

2. Pre-Tryout
   - A. Study the script
     1. Read and reread it
     2. Find the theme, conflict, etc.
     3. Study the characters, their relationships, and their backgrounds within the script

        4. Find the climax, high and low points, and transitions
    B. Study the overall background
        1. Study all the available research on the playwright, the script itself, the productions, and the critics's reactions
        2. Research the playwright's other works, his personal background, etc.
        3. Find the historical background (if any) of incidents, characters, and period setting of the play
        4. Study all available information on the author's style, sources for ideas, etc.
        5. Speak to the director about his interpretation
    C. Practice the roles
        1. Have one or two characterizations especially well in mind
        2. Read the lines of those characters aloud, and again and again
        3. Know exactly what the characters mean by what they say
        4. Understand the characters' relationship to the whole play, and their physical and emotional characteristics
        5. Try to understand what the characters feel or think as they speak, or the subtext of their lines

3. Tryouts and Casting
    A. Pay careful attention to the director and his interpretation during auditions
    B. Watch others to get pointers and ideas on what is and is not effective characterization
    C. Attend all auditions (if possible) to watch others and listen to the director's instructions (an actor picks up pointers this way and is always on hand if needed)
    D. Be on time
    E. If called back, be there promptly and study the script
    F. Learn the cast list and the rehearsal schedule

4. Early Rehearsals
    A. Be prompt, and always notify the director if you are

detained or unable to attend a rehearsal

B. Pay close attention to the director's blocking and the various rules and regulations
C. Always have a pencil and your script
D. Memorize your lines, blocking, gestures, "business," etc., and study the script for innovations
E. Get sufficient rest and observe basic health habits
F. Be in the frame of mind to work and follow directions; be alert and attentive
G. Respect and obey your superiors
H. Learn to take direction, suggestions, and criticism, and be mature in relations with the director and the other theatre people
I. Use rehearsals as a training ground for the play, not as a social club or opportunity for pranks
J. Integrate the director's comments and criticism into your characterization
K. Take breaks only at scheduled times and for no longer than the director specifies

5. Dress and Technical Rehearsals
   A. Be in the wings or where you can be easily reached when you are not on stage
   B. Be prompt and always willing to work
   C. See that costumes, props, and makeup are where they belong and are put away after use
   D. Be attentive to the director's criticism and technical problems
   E. Follow the stage manager's directions from dress rehearsal to the last performance
   F. Work for the good of the show
   G. Hang up costume and put away your makeup

6. Performances
   A. Arrive at the theatre so that you have adequate time for makeup, dressing, and other preparations
   B. Never drink alcoholic beverages prior to a performance
   C. Be in the proper frame of mind and capable of doing your best
   D. Be sure of each detail of performance, blocking, lines,

problems to be wary of, etc.
   E. Be professional; take responsibility
   F. Properly anticipate all entrances and cues
   G. Pay strict attention to the stage manager
   H. Take care of your makeup and costume after performance

7. Post-Production
   A. Fulfill your "strike" responsibilities
   B. Return all costumes, scripts, and makeup to the theatre department
   C. Leave the dressing room in orderly shape
   D. Evaluate your own performance: How could it have been better? Were you satisfied? What are your most personal feelings about what you did?

THE ASSISTANT DIRECTOR

The assistant to the director is immediately responsible to the director, and in turn, is in complete charge of the actors (see figure 3-1). The assistant keeps discipline in the group, gives orders, checks on absences, and in short relieves the director of as much routine work as possible. He should have the name, address, and telephone number of every actor.

The director gives his assistant orders and he passes them on to the rest of the group. The main purpose of the assistant director is to help the director with tryouts and rehearsals. One of his main functions is to prepare the promptbook and keep it up to date. He also cues the actors, takes over for an absent actor, and takes the notes given him by the director. The assistant director should also be encouraged to make original contributions to the artistic development of the production through suggestions, criticisms, and comments.

The following are suggestions that the assistant director may want to make use of during the different stages of the play production process.

1. Pre-Tryout
   A. Read the script to get a full understanding of the play
   B. Confer with the director.

1. Discuss the meaning of the play, theme, plot, characters, etc.
2. Do any necessary research on the author, period, or the play itself to further an understanding of the play

C. Prepare a promptbook for yourself and the director. (A promptbook contains the rebound script, a copy or copies of the floor plan of the set or sets, rehearsal schedules, a list of actors' names, addresses, and phone numbers [plus the names and phone numbers of other important personnel], notes, cues, and other pertinent information)

1. Rebind the script
   a. Use of a single script involves cutting an area slightly smaller than the pages of the script in plain sheets of paper and pasting the pages to the sheets so that both sides of the script page will be legible
   b. Use of two scripts involves pasting each page of the script on a separate sheet of paper
2. Opposite each page insert sheets of 8½″×11″ typewriter paper (the same size as the rebound manuscript) to use as a note pad for recording stage directions, inserted dialogue, etc.
3. Index the rebound script with tabs
4. Mark the cues and actors' entrances with pencils of different color

2. Tryouts and Casting

A. Prepare tryout sheets that include all names, phone numbers, addresses, height, weight, hair and eye colors, outside activities and work commitments, experience, and statements that the persons trying out will accept any role

B. Help with general tryout methods

1. Hand out, and collect, tryout sheets
2. Make sure that sufficient scripts are available
3. Answer general questions about tryout procedures and tryout sheets

4. Take notes if the director requests it

C. If allowed by the director, help in making casting decisions

3. Early Rehearsals
   - A. Keep the rehearsals running smoothly
     1. Attend every rehearsal
     2. Take the notes given by the director
     3. Follow along carefully in the promptbook
     4. Cue the actors when necessary
     5. Help actors rehearse lines
     6. Take over for absent actors
     7. Take over rehearsals when necessary
     8. Run errands; make phone calls; post notices, etc.
     9. Make sure people are where they are supposed to be when they are supposed to be
     10. Make suggestions concerning blocking, acting, and interpretation to the director as rehearsals progress
   - B. Keep promptbook up-to-date and accurate
     1. Mark down all blocking
     2. Mark in the promptbook all additions and deletions from the script
     3. Write in all business and positions on stage that the director gives the actor

4. Technical and Dress Rehearsals
   - A. Technical Rehearsals
     1. Check attendance of actors
     2. Take notes on acting and technical problems
     3. Watch promptbook
     4. Run errands
     5. Give notes and criticisms to the director after every rehearsal
   - B. Dress Rehearsals
     1. Check attendance of all actors and crews
     2. Watch promptbook
     3. Take notes on acting, costumes, lighting, and sound
     4. Run errands
     5. Give notes and criticisms to the director

5. Performances

- A. Check attendance at the time of company call and immediately check on absences
- B. Run last-minute errands if necessary
- C. Make suggestions to the director about the performances

6. Post-Production
   - A. Help with striking
   - B. Give the completed promptbook to the director
   - C. Write evaluations of the production process, the performances, and the overall experience from the educational view of assistant director

THE STAGE MANAGER

The stage manager's main function is to see that all jobs are carried out before and during a performance; he is the main link between all the specialized crews. During the performance he is in charge of the production and checks all technical aspects on the stage. He is responsible for a smooth-running production, and the production is entirely his responsibility. Prior to performance, he sees to the technical problems of the rehearsals.

The following are suggestions that the stage manager may want to use during the different stages of the play production process.

1. Pre-Tryout
   - A. Read the script to get a full understanding of the play
   - B. Take particular notice of technical difficulties: unworkable situations, such as entrances from the wrong side, time discrepancies, and difficult costume changes
   - C. Make preliminary plans for actors, costumes, lighting, sound, and props
     1. Record the characters' names and the scenes in which they appear
     2. Have a general idea of the costuming
     3. Prepare ample notes and descriptions of overall requirements for lighting and sound
     4. Make a complete property list
   - D. Obtain a ground plan showing the location of furniture

E. Discuss the theme, interpretation, style, props, scene changes, lighting, etc., with the director
F. Discuss the play's technical requirements and problems with the scene designer and technical director

2. Early Rehearsals
   A. Attend every rehearsal
   B. Set up the rehearsal room with the assistant director, including furniture, props, etc.
   C. Mark the rehearsal floor with tape according to the exact measurements that will be used on the stage (this gives the actors a clearer perspective of the area within which they have to work)

3. Dress and Technical Rehearsals

   Dress and technical rehearsals depend to a large extent upon the stage manager. Careful organization, control, and thorough knowledge of the production will do much to smooth over the many problems that will arise. The stage manager should work closely with the director and the technical director as he supervises the various production crews during the technical rehearsals. He should always be within conversing distance of the director and the technical director. Meetings with the director prior to each technical rehearsal are a must.
   A. Take complete charge of backstage
      1. Mark the position of the furniture on the stage
      2. Check with the head of props to see that all props are ready and in the proper places
      3. Record all technical cues in the promptbook
      4. Make sure that all actors are ready for their entrances
   B. Supervise the technical rehearsal, which is held so that the crews can work out the routine of scene shifts, sound effects, cues, and other technical features of the production (such as setting light levels, etc.)
   C. Run the final dress rehearsal as if it were a performance

4. Performances
   A. Check in at least one hour before performance time
      1. Check the actors' sign-in sheet and any absences
      2. Check with the stage and crew heads to make sure that

everything is in working order
3. Check the communications system
4. See that the curtain works
5. Get a report from the lighting crew to make sure all dimmers work and the positions of instruments have not been changed
6. Make sure all props are ready

B. Set up for the first act
1. No lights should be on except the work lights
2. See that all people except crews are kept off the stage
3. Call time to the dressing rooms: "Half hour," "Fifteen minutes," and "Five minutes," and "Places!"
4. Make sure that all actors who are on stage when the curtain opens are on early
5. Wait for go-ahead signal from the house manager
6. See that all actors are in place
7. Make sure that curtain man is in place
8. Call "Work lights out!"
9. When house manager signals, give cue to lighting crew to light the stage and dim the house. Give sound cue if there is one
10. Signal "Curtain!"
11. Note time at start of act

C. See that silence is maintained backstage
1. Again make sure that actors are where they are supposed to be
2. See that all the technical backstage personnel are where they are supposed to be
3. Give cues and warning cues for all technical cues
4. Give warning cue to curtain man and all others about eight speeches before the end of the act
5. Note the time at the end of each act, and follow the calling procedure again after eight minutes of intermission

D. During intermission
1. Turn on work lights
2. Supervise the changing of scenery
3. Make sure all unnecessary props are removed and necessary props are added

   4. Enforce silence backstage
   5. Repeat the calling procedure
   6. Call places
   7. Cue lights, sound, and curtain
E. After each performance make sure everything is in its proper place and ready for the next performance
F. Make sure safety light and fire curtain are set

5. Post-Production
   A. Help with striking
   B. Give promptbook to director
   C. Write an evaluation of the production, the technical problems, the conduct of the actors, and the experience from the educational view of the stage manager

THE TECHNICAL DIRECTOR

The technical director of a theatre is defined as a person who organizes and maintains the theatre workshop under the authority of the director and the designer. He supervises all technical aspects of play production: the construction of sets and props; lights, sound, and props during technical and dress rehearsals; the repair of broken fixtures; the shifting of scenery; and the strike (see figure 3-1).

The following are suggestions the technical director may want to follow during the different stages of play production.

1. Pre-Season
   A. Read all of the plays to be produced during the season
   B. Confer with the director (or directors) and designers of the plays regarding design concepts, schedules for setup, technical problems, special effects
   C. Clean up the scene shop
   D. Take inventory of the materials on hand
   E. Order basic materials for the season (nails, lumber, hardware, muslin, etc.)

2. Pre-Tryout
   A. Check with the business manager on the production budget
   B. Confer with the director, designer, crew heads of lights, props, and sound, and the stage manager regarding work

schedules, deadlines, floor plans, sketches, etc.)

1. Secure a rehearsal schedule and note all completion dates for props and sets
2. Secure a floor plan (drawn to scale) and a sketch of each completed set from the designer
3. Secure drawings of all special props from the designer

C. Make working drawings of all flats and props with the following information:

1. Size and measurements
2. Quality and type of materials
3. Instructions for joining flats, etc.

D. Prepare a list of the materials needed for construction

3. Early Rehearsals

A. Supervise the construction crew in measuring, marking, and cutting the lumber

B. Arrange for the purchase or rental of special props with the property chairman

1. Check out all proposed prop purchases or rentals with the designer
2. Order purchased or rented props and arrange for their arrival before the date of rehearsing with props

C. Begin construction of all other props

D. Consult the prop chairman on rehearsal props

E. Begin painting props and set pieces

F. Conduct trial setups in the scenery shop

G. Continue to attend production meetings with the director, designers, stage manager, and crew heads

H. Place the sets on the stage

I. Plan the technical rehearsals

4. Technical and Dress Rehearsals

A. Arrive early for technical rehearsals and check out the lights, sound, stage, etc.

B. Supervise the stage manager on running the show with the added elements of lights, sound effects, and scene and prop changes

C. Establish all cues with the director and stage manager

D. Rehearse all technical cues with the stage manager and technical crews

- E. Work with the construction crews in the final preparations of the sets

5. Performances
   - A. Arrive early so as to supervise the stage manager as he checks out all technical equipment
   - B. Be on hand during performances in case of technical trouble of major significance
   - C. If repair work is needed the technical director should supervise it. (Even though the stage manager is in complete control of the production during performances, the technical director, who is usually a faculty member, should be on hand. Because students should not be in complete charge, at least one faculty member should be close by.)

6. Post-Production
   - A. Organize a strike crew to dismantle the set immediately after the last performance
   - B. Clean the stage area
   - C. Return all props and set pieces to the scenery shop and storage areas
   - D. Check the budget with the business manager

7. Post-Season
   - A. Clean up the shop and storage areas
   - B. Begin reading next season's plays

THE LIGHTING CHAIRMAN

The lighting chairman is the master electrician and is in charge of the lighting crew, which is responsible for the maintenance and use of all electrical equipment. The lighting crew chairman is responsible to the technical director and the scene designer prior to the opening of the show (see figure 3-1) and to the stage manager during the run of the show (see figure 3-2).

The following are suggestions the lighting chairman may want to make use of during the different stages of the production process.

1. Early Rehearsals
   - A. Meet with the designer, technical director, and director
     1. Discuss, the theme and interpretation of the play

2. Discuss the blocking of the play and special effects
3. Develop cue sheets and special effects

B. Prepare the lighting plan
1. With the scene designer, design the lighting plan
2. Prepare the light-cue script
   a. List the light cues and specific effects chronologically
   b. Allocate responsibilities to the crew

C. Prepare the materials
1. Clean, adjust, and install the lights
2. Hang and connect the units
3. Cut and install color gelatines or color media
4. Imitate natural phenomena with general and specific lights
   a. Make the actors and settings most advantageously visible
   b. Color the stage picture
   c. Establish the proper mood
   d. Focus the attention of the audience through use of varying intensity
5. Check the exit, aisle, corridor, foyer, and stairway lights
6. Test the stage lights (with people on stage) for evenness and spread of light
7. Allocate light-operating responsibilities to crew

2. Dress and Technical Rehearsals

A. Supervise lighting during rehearsals under the direction of the director, stage manager, and technical director
1. Regulate dimmers
2. Operate switchboard
3. Work spotlights and followspots

B. Make necessary adjustments and additions
1. Recheck changes with designer and director
2. Enter changes in cue script

3. Performances

A. Supervise all equipment for proper maintenance
1. Check all equipment before curtain time
2. Report to stage manager when everything is ready

3. Operate switchboard and dimmers
4. Supervise operation of followspots, etc.

B. Operate house lights before curtain, at intermissions, and at final curtain

4. Post-Production
   A. Turn in cue book to director
   B. Replace and repair damaged or burned out equipment
   C. Return all borrowed and rented equipment
   D. Store all equipment which is not permanently hung

THE SOUND CHAIRMAN

The sound chairman is in charge of the planning and execution of all sound effects. He is responsible to the technical director and the designer prior to the run of the play (see figure 3-1), and to the stage manager when the run of the play begins (see figure 3-2).

The following are suggestions that the sound chairman may want to use during the different stages of the play production process.

1. Early Rehearsals
   A. Meet with the director, designer, technical director, and musical director (if the production is a musical)
      1. Discuss the style and interpretation of the play
      2. Discuss the required sound effects
      3. Prepare cue sheets
      4. Prepare technical-sound-cue scripts
   B. Collect or make the necessary equipment to produce each sound
      1. Tape special effects and music
      2. Collect effects from commercial discs
      3. Allocate responsibility for live effects
      4. Plan musical continuity for brief scene changes or breaks.

2. Dress and Technical Rehearsals
   A. Set up materials before rehearsal
      1. Mount the speakers
      2. Test all equipment

        3. Check out source, creation and preparation of live effects
    B. Add sound effects and background music at first technical rehearsal
    C. Make necessary adjustments and additions
        1. Set the sound level in relation to actors' voices
        2. Enter all changes in the sound-cue script
        3. Recheck all changes with the director

3. Performances
    A. Test all equipment before the doors are opened and tell stage manager when everything is ready
    B. Play mood music for audience prior to curtain
    C. Supervise execution of all sound effects
    D. Mark any adjustments in cue script
    E. Store equipment for the next performance

4. Post-Production
    A. Turn in cue script to director
    B. Mark all tapes and file them in sound lab
    C. Return all borrowed or rented materials
    D. Store all equipment

THE PROPERTY CHAIRMAN

The property chairman is responsible for the crew which acquires and arranges all the hand and set props used in production. He is responsible to the technical director prior to the run of the play (see figure 3-1), and to the stage manager during the run of the play (see figure 3-2).

The following are suggestions that the property chairman may want to make use of during the different stages of the play production process.

1. Early Rehearsals
    A. Meet with the director, designer, and technical director
        1. Discuss the style and interpretation of the play
        2. Acquire a property list at these meetings
        3. Learn the moods and atmosphere of the play to simulate authenticity

- B. Prepare a property list
  1. Recheck property list with the director
  2. Make a list of possible sources for props (borrow, buy, or construct)
  3. Allocate responsibility of props to crew
  4. Acquire props
- C. Prepare rehearsal props
  1. Acquire list of props needed during rehearsals from the director
  2. Acquire or make prop facsimiles for rehearsals
- D. Prepare production properties
  1. Make prop box or prop table
  2. Make a chart to indicate the location of all props and prop tables
  3. Mark props with tape, according to location
  4. Note the location of each prop at the beginning of each scene
  5. Allocate responsibility of hand and set prop placement to individual crew members

2. Dress and Technical Rehearsals
   - A. Supply rehearsal with actual show props
     1. Recheck all prop locations before curtain
   - B. Supervise property traffic
     1. Take props to proper entrance to give to actor
     2. Collect props at exits and replace in prop box
     3. Change props between scenes
     4. Report to stage manager when props are ready, before each scene
     5. Collect hand props at end of rehearsal
     6. Repair or make necessary changes in props after each rehearsal

3. Performances
   - A. Recheck all preparations before curtain time
     1. Double check first scene setup
     2. Inform stage manager when props are ready
   - B. Supervise property control traffic
     1. Follow same procedure as during technical and dress rehearsals

4. Post-Production
   A. Collect all props
      1. Return borrowed or rented props
      2. Store theatre's props in prop room
   B. Turn in prop cue script to director

THE COSTUME DESIGNER

The costume designer designs and/or supervises all costumes for the season; it is his (or her) responsibility to see that the actors appear on stage in suitable costumes which also "fit" the characters they play. And not only is the costume designer in charge of costumes and makeup, he is responsible for the appearance of each actor on stage. Undoubtedly, the costume designer is one of the most important artists and technicians in carrying out a production. He works under the jurisdiction of the director and the artistic director (see figure 3-1).

The following are suggestions that the costumer may want to follow during the different stages of the play production process.

1. Pre-Season
   A. Inventory the costumes and makeup, and clean the former for the upcoming season
   B. Make all necessary repairs
   C. Order any necessary items

2. Pre-Tryout
   A. Read and become familiar with the plays for the season
   B. Devote special concentration to each play in turn
   C. Visualize the settings, characters, and costumes and analyze the characters to interpret their most appropriate costumes
   D. Meet with the director and artistic director (scene designer)
      1. Discuss the style and interpretation of each play
      2. Discuss all visual aspects of production
      3. Discuss the colors of sets and costumes
      4. Discuss the characters and their interpretations
      5. Discuss, in general, the costume plan
   E. Do research and rough sketches for each character

3. Tryouts and Casting
    - A. Organize the costume crew
    - B. Supervise measurement taking
    - C. Appoint a makeup chairman
    - D. Meet with the director and discuss all makeup problems

4. Early Rehearsals
    - A. Learn the stage groupings and the playing patterns of actors
    - B. Learn the light plot
    - C. Rent costumes for historical plays (if they are not to be made)
    - D. Design whatever costumes must be made
    - E. Meet with the director and discuss designs
    - F. Revise the designs if necessary and meet again with the director for final approval
    - G. Borrow costumes, accessories, and materials if possible
    - H. Buy any needed materials and supervise the making of costumes
    - I. Meet with costume committee and describe how it will accomplish its task
    - J. Schedule and assign duties to costume crew
    - K. After costumes have been made, call for actors' fitting
    - L. Alter costumes if necessary, and fit again

5. Dress and Technical Rehearsals
    - A. Organize the costume crew for dress rehearsals. (A member of the costume crew should be assigned to each actor or small group of actors to assist in dressing and be responsible for the costumes)
    - B. Sit in the house and view each scene critically under the stage lights
        1. Consider the total stage picture as a color unit and determine if it is harmonious, if substitutions or changes would improve the ensemble effect
        2. Check the appearance of each costume to see if it is successful or needs changing
    - C. Make last-minute adjustments

6. Performances
    - A. Keep costumes in good condition with help of wardrobe

committee

B. Make sure actors are properly dressed

C. Begin production activities for the next show

7. Post-Production

A. Instruct wardrobe committee on cleaning and storing costumes

B. Return all rented costumes as soon as possible

C. Check with the business manager about paying rental fees

D. Clean all costumes; return borrowed ones to owners

8. Post-Season

A. Inventory costumes, and see that all are cleaned and repaired

B. Send thank-you notes to all who donated or loaned costumes for shows

THE WARDROBE COMMITTEE

The wardrobe committee is a group of individuals who must carry out the ideas and desires of the costume designer in preparing or providing costumes for a play. This committee is under the direct supervision of the costume designer, who acts as its chairman prior to the opening of the show (see figure 3-1). During the production, the wardrobe crew is under the supervision of the stage manager (see figure 3-2).

The following are suggestions that the costume committee may want to make use of during the different stages of the play production process.

1. Tryouts and Casting

A. Measure each actor for his costume as soon as the cast is chosen

B. Meet with the costumer for plans and instructions

2. Early Rehearsals

A. Prepare the costumes under the supervision of the costumer

3. Dress and Technical Rehearsals

A. After the costumes are made, they should be pressed and carefully stored for rehearsal

B. Committee members assist the actors to whom they are

assigned

C. The committee is responsible for checking the costumes after each rehearsal and seeing that they are hung up and properly stored

D. Committee members should be available to the costumer and director for instructions on changes and alterations

4. Performances
   A. Everything should be ready by opening night
   B. A member of this committee should be backstage during the entire production with needle, thread, safety pins, iron, etc. (If the cast is a large one, several costume committee personnel will be needed)
   C. Continue dressing and checking each actor before he goes on
   D. Keep costumes in good, clean condition
   E. Make sure that each costume is hung up after each performance

5. Post-Production
   A. Clean the costumes after the close of the run and inventory them
   B. Box and return rented costumes
   C. Clean and return borrowed costumes
   D. Help with general strike

THE MAKEUP COMMITTEE

The chairman of the makeup committee is the costume designer, and he is charged with highlighting the external characteristics of the actors for the audience with innumerable makeup materials. The makeup committee works under the costume designer prior to the run of the play (see figure 3-1), and under the stage manager after the play opens (see figure 3-2).

The following are suggestions that the members of the makeup committee may want to follow during the different stages of the play production process.

1. Tryouts and Casting
   A. Meet with the designer and director to hear their interpretations of the style of the play

B. Meet with the designer to discuss the specific characters
C. Decide upon the type of makeup to be used and the manner in which it will be applied

2. Early Rehearsals
A. A manager of makeup is chosen and is given a makeup chart. After checking the makeup on hand, he arranges purchases upon the advice of the costume designer and the business manager

3. Dress and Technical Rehearsals
A. One complete makeup rehearsal is usually enough (except for special, elaborate makeup), and usually coincides with the final dress rehearsal (since makeup cannot be adequately judged until all the lights are set and full costume is worn)
B. Having selected makeup that fits the character and costume of each actor, arrive early and make all preparatory arrangements
C. Help each actor put on his makeup so that he will be able to apply his own during the run of the show
D. Assist actors who need to change hair styles
E. Keep makeup supply well stocked
F. Clean up the makeup room after rehearsal and put makeup away

4. Performances
A. If all actors can apply their own makeup, there should be only one makeup person at each performance
B. Arrive early and put makeup out neatly
C. Assist each actor as needed
D. Check each actor before he goes on stage
E. Clean the makeup room and lock it after each performance

5. Post-Production
A. Clean makeup rooms and put all makeup away
B. Inventory the makeup and supplies
C. Order the needed materials and give the list to the designer

THE CHOREOGRAPHER

The choreographer, working closely with the director and the musical director, is the person who stages all of the dances and may also block and stage all musical numbers in the show. He is directly responsible to the director (see figure 3-1).

The following are suggestions that the choreographer may want to make use of during the different stages of the play production process.

1. Pre-Tryout
   - A. Meet with the stage director to ascertain the use of dance numbers
     1. Work out their time limits
     2. Get the stage director's interpretation and adapt it to the dance movements
     3. Study the ground plans to learn how much stage space will be available
     4. Learn how the director wants to cast the show in relation to the dances
   - B. Secure the musical scores and make sure the arrangements are feasible
     1. Begin working on dance outlines and ideas
     2. Note the length of dance arrangements and any incidental problems

2. Tryouts and Casting
   - A. Arrange with the stage director and musical director, and hold dance auditions
     1. Arrange with the musical director for a rehearsal pianist
   - B. After auditions, meet with the stage director and the musical director to cast the play

3. Early Rehearsals
   - A. Have the stage manager arrange space for dance rehearsals
     1. Make sure that a piano is available
     2. Make sure that the sets are outlined on the floor with tape
   - B. Coordinate the rehearsal with the stage director and the musical director
   - C. Make arrangements with the musical director for a rehearsal pianist
   - D. Begin blocking the dances

- E. Meet with the director periodically to brief him on progress and problems
- F. Add to or subtract from the dance score as needed, in cooperation with the musical director and the stage director

4. Dress and Technical Rehearsals
   - A. Work with the stage director and musical director in making cuts or changes
   - B. Help the stage director integrate the blocking and choreographed scenes
   - C. Be prepared to reblock musical numbers or dances at the last minute
   - D. Work with the set designer to make minor changes in dance space, set props, platforms, etc.
   - E. Make sure that all dances and musical numbers are blocked and polished prior to continuity rehearsals
   - F. Note any errors and bring them to the attention of the proper persons
   - G. Select a dance captain to take over during performances
     1. The captain should be a well-trained and experienced dancer
     2. Familiar with all the dances and movements, he should also be able to work well with people. (In theory, he is responsible for the dancers and dancing during the run of the show; he works directly under the stage manager.)

5. Performances
   - A. The dance captain takes over
     1. He assumes all the responsibilities previously held by the choreographer
     2. He holds additional rehearsals, according to need, with the cooperation of the stage manager

6. Post-Production
   - A. Confer with the director for evaluation and recommendations

THE MUSICAL DIRECTOR

The musical director handles and arranges all the musical elements of a musical production. He coordinates all the musical elements with the stage director and choreographer so as to round out the entire production. He is directly responsible to the director (see figure 3-1).

The following are suggestions the musical director may want to make use of during the different stages of the play production process.

1. Pre-Tryout
   - A. Meet with the stage director as soon as possible
     1. Discuss the theme, interpretation, and style of the production
     2. Find out how much music there will be and how the director wants to use it
     3. Decide upon the size of the orchestra and the type of accompaniment
     4. Make sure the proper number of scores and vocal arrangements are ordered through the business manager
     5. Find out how the director wants to cast the show musically
   - B. Begin working with the music
     1. Play the entire score through
     2. Note the problem areas
     3. Make sure that the arrangements will "work"
     4. Make audition selections either by voice part or character part
   - C. Check with the director on a pianist for the auditions
   - D. Prepare a musical audition sheet with the cooperation of the director and the assistant director

2. Tryouts and Casting
   - A. Hold musical auditions (usually in conjunction with the director and the choreographer)
   - B. Meet with the director and the choreographer after auditions and cast the play

3. Early Rehearsals
   - A. Meet with the cast and distribute the scores
     1. Explain how the music will be used
     2. Explain the director's interpretation

B. Set up a schedule of music rehearsals in conjunction with the director and the choreographer
   1. Make sure that the rehearsal schedule includes the vocal coaching of the lead character
      a. Meet with these people individually
   2. Organize and schedule chorus rehearsals
   3. Arrange for a pianist for all music rehearsals
   4. Check with the stage manager and make sure that a piano is available for all music rehearsals

C. Begin music rehearsals
   1. Rescore songs if voices do not fit the score adequately
   2. Brief the director on progress and problems
      a. Advise him if a number is not working out and should be cut

D. Select a conductor (if the musical director is not a conductor)

E. Select the musicians
   1. Sign A.F. of M. union contracts if union musicians are required and there is no union waiver
   2. Work with the business manager in signing union contracts and selecting salary ranges
   3. Work with the music department in securing qualified players

F. Set up an orchestra rehearsal schedule and distribute the scores

G. Meet with the business manager and tell him what musical equipment is needed and when it will be needed

H. Begin orchestra rehearsals
   1. Work out any problems, and restructure the score if necessary
   2. Be prepared to add dance bars or delete measures as requested by the director or choreographer
   3. Be prepared to revise change-of-scene music

4. Dress and Technical Rehearsals

A. Oversee all musical features
   1. All talent and musicians should be thoroughly prepared
   2. Work with the choreographer and director on any additional changes

        3. Note the musical errors and bring them to the attention of the proper persons

5. Performances
    A. The conductor takes over, and
        1. Brings errors to the attention of the proper persons
        2. Calls additional rehearsals as needed

6. Post-Production
    A. Collect the scores
    B. Arrange with the business manager to have equipment returned
    C. Meet with the director to evaluate the production
        1. Make recommendations for the next production

THE PRODUCER

The producer has ultimate control and authority over all aspects of theatre production (see figures 3-1, 3-2, and 3-3). In educational theatre on the secondary level, this person is the school principal, and the president on the college and university level. The principal or president usually delegates and assigns the particular duties of the operation of the theatre to faculty and staff members, but he always retains complete authority and the ultimate responsibility. For all practical purposes, the departmental chairman normally functions as the producer in the day-to-day activities of the theatre.

It is the producer's responsibility to see that all school rules and regulations are carried out and that the image of the school is enhanced. It is also his duty to approve or establish the budget and see that the school is properly insured against all contingencies that might arise from a public theatre program. Thus in educational theatre the producer is primarily concerned with three areas: (1) policy, (2) finance, and (3) image.

Policy

It is the right and the duty of the producer to establish or approve the overall policy or purpose of his school's theatre and to see that this policy is in accord with the policy of the school. It is his responsibility, therefore, to see that this policy is carried out in the theatre's artistic and commercial practices. The theatre staff has an obligation, as well as a right, to attempt to influence those policies, to advise and to recommend, but the principal or the president must, in the last analysis, establish the policy. Once the policy has been established, the season should be decided upon and approved by the producer. He should analyze and assess the season in terms of the overall policy and purposes of the theatre and the school.

As the season progresses, the artistic and commercial practices of the theatre staff should be evaluated by the producer in terms of how well the policy is being upheld and whether the purposes of the theatre are being achieved.

At the end of the season, both the policy and its implementation should be evaluated by the producer and the theatre staff to discover discrepancies and desirable changes. New directions should also be discussed at this time.

Finance

The producer exercises ultimate authority in the formulation of and adherence to a budget. He has final approval over expenditures, purchases, and salaries. He also decides the minimum income goal. As part of his financial responsibilities, the producer must see that the school is sufficiently insured against all contingencies, including public liability as well as insurance for students who might become injured while participating in a production. The theatre manager should resolve these problems with the producer.

Image

The producer (the principal or president) serves as a liaison between the school and the community. It is therefore necessary for him to see that the school develops or maintains the respect of the community. Since the theatre deals with the public and the community in its public performance program, the school has an important stake in that program. While departmental chairmen, principals, and presidents delegate various responsibilities to the faculty and staff, they must retain their authority for protecting the image of the school. They should therefore be concerned with play selection, casting, etc., inasmuch as these reflect or form the image of the school. Constant communication between the producer and the theatre staff will help keep this problem in hand.

THE MANAGING DIRECTOR

The managing director is the supervisor of all the commercial functions of the theatre production program, though sometimes this job is combined with that of the business manager (see the "Business Manager" section below). When the jobs are separate, the managing director serves as a liaison, as well as supervisor, between the various commercial functionaries of the theatre. In either case, he is totally responsible for the commercial functions. He carries out the producer's policies, delegates responsibilities, takes part in play selection, and supervises budget preparation and control, purchasing, advertising and publicity, ticket sales, and house management (see figure 3-3). His goals must be the following.

1. To facilitate the operation of all commercial aspects of play production and see that they are handled in an efficient and responsible manner
2. To coordinate all the business purchases, sales, and publicity activities
3. To facilitate the jobs of the director, scene designer, costume designer, and technical director when these persons are involved in commercial matters
4. To carry out the basic theatre policy
5. To serve as a liaison between the producer and the theatre staff
6. To contribute to the overall aesthetic impression of each production

THE BUSINESS MANAGER

The business manager is in charge of carrying out and/or supervising all business activities of the theatre. He is directly responsible to the managing director and the producer (see figure 3-3). The publicity director, house manager, and box office manager are under his direct supervision. It is his responsibility to pay all invoices, deposit all monies collected, and keep the financial books for the entire year.

In most school theatres the business manager is a student, while the managing director is a staff member. The managing director, in this case, should keep tight control and supervision over the activities of the business manager. He should be sure that the position has a certain amount of controlled authority, and yet make sure that the experience is meaningful and educational.

The following are suggestions that the business manager may want to use during the different stages of the play production process.

1. Pre-Season
   A. Consult with the artistic director (scene designer), costume designer, technical director, musical director, and managing director
      1. Discuss the productions to be presented
      2. Determine what costs may occur in
         a. Capital equipment
         b. General operation
         c. Technical expenses
   B. Prepare a preliminary budget
      1. Estimate income
      2. Estimate expenses
   C. Meet with the theatre staff to discuss and revise the budget
   D. Prepare the final budget and submit it to the producer
   E. Obtain production rights and pay royalty fees
   F. Revise (if necessary) internal business policies and practices
   G. Employ or engage the services of any new personnel needed for carrying out the business functions
   H. Have the tickets printed
   I. Supervise the design and publication of the season brochure with the managing director
   J. Purchase the necessary supplies
   K. Purchase the necessary scripts for the entire season
   L. Set up the bookkeeping for the season

2. Pre-Tryout
   A. Deposit all monies collected from
      1. Season sales
      2. Subsidies

B. Purchase supplies as they are requisitioned by the theatre staff

3. Early Rehearsals
    A. Purchase supplies and materials as requested
    B. Print the programs
    C. Keep the books up to date

4. Performances
    A. Supervise the box office manager's operation
    B. Deposit the money
    C. Record the box office reports in the books

5. Post-Production
    A. Prepare and distribute financial reports on a production's income, expenses, and balance
    B. Review the budget with the theatre staff
    C. See that all rented materials are returned

6. Post-Season
    A. See that all bills have been paid
    B. Prepare and distribute the final financial report
    C. Evaluate all business areas
    D. Have an external audit made of the financial books
    E. Send letters of appreciation to those who volunteered their services
    F. Recheck to see that all rented materials have been returned
    G. Prepare a scrapbook of the year's activities

THE BOX OFFICE MANAGER

The box office manager is responsible for the sale of season tickets and the operation of the box office. He is directly responsible to the business manager and the managing director (see figure 3-3). In small theatres, where the managing director also serves as the business manager, the box office manager is responsible only to the managing director.

The following are suggestions the box office manager may want to make use of during the different stages of the play production process.

1. Pre-Season

A. Revise, if necessary, the box office policies and procedures
B. Submit requests for purchases to the business manager—for
   1. Season tickets
   2. Individual admission tickets
   3. Envelopes for ticket reservations
   4. Forms and other supplies
C. Employ or engage the services of any new personnel needed
D. Instruct the box office personnel in procedures for selling season tickets and running the box office
E. Establish a sales campaign
   1. Confer with the managing director and the publicity director
   2. Contact previous-season patrons
   3. Direct the sales of season tickets
F. Submit daily reports and the monies collected from sales

2. Early Rehearsals
   A. Set up the box office
      1. See that all supplies are on hand and accounted for
      2. Determine the box office hours
      3. Assign personnel to run the box office
   B. Rack the tickets
   C. Pull complimentary tickets and house seats
   D. Fill mail orders
   E. Obtain sufficient change
   F. Open the box office
   G. Sell tickets
   H. Prepare a box office report at the close of each day
   I. Give the box office report, money, stubs, and season ticket coupons to the business manager at the end of each day

3. Performances
   A. Operate the box office in the same manner as above and on the evenings of the performances

4. Post-Production
   A. Box and file the stubs and other "deadwood"
   B. Prepare and distribute the final box office report for the run of the play

THE PUBLICITY DIRECTOR

The publicity director is under the supervision of the business manager (see figure 3-3). Directly in charge of generating public interest in the theatre, he alerts the public to a theatre event in order to create a public opinion which is intelligent, informed, and favorable.

The following are suggestions the publicity director may want to use during the different stages of the play production process.

1. Pre-Season
    - A. Become personally acquainted with newspaper editors and theatre writers and critics
        1. Find out what kind of material they want
        2. Find out when notices should be received and how much free space you can expect to get per show
        3. Make a file of all the information about each newspaper
            - a. It should contain the names and addresses of the newspapers, the deadline for articles, and other pertinent information
    - B. Send the newspapers publicity releases that contain the entire season of plays, the performance dates, and information for obtaining season tickets. Also, mention the staff members and new plans
    - C. Purchase advertising
        1. Ads should describe the entire season, specify the dates of plays, and tell how and where season tickets may be purchased and the prices
        2. Include a mail order coupon in the ad
    - D. Place posters around the town and on the campus
    - E. Send out brochures or flyers to a selected mailing list

2. Pre-Tryout
    - A. Send publicity release telling when and where tryouts will be held
    - B. Place posters around the campus telling when and where tryouts will be held

3. Early Rehearsals
   A. Send out publicity releases with a list of the cast and the parts they will play
      1. Include biographical material on the major roles
      2. Send out information on group rates to schools or special groups
   B. Make sure that posters have been ordered and printed

4. Later Rehearsals
   A. Toward the end of the rehearsal period, send releases to the town papers. (It is best if they are printed in the Sunday issue just before the box office opens)
   B. At the same time, place ads in the local newspapers
   C. Place ads in the school newspaper
   D. Make sure that the publicity releases are interesting and that they complement the paid ads
   E. Send out publicity releases or fact sheets to the local radio and television stations two weeks before opening night
   F. Place more posters around town and on campus one week before opening night
   G. Set up a picture-taking session with the director of the play
   H. Set up a lobby display in the theatre and close to the box office

5. Performances
   A. Invite a reviewer from the town newspaper
   B. Invite a reviewer from the school newspaper
   C. Take an opening night photo for the next day's paper

6. Post-Production
   A. Hold a discussion of the production that is open to the public
      1. List the date and time in the program
   B. Give the business manager a list of the persons to be thanked for their support
   C. Give the business manager a complete record of all publicity for the play: ads, posters, flyers, articles, etc.

7. Post-Season
   A. Give the business manager a file that contains all the ads and publicity for the year

B. Make a file of all publicity ideas so that the next year the publicity director can more easily decide upon effective methods of publicity

THE HOUSE MANAGER

The house manager works under the direct supervision of the business manager and the managing director. He is in charge of seeing that the physical plant, from the curtain to the front doors, is in order. It is his responsibility to see to the comfort and well-being of the audience at every theatre event. The ushers are under the jurisdiction of the house manager (see figure 3-3).

The following are suggestions that the house manager may want to follow during the different stages of the play production process.

1. Pre-Season
   - A. Secure ushers and ticket takers for the upcoming season
     1. Canvass sororities, honorary organizations, service clubs, etc., for volunteers
     2. Check the file for last year's volunteers
   - B. Check the theatre building
     1. See that heating and ventilation are adequate
     2. See that the exits are well lit and easily accessible
     3. See that all seats are sturdy and usable
     4. Report all needed repairs to the theatre business manager, who will report them to the school officials
   - C. Have the materials needed for emergencies
     1. Check the fire extinguishers
     2. Secure several first-aid kits
     3. Have a file with a list of numbers to use for various emergencies
        - a. Have a reputable doctor available
        - b. Notify the police and fire departments of the performances

2. Dress and Technical Rehearsals
   - A. Train the ushers
     1. Teach them the seating plan of the theatre
     2. Explain the proper way to seat patrons

a. Tell them to be courteous and attentive to the comfort of the audience

3. Explain to ushers the method of distributing programs to the audience
4. Make sure they know what to do in emergencies
5. Be sure they dress properly for performances
6. Establish an usher schedule for the run of the play
7. Have them arrive twenty minutes before the doors open

B. If there are ticket takers, train them
1. Make sure they know how tickets are to be secured and validated
2. Prepare a schedule for the run of the show
3. Make sure they know what time to arrive and how to dress

C. Check supplies
1. See that an adequate number of flashlights and batteries are available and in good working order
   a. Have extra personnel on hand
2. Obtain the programs for the play

3. Performances

A. Meet with ushers and ticket takers twenty minutes before the doors open
1. Go over the policies and procedures
2. Distribute the programs and flashlights

B. Stand in rear of theatre and be available to handle last-minute problems

C. Close theatre doors when curtain time is at hand

D. Signal stage manager to start play when the audience is seated

E. Turn off lobby lights

F. Remain in lobby during the performance to admit late-comers

G. Open theatre doors at intermission time and turn lights on in lobby

H. Signal the audience that intermission is over by flashing lights or ringing buzzer or bell

I. Close theatre doors and turn out lobby lights when audience is seated

J. Clean lobby during the acts
K. Open doors and turn on lights at curtain
L. Thank ushers and ticket takers
M. Check house before leaving
    1. Make sure lights are off and doors and windows are closed

4. Post-Production
    A. Collect all equipment from ushers
    B. Supervise and assist with strike and auditorium cleanup
    C. Give names of ushers and ticket takers to business manager for thank-you notes

4 Selecting the Theatrical Season of Plays

THE PLAY'S THE THING

COMMERCIALLY or artistically, one of the most important aspects of any successful theatre program in high school or college is selecting the proper plays for production. No matter how good the actors or how talented the director, or how beautiful the theatre or settings, if the vehicle for all of the theatrical elements and activity has not been selected with care and intelligence, success can be illusive. Audiences normally go to the theatre to see a play—not an actor, a set, props, or costumes. It is the play which must be "sold," publicized, advertised, and eventually "bought" by the public. It is the play which actors, technicians, director, and designers must spend days, weeks, and months perfecting. In short, the play is, and always has been, the heart of theatre.

Selecting a play for performance is a difficult task, but selecting an entire season of plays—three, four, or five—is really a monumental task. It cannot be done hastily or in one meeting. This director consistently spends month after month with his colleagues talking over a single prospective season—listing plays, evaluating each, evaluating them as a group, rethinking technical and casting problems, sales possibilities, variety, balance, etc. Three months of consideration just to select a four-play season might seem an unduly long time, but in the long run they are probably the most crucial three months of work in the entire play production process. It is difficult to make a production better than the material out of which it is made, and the material of a production is the drama itself.

An important point to be clarified here is the role of the theatre manager in the process of play selection. It is, after all, the manager and his staff who will attempt to "sell" the production to the public. It is the management staff which has the responsibility for building and maintaining an audience for the theatre program. The management staff also has a stake in seeing that the overall philosophy of educational theatre is carried out in practice.

Play selection is one of the methods by which the management staff can develop an audience and carry out the aims and objectives of the theatre. This does not mean that the theatre manager should dictate the selection of a play, but that he should enter into the discussions, know the plays and the directors, be able to make suggestions as to schedule, number of performances, the order of the plays, and, in general, make certain that the package (1) will be attractive to an audience and (2) will assist the staff in carrying out the aims and objectives of educational theatre.

SELECTING A PLAY

There is really only one criterion for selecting a play for production in any type of theatre situation: select a *good* play. In general, in considering what is a good play for production, the director must take into account (1) a play's inherent dramatic and theatrical values, and (2) the particular production problems which the play presents for a particular theatre.

Dramatic Values

The essential dramatic elements which must be considered in evaluating a play for production are (1) conflict, (2) theme, (3) dramatic action, and (4) characters. While these are not all of the essential elements of drama, they do serve as a starting point in looking at a play from a production point of view.

Conflict. Good dramas have well-defined, exciting, and clear conflicts.

A play is the narration of the beginning, the middle, and the end of a conflict. In every good drama there must be a least one central conflict around which all of the characters act. A conflict, in turn, is usually defined as the direct opposition of two forces. It makes little difference what these two forces are, or why they are in conflict with each other: what is important is that a conflict—a direct opposition of whatever nature—exists. A force may be a man, nature, God, a group of men, an ideology, an idea, or even a philosophy.

Conflicts, then, can be expressed in terms of man against man, man against society (a group of men), man against nature, society against society, ideology against ideology, man against God or even god against god, or any combination of forces. All of these are valid dramatic conflicts, and have been used in thousands of dramas from Aristophanes to Albee.

The two forces which are in conflict with each other in dramas are the *protagonist* and the *antagonist*. The protagonist is the person or force with whom the audience sympathizes, usually the main character or "hero." The antagonist is the force which is against the protagonist, which works against his well-being. This "anti-force" may be a force outside the hero, or it may be a force within the personality of the protagonist himself. If the antagonist is a force outside the protagonist (another character or group of characters), the conflict is said to be an *external* conflict. If the antagonist is a force within the structure of the hero, the conflict is called an *internal* conflict.

In the case of an internal conflict, the antagonist is described in terms of a weakness or flaw within the makeup of the leading character's personality complex. The conflict then revolves around the hero and his flaw, with the former striving to maintain life in harmony with himself and society, and the latter trying to destroy that peaceful, harmonious existence. It is, in effect, a struggle between two facets of a character's personality.

This idea of conflict—whether it be external or internal—is the heart of drama; it is, in essence, what makes a drama dramatic. It captures and sustains interest; it is the vehicle for suspense; it allows the audience to become involved in a struggle and to "root" for a victor and secretly desire a loser.

Conflict, after all, is what makes football, baseball, basketball, and other sports exciting. Conflict invests interest in the mountain climber, the swimmer, the political convention, and the tight-rope walker. Drama in sports or athletics, politics or theatre does not exist without conflict. A well-defined, clear, and exciting conflict is a basic requirement for a good play.

Theme. Good dramas have meaningful, worthwhile themes.

After analyzing what was said about the nature of conflict in drama, we can say that conflicts occur because the protagonist and the antagonist set certain goals for themselves which, by their very nature, are mutually exclusive. That is, the attainment of the two goals is impossible at one and the same time: the protagonist wants something and the antagonist wants something else, and if the protagonist attains his desire, the antagonist cannot attain his. Conversely, if the antagonist attains his goal, it is impossible for the protagonist to attain his. This idea of the attainment—or non-attainment—of mutually exclusive goals is what causes conflict in drama.

As a drama progresses, the two forces get closer and closer to their respective goals. But at the end of the drama, either the protagonist attains his goal or the antagonist attains his. The conflict is over; there has been a victor and a loser. Thus the theme of a drama is the statement of the conflict *in terms of its final outcome.* They may be stated in very general terms, such as conformity defeats individualism (*An Enemy of the People*), or in the more specific terms of the plot, such as the desire of a community to force its will and values upon a strong-willed member of that community.

While this might seem like too analytical a method of approaching the thematic content of a drama, it can assist the director and theatre staff in stating and comparing themes. However, it must always be remembered that quite often the discovery of themes is an individual, personal, and somewhat intuitive task. The theme, after all, is a statement of the idea of a drama—the meaning and intuitive inspiration which prompted the writing of the script by the dramatist. It is his vision of an inner meaning of life and the human situation which the dramatist, as artist, discovered in nature. And being an emotional, personal response to life, the discovery of themes must also be, to some extent, an emotional problem or venture.

In any case, the discovery of meaningful, emotional, and important statements about the human situation should be an important guide to the evaluation and selection of worthwhile dramas for production.

Dramatic Action. Good dramas contain a significant quantity of dramatic action.

Dramatic action, one of the essential elements of drama, is often what distinguishes drama from poetry or prose. When we say that a drama has action, we mean that it "goes someplace"—that it progresses from one situation to another, always moving toward a definite conclusion and resolution.

Action, therefore, means a change from one relationship to another or from one circumstance to another. Do the characters change? Does the relationship between the conflicting forces change? Is there forward progression, from one situation or circumstance to another? Is the concluding situation or circumstance substantially different from the opening one? If these questions can be answered in the affirmative, the drama "goes someplace"; it has dramatic action.

Dramatic action is directly related to incidents or episodes, which are actions by either the protagonist or the antagonist which place him closer to his goal. Incidents, therefore, are those actions which create change and are directly responsible for dramatic action.

It is not true, however, that the more incidents in a drama the more action that drama will have. The dramatic action of a drama is related to the total amount of change (progression) in the characters or situations; it does not consist in the number of steps (incidents) it takes for that change to be made.

As indicated, it is very important that dramas have action. And as can be seen from the nature of dramatic action, action does not mean mere physical activity on the part of the characters on stage. A duel, a murder, a fight, a love scene are all very exciting and "active" moments on the stage, but that does not mean they can be classified as incidents or that they produce dramatic action. A dramatic incident has nothing to do with physical, or theatrical, activity. An incident which moves the plot forward, and produces change and dramatic action, may be a thought, a duel *or* a quiet decision, a death, a birth, or the falling in or out of love. It can be violent physical action or the internal, quiet change brought about by a mental decision.

While all of these actions and changes are possible, a director should view dramas in terms of their translation into theatrical, visual, physical terms. Indeed, the art of theatre production is to a great degree a visual art. People go to the theatre to "see," not to "hear," a play; and the dramas that are selected for production must be not only dramatic but theatrical. In other words, the incidents should lend themselves to exciting and moving physical actions which will allow directors, designers, and actors to make maximum use of all the theatrical elements at their disposal.

In general, good plays contain dramatic action in the form of incidents which move the plot forward (plot, in this sense, consisting of the orderly arrangement of incidents into a story form). Good dramatic action is both dramatic in terms of the change which is brought about and theatrical in terms of the visual aspects of theatre production.

Characters. In analyzing a drama with a view to production, it is important to consider the central characters and to determine whether or not they are (1) clearly developed and described, (2) believable, and (3) consistent.

One of the most important tasks of the dramatist in the creation of his characters is to make them *clear* to a potential audience member. The spectators must "know"—really know—a character if they are to understand the plot and empathize with the character. When one stops to realize that, within the space of only several hours' time in the theatre, a dramatist must not only present all the intricate details of conflict, action, theme, and story but must also "describe" some ten, twelve, or more different characters (all of whom the auaience has never before seen) in sufficient detail that they are fully understandable to a diverse audience, we can realize just what a task good playwriting really is. Nevertheless, in thinking about characters in a play under consideration for production, attention must be given to whether they are easily understood and clearly described.

In many cases a dramatist utilizes type characters; that is, characters who are immediately recognizable as similar to certain types or kinds of persons in real life. In general, the use of type characters is not normally detrimental to the quality of a drama, and even the use of stereotype characters (those types which have been used over and over in drama and literature and thereby become fixed and practically unalterable) is necessary at times. The principal criterion for a director's or producer's judgment should be whether the characters can be easily grasped by the audience and yet particular enough to be distinctly remembered—characters with whom an audience can empathize.

In addition to being clearly described and recognizable, characters must also be believable. The degree to which characters appear believable to an audience depends to a great extent upon the quality and strength of the motivation of each character. People usually don't act unless they have some reason for acting, and an audience which sees a character acting without sufficient reason will not readily accept that character as true to nature. Thus three types of motivational factors are used in dramas: (1) basic psychological drives, (2) social situations, and (3) the "built-in" action of the plot.

Psychologists can give us a long list of the basic drives of men: self-preservation, security, novelty, peace of mind, gregariousness, moral respect, family ties, competition, etc. And if one or more of these drives are threatened or challenged, a person (or character) will usually be forced into action.

While this form of psychological motivation is often used in dramas, it is not the only motivation a character may have. Many characters in dramas act in a certain manner because of the physical or social situation in which they find themselves. And so a comprehensive evaluation of the physical or social environment in which those characters are placed might yield a different sort of character motivation. From the time of Ibsen and Strindberg, our popular realistic, and especially naturalistic, drama has put much emphasis upon this idea of environmental or social character motivation. During the past one hundred years, many dramatists have believed that man, to one extent or another, is a product of his heredity and environment, and these concepts have been dominant as character motivations and drives.

A final reason for the action or actions of characters in a drama is the action of the plot itself. Quite often a character's action is prompted by the action of another character. For example, the protagonist does action A, and because of A the antagonist does B. In this case the reason for B is A, a cause-and-effect motivational explanation in which a character reacts to the actions of other characters. This is quite often a very practical method of discovering the motivational pattern of a drama.

It makes little difference which means of motivation appears in a drama (and often all types are used). What is important is that a clear, well-established, adequate motivation is available to the audience to explain the human actions of characters on stage. Thereby, the believability of characters is greatly enhanced.

A final quality for judging characters is consistency. As a general rule, the actions of characters should accord with their basic nature, as described by the dramatist. Characters in dramas should be drawn in such detail that their actions can be easily seen and judged as essentially consistent and coherent, and to an extent predictable.

Theatrical Values

It is possible, indeed quite likely, that a drama which is under consideration for production contains all the dramatic elements which constitute a piece of good dramatic literature and yet, when produced, will fail as good theatre. The reason for such failure might not be an inadequate production staff but, rather, the fact that the drama does not have high value as a piece of theatre.

In addition to measuring up to the criteria of good dramatic literature, a play also must measure up to the high standards of the theatre. This involves being playable to a specific audience, and being well suited to such production elements as those in "spectacle," which includes movement, pace, scenery, lighting, costumes, and sound.

The Audience. Plays are produced for the benefit of an audience—to entertain. The wise theatre director and producer will know not only the dramatic literature but his potential audience as well. *Oedipus Rex* or Racine's *Phaedra* might be great pieces of dramatic and theatrical literature, but they might fail as theatre in Podunk Junction if the audience is unable to grasp and appreciate their thematic and emotional content. And if such is the case, the audience must not be blamed, for it is the responsibility of the director and the producer to select dramas which will suit the general intellectual level of the audience.

The appeal of any play will vary from audience to audience and from community to community. In order to know what a given community will accept as theatrical entertainment, the following suggestions are given.

1. Obtain a list of all the plays done in the community by other theatrical groups (both professional and non-professional) during the preceding five or six years for determining the type of plays to which the community has been exposed. An analysis of the attendance figures for each of those plays might give the prospective director and producer a good idea of the type of plays the audience accepts.

2. Investigate the other forms of cultural activity available to the community. Does the school or town have a concert orchestra? Are the concerts well attended? Is there a symphony orchestra? Are there art shows? Is there a well-used art or cultural center? Do any movie theatres show quality films on a regular schedule? Answers to these types of questions and knowledge of the attendance at these events should help form a picture of the potential audience.

3. Discover the mores, prejudices, beliefs, and religious tone of the school and town. Although such deep, personal beliefs and attitudes are sometimes very difficult to assess without a concerted, deliberate, long-term effort, it is possible to make meaningful initial judgments in this area by seeking out and talking with neighbors, administrators, and various members of the community, by reading the school catalogue, paper, and literary magazine, and from the community newspapers and chamber of commerce publications.

The audience is important; indeed, it is the sole reason why dramas are produced. The better your knowledge of the particular audience, the better your chance of success in selecting a drama which will appeal and entertain.

Spectacle. Good plays lend themselves to all the advantages of production which contemporary theatre technology can produce. The plays that are selected for production, in addition to being good dramatic literature, should make full advantage of scenery, color, lighting, costumes, movement, and sound. To be truly theatrical, productions should have visual and aural excitement and action. Because people go to "see" a play, the play should project itself—characters, plot, empathy, and emotion—over the footlights and into the audience. It should invite empathy, and should have sufficient action, excitement, and suspense to make the audience vicarious participants in the flow of dramatic action. If the audience does not become involved in the excitement, the lines, the fate of the characters, or the suspense, it will not "care about" the play. Emotional involvement in the theatrical spectacle of staged events is the meaning of "good" theatre.

Practical Problems

In addition to the inherent dramatic and theatrical values of a script, numerous practical considerations are often more important in determining the plays that should be produced. These include the evaluation of (1) available talent, (2) physical facilities, (3) cost, and (4) a play's personal challenge.

Cast. "You can't win the race if you haven't got the horses." And in a sense, this is also true of theatre productions; it is very difficult for a production to rise above the limitations of its acting talent. One of the practical problems of play selection, then, resides in the questions Can the play be cast? Are the roles too difficult for the quality of the available talent? Is the cast too large for the number of students who might normally be expected to audition? Will the play encourage maximum participation?

Before a play is selected, a director must be reasonably certain that the demands of the roles can be met with the available acting talent. It would be sheer folly to select *Oedipus Rex* or *Macbeth* if suitable actors are not available, in the hope that someone will happen along for tryouts who could play the lead roles. Nine out of ten times it will not happen, and it would be better not to do either of these plays than to do them without the proper depth of talent. This does not imply that roles must necessarily be "precast" months or a year in advance; it means simply that, for plays in which the major roles are so important and difficult, the director should have people in mind whom—if no one else satisfactorily auditions—he can fall back upon.

Physical Facilities. When a director or theatre manager asks whether a drama under consideration can be staged, he is asking whether the stage can accommodate the theatrical and spacial demands of the script and whether the physical equipment and technical facilities are adequate.

In determining the adequacy of the stage, a director must consider (1) the size of the cast, (2) the number of necessary set changes which can be accomplished in the available wing space and fly area, and (3) the proscenium height (if a realistic interior with more than one story is required).

Some scripts demand particular physical facilities and technical equipment, such as traps, projections, simultaneous sets, full box sets with ceilings, or large staircases. An analysis of these problems, and the special effects a play might require, before the selection is made will substantially reduce production headaches.

Along with the proper physical facilities, a theatre needs the proper manpower to work on the production and the technical problems, and adequate time. Careful analysis of the time available for construction and the labor required to build the setting should also be undertaken at this time.

Cost. Another practical consideration in the selection of a play is the cost required to produce it. The areas of play production in which the cost is highest are (1) royalties, (2) costumes, and (3) scenery.

In general, royalty payment in amateur theatre is determined by the popularity of the drama and the amount of revenue the copyright holder can reasonably expect the theatre to receive. Thus the more popular "in demand" dramas require higher royalty payments than less popular or more obscure plays. Recent Broadway musicals and plays by major contemporary dramatists, for example, are quite costly. But copyright protection on a drama expires in fifty-six years, and thus plays which were written over fifty-six years ago can be done without the payment of royalty. Before a play is selected, the royalty for the total run of the production should be known. (A more detailed discussion of royalties is included in chapter 5.)

Period plays, which require the actors to wear clothing other than contemporary dress, are more expensive than present-day plays. Costumes are both expensive to rent and expensive to make. In general, however, a theatre is better off if it can make its own costumes and, after the production, put them in its costume collection for possible use in succeeding productions. Rented costumes must be returned, and a theatre has no tangible asset for the expense (costume rentals vary from $20 to $30 per costume, depending upon their style and the length of time for which the theatre rents them). Thus, while a production of *Hamlet* would not pay royalties, rented costumes would make it an expensive production. The rental of costumes for *Hamlet* in a recent production at Bradley University ran slightly over $1,100. (A full discussion of costume costs and estimates is also included in chapter 5.)

Another major production expense occurs in the area of setting, including props, lighting, sound, and the physical settings. In general, dramas which demand realistic treatment (box set, detailed props, and furniture) and musicals with a number of sets are more expensive than dramas which can be produced without scenery or in front of curtains and drapes with space staging or against borders and legs. (A full discussion of budget problems in technical production is included in chapter 5.)

Personal Challenge. A great deal of time, energy, emotional involvement, sacrifice, and plain hard work go into the production of a play in educational theatre, and students and director alike give up many hours of their time. Since the very activity of play production has certain educational implications for the students who participate, it is important that all of this time and effort is not wasted on a vehicle which offers them no intellectual, artistic, or creative challenge. And if a director is to demand so great an amount of time and energy from the students and production crews, one of the results ought to be the personal growth of the students.

What better way is there to come to grips, intellectually and emotionally, with a great piece of dramatic literature than to work for five weeks, six days a week, and three to four hours each day preparing it for production? There is no substitute for this type of detailed study and analysis of a script. Any English class cannot begin to approach the in-depth appreciation and knowledge one gets of a play when he rehearses and produces it. Therefore all of this time ought to be spent in learning something significant—something worth learning.

In addition, there should be a certain challenge for the cast in the roles in the play. One of the benefits of working as a cast member is the opportunity it provides for creative and personal self-expression. If, in an inferior drama, there are no creative, personal challenges, this very important value of educational theatre cannot be attained.

Finally, because one of the functions of educational theatre is to raise the general public's level of taste, appreciation, and standards in dramatic literature, the dramas selected for production should also offer an intellectual, emotional, and aesthetic challenge to the audience. This, of course, does not mean that every play must be over the heads of the audience but, rather, that if a person gives up one of his evenings and a dollar or two for the theatre, it ought to be worth that time and money. Thus there is a corollary responsibility not to waste an audience's time and money on an unchallenging and unentertaining piece of material.

SUMMARY OF CRITERIA FOR SELECTING A PLAY

In summarizing the dramatic and theatrical values of a drama being considered for production, the following questions should serve as guides.

1. Does it have conflict?
   a. Is that conflict well defined?
   b. Is it an exciting conflict?
   c. Is it meaningful?
   d. Is the conflict portrayed in terms of a strong protagonist and antagonist?

2. What is the theme of the play?
   a. Is it meaningful, significant, and worthwhile?
   b. Is the theme clear?
   c. Does it have emotional content?

3. Does the play have sufficient dramatic action?
   a. Does the play progress or move forward?
   b. Are there interesting changes in the dramatic situation?
   c. Does the nature of the relationships between characters change?
   d. Are those changes exciting, suspenseful, theatrical?
   e. Does the progression build to climaxes?
   f. Are the incidents which produce the dramatic action logical and believable?

4. Are the characters clearly developed and described?
   a. Are they well motivated and believable?
   b. Can the audience empathize with them and care about

their fate?

c. Are they consistent?
d. Do they seem real?
e. Are they unique or colorful?
f. Will they be remembered?

5. Is the play theatrical?
   a. Does it take advantage of all the elements of the the- including color, sound, movement, spectacle, and the theatre environment?
   b. Is it visual?

6. Will the play "fit" the audience?
   a. Is it timely?
   b. Is it similar to other plays to which this audience has been exposed?
   c. If the play contains moral, religious, or political ideas, will the audience accept them?
   d. Are the language and ideas in "good taste" for this particular audience?
   e. Will it "involve" the audience?

In assessing some of the practical problems involved in the production of a script, the following questions should prove helpful.

1. Can the play be cast?
   a. Is the proper level of talent available for the lead roles?
   b. Are there enough roles for the talent which will audition?
   c. Will the play encourage maximum participation?
   d. Are the male and female roles distributed more or less according to school population?

2. Can the play be staged?
   a. Is the stage adequate for the size of the cast?
   b. Can the stage house the required number of sets and set changes?
   c. Does the stage aesthetically "fit" the sets and the play?
   d. Is there adequate time to rehearse the play and construct the sets?
   e. Is there an adequate technical staff?

3. Can the production costs be met?
   a. How much is the royalty, and is the play available for production in your school?
   b. How much will the costumes cost?
   c. What are the cost requirements for set construction, lighting, props?

4. Is the play challenging?
   a. Does it challenge the actors?
   b. Does it challenge the director?
   c. Will it challenge the audience?

In general, all of these questions revolve around four criteria: (1) Is it a good drama? (2) Is it theatrical? (3) Can it be done in this theatre at this time? (4) Is it worthwhile spending five weeks of work on? If the answers are yes, go ahead!

SELECTING A SEASON OF PLAYS

Most educational theatre programs offer more than one play during the academic year, from September through May. In addition, the vast majority offer these plays as a package, for which the audience can purchase a season ticket (usually at a reduction in price over the cost of purchasing a ticket for each play).

There are many advantages to offering this type of "package season" at the start of the year. First, by selling all the shows in advance, the theatre is provided with operating income early in the year. Second, it assures a rather general basic attendance figure for the plays. Third, it provides the patrons a well-rounded theatre diet—exposure to diverse types and styles of drama. Fourth, it helps instill the theatre-going habit in the patrons. And fifth, by purchasing a season ticket the patron usually sees plays he might not have seen if he had purchased tickets on an individual basis.

Adoption of a seasonal plan makes the problem of selecting plays more complicated or complex than the selection of a single play. Each selection must be analyzed and must be seen not only as an entity in itself but also in terms of the package, so that the prospective theatregoer, contemplating the purchase of a season ticket, will have the inducement of a well-balanced variety.

Seasonal Variety

In attempting to give the audience a variety of plays in the seasonal package, the director or theatre manager has very wide latitude in the various categories from which he can make his selections. Wise use of these categories should enable any theatre to present an appealing season for all tastes and interests. (Again, one of the functions of educational theatre is to give audiences a broad look at world drama.) Some of the categories from which a variety of plays might be chosen can be denoted by type, style, period, setting, and cast.

Types of Plays. The conventional type-divisions of plays are tragedy, comedy, melodrama, and farce. Tragedies and melodramas are essentially serious—plays in which the dramatist views his subject matter, the conflict, and resulting complications as serious. Comedies and farces are essentially non-serious; that is, the dramatist views his subject matter, conflict, and resulting complications as funny, amusing, or frivolous.

Musical comedy has recently become an important type of drama, and must also be considered in selecting a season's plays. Vast numbers of people would rather see a musical comedy than almost any other type of play. The popularity of the musical in the American theatre during the last quarter of the century attests to the desire of audiences to be lightly entertained.

Some of the popular tragedies are *Oedipus Rex, Macbeth, Death of a Salesman,* and *Mary Stuart.* Some examples of good melodramas are *No Place to Be Somebody, The Visit, Who's Afraid of Virginia Woolf?, Child's Play,* and *All the Way Home. The Odd Couple, The Would-Be Gentleman, Ah! Wilderness, The Skin of Our Teeth,* and *School for Scandal* are comedies, while *Charlie's Aunt, The Bedbug,* and *The Importance of Being Earnest* are farces. A well-balanced season should contain a good variety of these different types of plays.

Style of Plays. Style, in general, is a characteristic or distinctive manner of selecting, arranging, distorting, and emphasizing the materials and surface elements of dramatic construction. Specifically, style can be directly related to a dramatist's treatment of plot, characters, language, etc. The selection, pattern of arrangement, and emphasis and distortion a dramatist employs in his treatment of the elements of drama constitute the style of a play. (See figures 1-1 and 1-2 for the relationship between the artist's work and the art object.)

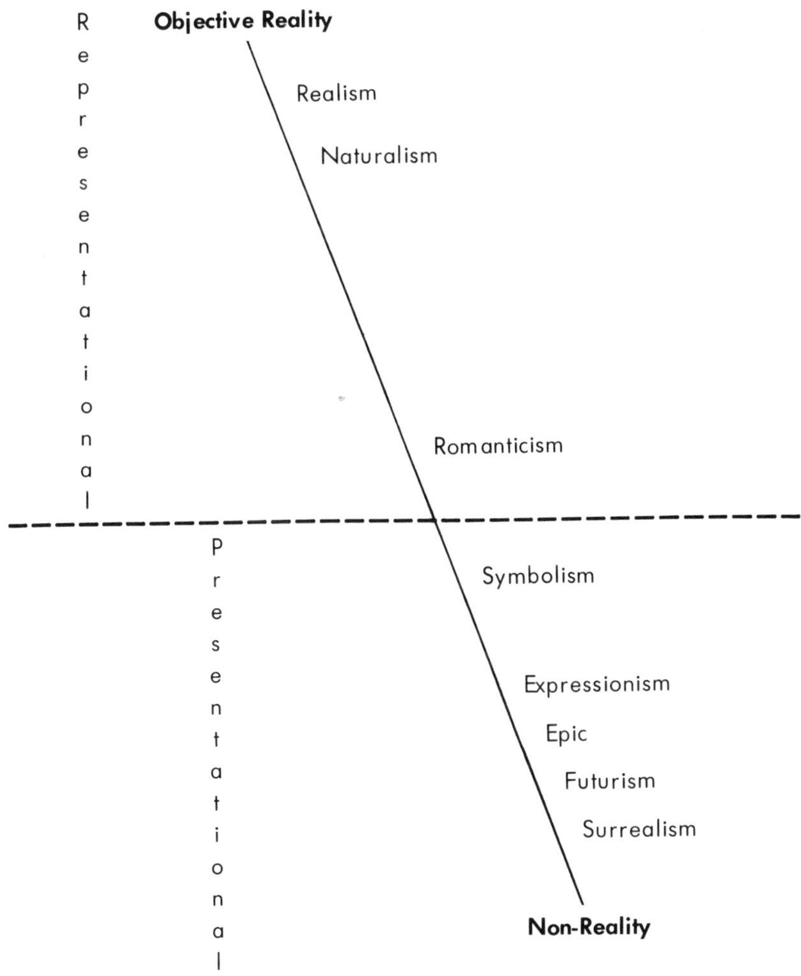

Figure 4-1. Theatrical Styles and Their Relationship to Reality

A general way of classifying style in drama is in terms of the so-called generic styles, by a drama's "illusionistic" or "non-illusionistic" manner of presentation. Because of the particular treatment of elements of drama taken from objective reality, the resultant play can be seen as tending toward or away from the presentation of an illusion of reality. All styles can be seen, then, as approaching either reality or non-reality (complete abstraction), as in figures 4-1 and 4-2.

1. Representational Styles
   - A. Representational Dramatic Styles
     1. Realism
     2. Naturalism
     3. Romanticism
   - B. Representational Production Styles
     1. Realism
     2. Selective realism (suggestive realism)
     3. Impressionism
     4. Naturalism
     5. Romanticism
2. Presentational Styles
   - A. Presentational Dramatic Styles
     1. Symbolism
     2. Expressionism
     3. Epic
     4. Futurism
     5. Surrealism
   - B. Presentational Production Styles
     1. Symbolism
     2. Expressionism
     3. Epic
     4. Surrealism
     5. Constructivism
     6. Cubism

Figure 4-2. List of Representational and Presentational Dramatic and Production Styles

The illusionistic mode of drama is sometimes referred to as the "representational" style, in which a play is presented in the same manner and sequence as actual life. Illusionistic plays and production techniques aim at representing normal, everyday human experience in recognizable and natural settings, with the characters speaking in ordinary-sounding conversation.

The non-illusionistic mode is also called the "presentational" or "theatricalistic" style of drama, in which the aim is to project the play's content, frankly and directly, to the audience. Non-illusionistic plays have little conformity to the way people behave and talk in real life. Theatricalism, the non-illusionistic tendency in production, attempts to make the audience clearly aware that it is witnessing a play and not an excerpt from real life. The ideal of theatricalistic drama production is experience that is free from all pretense of reproducing reality.

In summary, the two general stylistic trends in drama are toward, and away from, illusion. Plays are generally classified as typifying one of these tendencies, and hence the generic styles of representationalism (illusionism) and presentationalism (non-illusionism or theatricalism). Figure 4-2 lists specific styles as either representational or presentational.

The following list of plays, classified by style, might serve as a guide in selecting plays with a view toward finding variety in style.

Realistic Plays
- Ibsen's *Ghosts, An Enemy of the People, A Doll's House*
- Williams' *The Glass Menagerie*
- Howard's *They Knew What They Wanted*

Naturalistic Plays
- Gorki's *The Lower Depths*
- Strindberg's *Miss Julie*
- Rice's *Street Scene*

Romantic Plays
- Hugo's *Hernani*
- Synge's *Playboy of the Western World*
- Schiller's *Mary Stuart*

Symbolistic Plays
- Maeterlinck's *Pelleas and Mellisande*
- Hauptman's *The Sunken Bell*
- Sherwood's *The Petrified Forest*

Expressionistic Plays
- Toller's *Man and the Masses*
- Rice's *The Adding Machine*

Strindberg's *The Dream Play*

Epic Plays
Brecht's *Galileo*
Weiss's *Marat/Sade*

Period Plays. Variety in a season's program can also be obtained by selecting plays which represent the great diversity of historic periods of dramatic literature. In other words, contemporary dramas are not the only dramas which can be successfully produced for contemporary audiences. The vast heritage of great Western drama, from the Greeks to the present time, is still capable of moving audiences to tears and laughter.

Educational theatre directors and managers, aware of their special obligation of preserving the literary and dramatic heritage of the Western world in living, theatrical form, should pay special attention to the period from which each play is selected. The major dramatic periods from which a variety of selections is possible are the (1) classic Greek, (2) Roman comedy, (3) medieval, (4) Italian renaissance, (5) Elizabethan and Jacobean, (6) Restoration and eighteenth-century England, (7) Spanish golden age, (8) French seventeenth century, (9) German and French romantic, and (10) modern.

Settings and Costumes. In addition to all the types of drama which are available to a director or theatre manager, production and staging techniques should also be considered in evaluating the variety of offerings for a season. An entire season of plays produced with box sets provides neither the audience nor the student participants a proper perspective of theatre production techniques, whereas a full range of staging methods will enhance a season from both an audience and a participant point of view.

In addition to considering staging methods, it is also wise to provide variety in costumes. All plays, of course, should not be done in costume, nor should all be done in contemporary dress. Practically, the theatre staff can be expected to make and/or supervise the acquisition of costumes on a limited basis, and therefore a variety of costume shows is desirable.

After checking the season repertory for variety in type, style, and period of drama, the director or theatre manager should look at the staging of each play and its scenic requirements. Box sets, drop and wing sets, multiple staging, formalistic sets, space stages, revolving sets, platform stages, and thrust and proscenium stages are some of the variations which can create a meaningful technical and design production program for a season of plays.

Cast. Finally, in building a varied season the size and composition of the cast should not be overlooked. A judicious mixture of small-cast shows (ten to twelve actors) and large-cast shows (over fifteen) and male- and female-dominant shows is always desirable. Even though the vast majority of plays are written for male leads, it is possible to select at least one play every season in which the school's female talent can be featured. And from a practical point of view, it is easier to cast a large-cast show if it directly follows a small-cast show, and easier to cast a predominately male show right after a female-dominated show.

SUMMARY (A)

If in the selection of a season of plays there is a variety in (1) the type of plays, (2) the style of plays, (3) the periods of dramatic literature, (4) the type of staging and costumes, and (5) the size and makeup of the casts, a theatre manager can be certain he is offering the public "something for every taste" and is fulfilling the obligation of an educational theatre to provide the audience the best in all kinds of dramatic literature and theatre.

During the last four years at Bradley University, plays have been produced from the classic, Elizabethan, seventeenth-century, eighteenth-century, early nineteenth-century, and contemporary periods; from Greece, England, France, Germany, Sweden, Italy, Czechoslovakia, and America; and by such authors as Sophocles, Aristophanes, Shakespeare, Molière, Strindberg, Schiller, Capek, Giraudoux, Ionesco, Weiss, Albee, Simon, and Beckett. Any student who participated in the University Theatre programs during those four years of college life experienced almost every type of good theatre.

Balance in a Season

In attempting to provide a balanced season, the theatre director tries to weigh the values of each selection so that the end result is a season with proportion and harmony. This assumes that there is variety among the selections and that the variety of selections can be arranged into a pleasing package.

For example, seasonal balance can be achieved if a serious play is followed by a comedy, a costume play by a modern-dress play, a large-cast show by a small-cast show, or a drop and wing set by a box set. In other words, each play is "balanced" by the one which follows it. *Marat/Sade*, for example, should not follow *Hamlet*, but it might follow *The Odd Couple, Oh Dad, Poor Dad,* or *Luv*. In the same sense, *The Odd Couple* should not follow *Luv* or *A Majority of One*.

In addition, an educational theatre would usually select a large-cast show for its opening production. The first play of a new academic year normally attracts the largest, most enthusiastic group of students for auditions, and it is a good idea to involve as many of those students (many of whom are showing interest in the theatre for the first time) as possible. In that way there is not a large number of disappointed students, and a good working group can be established for the season. Besides, a large-cast show is usually rather spectacular and theatrical, which is a good way to start the season—with a bang!

If the first show is a large-cast modern comedy (*The Madwoman of Chaillot*), it might be a good idea to select a small-cast serious play for the second slot. And since *Madwoman* is a costume show, the second one ought to be in contemporary dress (*Who's Afraid of Virginia Woolf?*). The third show might be a classic—a comedy or serious play (*Mary Stuart*). A musical comedy might close the season (*A Funny Thing Happened on the Way to the Forum*). If such a season were analyzed according to balance, it would reveal the following: (1) a large-cast French comedy of the early twentieth century, with costumes and romantic or fantasy staging; (2) a small-cast, serious, contemporary American play in modern dress, with box set; (3) a small-cast, non-royalty nineteenth-century German tragedy in period costume, with multiple staging; and (4) a large-cast American musical comedy in Roman costume, with a unit set. Variety and balance!

Although a perfectly balanced season is probably impossible, the theatre director who is genuinely interested in attracting and holding a theatre-going public can, through hard work and thought, arrive at an attractive package which will please almost all tastes. It's well worth the trouble!

Selecting the Dates

An educational theatre has special problems in selecting the dates for its productions—problems that are not normally faced by the managers of professional and/or community theatres. These problems include (1) the opening and closing dates of the academic year, (2) school vacations and holidays, (3) athletic programs, and (4) special events, such as homecoming, Greek Week, Dads' Day, lecture-concert series, proms, formals, convocations, guest speakers, etc.

Problems. The first task in scheduling a season is to obtain from the school administration the official opening and closing dates of the academic year and the dates for the Thanksgiving, Christmas, and Easter vacations and other holidays. In planning the schedule, the director must allow sufficient rehearsal and set construction time prior to each play, as well as a sufficient period prior to tryouts, to allow the students to read the plays and become familiar with the roles. It should be remembered that during the Thanksgiving, Christmas, and Easter breaks there can be no rehearsals or set construction activity, since most high schools close down during vacations and don't permit school activities during those times. In colleges it is very difficult to rehearse when so many students leave campus. Also, the actors can become quite stale if they go for a week or so without rehearsals. Therefore, it is not a good idea to schedule a play whose rehearsal and performance will be interrupted by a long break.

Similarly, it is advisable to meet with the athletic director to discover when home basketball and football games are scheduled. An educational theatre director must be aware that interschool athletic schedules are set far in advance, in many cases as much as five years, and that these schedules are not planned around the theatre. The theatre almost always comes second to athletic programs and schedules. If a school is small, with a small potential audience, it is unwise (even if allowed) to have the theatre compete with a basketball or football game.

Finally, the dates of all the special events that have been scheduled during the school year should be obtained from the administration.

If possible, the theatre should try to avoid conflicts with these events; however, it might be possible to plan a theatre production as a *part* of these events. A play, for example, can be one of the activities included in Homecoming Day, Dads' Day, Greek Week, or Religious Emphasis Week. It would be well to confer with the proper school officials and discuss the advantages (and disadvantages) of combining a theatre production with a larger activity or event.

After recording all holidays and special events on a calendar, the director is ready to try to schedule his season of plays. Some day, perhaps, schools will wait until the theatre has decided upon its schedule before scheduling football and basketball games, lectures, etc., but until that time (in a distant century) the educational theatre director had better be aware that his program does not come first. His problems of set construction, rehearsals, and performance dates have very low priority in the academic calendar.

Special Play Selection Techniques

In addition to the play-selection factors discussed above, there are a number of other reasons for selecting a play or a seasonal package of plays. First, it is sometimes possible to select a play to coincide with a holiday, school event, or particular season. *The Lion in Winter*, *Everyman,* or *The Messiah*, for example, might be apropos during December, and *Between Two Thieves* and *Thor, with Angels* might be appropriate during Lent or around Easter.

Second, while one of the important factors in selecting a season of plays is variety, a theatre might violate that principle in order to present a season of plays that have a common basis—the same style, type, period, country of origin, or thematic content. A full season of American plays, or European non-realistic plays, or of plays with racial, political, or social or religious themes, or of plays by French or Russian authors might provide an interesting and educational theatre season.

Third, a play might be selected for a special campus or community minority group—blacks, Jews, or Catholics. Also, a play that dramatizes the problems or accomplishments of a nationality or profession might involve special groups of students in a worthwhile educational and artistic project.

Finally, whatever the selections or package, the theatre must "sell" the season. A package of four or five obscure plays, no matter how dramatically and educationally worthwhile, usually will not sell. The wise educational theatre director and manager will look for at least one "hit" show, which because of its reputation or popularity will so strongly attract patrons that they will be persuaded to "buy" the whole season. The theatre does not have to be overly commercial, but it must, through the selection of its products, attract an audience.

SUMMARY (B)

After all the plays and tryout and production dates have been selected, the following questions should serve as guidelines in checking the overall quality and "practicality" of the season.

1. Is there variety in the season?
   a. In the types of plays?
   b. In the styles of plays?
   c. In the periods represented?
   d. In the settings and costumes?
   e. In the casts?
2. Is there balance in the season?
3. Is there enough time to rehearse the plays?
4. Are rehearsal periods free of vacation breaks?
5. Do the production dates conflict with other campus activities or events?
6. Is there one "hit" show which will help sell the season?

5 The Budget: Income and Expenses

"I'm an artist—a creative artist. I can't be tied down to the minutiae of facts, figures, addition, subtraction, keeping records, and all that."

"I have classes to teach and plays to direct. Leave the bookkeeping to an accountant, not a theatre director."

How many times I have heard these sentiments expressed—and sometimes even from my best friends. However praiseworthy it might be to be an artist of the theatre, unencumbered by the everyday, practical details of business and economics, the fact remains that—in a sense—the theatre *is* a business. No one can deny that the professional, commercial theatre must operate in a businesslike manner, and few will deny that most amateur community theatres must not only devote time and energy to the artistic aspects of production but must also attend to the commercial aspects with equal vigor. In the same way, but on a smaller scale, educational theatres must also spend time, energy, and devotion on the commercial aspects of production. Materials must be purchased, tickets must be sold, money collected and deposited, records kept, and a budget prepared and adhered to.

THE BUDGET

Simply put, a budget is a financial statement of the estimated income and expenses for a given period of time and in three general categories: (1) the income the theatre anticipates it will receive and the sources of that income, (2) an estimate of the amount of money it anticipates it will spend and specifically how it will be spent, and (3) the specific periods of time for which the estimates are made.

Most individuals and families, and all businesses, prepare and keep budgets. For the family, this involves preparing a monthly allocation of family income to family expenses. In other words, the head of the family usually knows how much money he will make during the month, and then he attempts to plan how the family should spend that money. Then, during the budget period, the family spends its income according to the allocations in the budget. Thus the budget can be looked at as the starting point of a plan, a forecast for a certain course of action. After its approval or acceptance, a budget becomes a guide, a method to be followed in economic activities.

Purposes

The reason why the head of a family decides to prepare and follow a budget is that he wants to keep his family economically solvent; he must satisfy its needs with the means available to him. He must, therefore, know the limits of his means, together with the family's needs. He then attempts to balance these two: to spend only what is available and yet satisfy, as best he can, all the needs of the family. In short, he can direct his family's economic activities best—in an intelligent, responsible manner—if he (1) realistically plans ahead and (2) sticks to those plans.

The educational theatre manager also operates his theatre's economic activities in an intelligent, fiscally responsible manner, consistent with the sound financial management of the school, if he—like the family breadwinner—realistically plans ahead and then sticks to those plans. The basic purpose in preparing and following a budget is to operate the theatre in a fiscally responsible manner, which is also consistent with all good educational management and administrative responsibilities, because every educational institution operates on a budget. The financial officer plans a school's expenses in advance, and during the school year he follows those plans.

The financial officer of the school makes his expense allocations on the information and instructions he receives during the planning stage from department heads and all those who expect to spend school funds—from estimates of their needs. With all these figures on hand and a knowledge of the total amount of money that is or will be available, the financial officer allocates to each department, operation, and activity a certain amount of money which can be spent during the academic year. Sometimes the allocations are equal to the original estimates of needs; most often, however, due to limited available funds, the final allocations are somewhat less than the original requests. Thus academic departments usually have less money to spend than they need. And thus if the school administration is to allocate funds to the theatre responsibly, it must have reliable estimates of the theatre's income, costs, and expenses. The preparation of a theatre budget is therefore necessary, if only for administrative reasons.

Types of Budgets

The father who sits down to estimate his family's income for the coming month and to formulate a plan for spending that income tries to make family expenses (including the amount allocated for savings) equal the family income. He is attempting, therefore, to devise a *balanced* budget—one in which expenses do not exceed income. If his budget shows that his expenses will exceed his income, it is an *unbalanced* budget. Thus a balanced budget is one in which total income and expenses are equal; an unbalanced budget is one in which total expenses are higher than the total income.

Budget Policy

The goal of all who plan budgets is to make them balance—to make expenses equal to income. It is expected that families and businesses, and professional and community theatres as well, will operate on a balanced budget. Only in this way can they remain fiscally solvent. However, it is not reasonable to expect educational theatres to operate on a completely balanced budget. Their expenses will always exceed their income when the former includes such major items as the salaries of directors, designers and technical staff, auditorium expenses, utilities and supplies, and production expenses, including capital equipment. Unless ticket prices are literally astronomical—way beyond the reach of the average student—schools should therefore be expected to subsidize a certain percentage of the overall cost of operating an educational theatre production and instructional program.

The major areas in which schools subsidize the theatre are instructional services. This includes the salaries for the professional education staff and the physical facilities of the auditorium, scenery shop, rehearsal space, utilities, and major capital equipment items. All of these items can be regarded as part of the instructional, educational functions of the school, and thus the cost of maintaining them should be borne by the school.

In addition, however, other expenses are incurred by the theatre in the production of a season of plays. Since an educational theatre has an "independent" income and can, through personal initiative, present a quality production program, the implementation of the aims and goals of educational theatre, together with the teaching of good theatre production, increases the income potential of the theatre.

It is reasonable, therefore, to expect an educational theatre to pay a share of its production expenses. This share should include all the usual production expenses, as well as a small portion of the capital equipment—although for the vast majority of small high school theatres the inclusion of capital equipment is not possible. In most colleges and universities, however, which have at least 5,000 students enrolled, the inclusion of a small portion of the capital equipment expenses within the theatre budget might be reasonable. In larger schools of over 10,000 enrollment, a balanced budget might include all capital equipment.

At least two advantages accrue to an educational theatre from operating a production schedule on a balanced budget. First, it provides an incentive for the staff and the students to work for the growth of the theatre in terms of audience potential. If it is true that quality theatre—good entertainment—attracts an audience, the incentive to attract larger audiences and thereby spread the influence of living theatre to more and more people should help produce quality theatre.

Second, it is just good theatre education to train future theatre practitioners to work for financial responsibility and independence in theatre. With less and less money available to the arts in both the schools and the community, those who are being trained in arts management (professional, community, or educational) should have a firm grasp of basic economic and financial responsibility.

Thus the budget policy for educational theatres should be to follow a balanced budget—to pay, through earned income, all usual production expenses and, depending upon the size of the school, some or all of the capital equipment. Keeping this policy in mind as a goal should strengthen the aims and standards of the educational theatre.

Income

In the preparation of the preliminary budget, the first step is to estimate the potential earned income for the season, for which there are seven potential sources: (1) season subscriptions, (2) individual admissions, (3) group-rate admissions, (4) concessions, (5) rentals, (6) program advertising, and (7) gifts and contributions.

Season Subscriptions. The advantages of an educational theatre's having some type of season subscription plan have been touched upon in chapter 4, and, in general, such a plan allows a person to purchase admission to an entire season of plays at a price which is normally substantially less than the cost of purchasing a ticket for each play in the season. (The various types of season subscription plans available to educational theatres will be discussed in detail in chapter 7.) In order to arrive at an estimate of how many season subscriptions a theatre can sell, and therefore what income can be expected from this source, it is best to look at the records of the previous season.

First, a comparison should be made of the previous season of plays with those of the projected season. Does the proposed season offer as many popular plays as the previous one? In general, does the season appear to be as attractive or appealing to the potential audience? In attempting to answer these questions the manager should compare the seasons play by play and then as a package. If the projected season appears to be at least as attractive as the previous one, it would seem reasonable to estimate that season sales should be as good as or better than last year's.

Second, examine the individual admissions for each of last year's plays. A theatre manager should assume that if a number of persons purchased individual admissions to plays and were satisfied with the productions, a certain percentage of them will return next season to purchase the entire package. If individual admission figures were low, raising the estimate for season subscriptions for the next year is not indicated.

Third, the theatre manager should examine the overall quality of the productions during the previous year—admittedly a difficult task. Nevertheless, an objective examination of the quality of the theatre's productions, the audiences, critical reactions, and the general reputation of the theatre are important considerations in determining how many subscribers will return for more of the same next year. Very simply, the manager needs to determine how many satisfied customers he thinks the theatre has made.

Finally, the manager should consider the school and the community to determine if there will be more competition in the entertainment area next year. If there is a new theatre group in town, he can figure that some people will choose to attend that theatre over his. And if the entertainment offered by the school is greater than last year, he can figure that people's budgets will not be able to absorb all the entertainment, and therefore he might expect that his sales increase will not be commensurately larger.

If all these indicators are positive and the manager believes all indications are that this season will be as good as or better than last year, he is in a position to estimate his season subscribers. Increasing last year's figure by 10 percent should be a safe estimate.

If the theatre manager is initiating a season subscription plan in the school for the first time, he will not have as accurate records to guide him. In this case it is much more difficult to arrive at a proper estimate, but even then it is not wise to guess, to pull a number out of a hat, because the risk is too great. Instead of merely guessing, a check of the individual admission figures for the past season should be made. Taking 60 percent of the lowest attendance figure should give the manager a reasonable figure to use as an estimate of season subscribers for the first year. For example, if the school produced three plays last season and the attendance figures show that 1,050 persons saw the first one, 1,100 saw the second

CARL A. RUDISILL LIBRARY
LENOIR RHYNE COLLEGE

one, and 1,300 saw the third one, the director could reasonably estimate that next year he can sell around 700 season subscriptions. This figure may seem to be too low; however, underestimating income is always better than overestimating it.

A word or two should also be said about the practice of overselling season subscriptions. A number of theatres (educational, professional, and community) regularly sell more season subscriptions than they could accommodate if all those subscribers were to attend any one play. For example, a play that is running for five performances in a 350-seat house can accommodate only 1,750 people, and thus if the theatre has sold 2,000 season subscriptions it is oversold. The reason managers do this is because, from experience, they have noted that no more than, say, 85 percent of all season subscribers used their tickets for any given play. Thus the manager figures that even if 85 percent of his subscribers were to use their tickets for a particular play, 50 seats would still be available.

Generally it is dangerous to oversell season subscriptions, because a theatre manager who does this may eventually be caught short. The danger is reduced, however, if accurate records have been kept for several years which show the percentage of subscription attendance for various types of plays. If these records indicate that 100 percent of season subscribers have never attended even the most popular plays, the practice of overselling can be justified. A novice educational theatre manager, however, should never do this, and even experienced managers had better be prepared to add a performance for a popular show.

Individual Admissions. The second source of income for a theatre is the money received from admissions for each production. Even if a theatre has a season subscription plan, there are sure to be a number of non-subscribers who will attend one or two plays, and will therefore pay the regular single-play admission price.

In making the individual-admission estimate, the manager estimates how many persons will pay to see each individual play. The records of individual admissions to similar-type plays will be very helpful here. Figure 5-1, for example, shows hypothetical individual-admission records for two seasons and an estimated individual-admission figure for a projected season. From the figures of the last two seasons, it is obvious that musical comedies have the greatest individual appeal and that classic or period serious dramas have the least appeal. In between these two extremes are contemporary serious plays and contemporary and period comedies.

Season's Presentations Two Years Ago

	Attendance
You Can't Take It with You	457
Miss Julie	159
A Taste of Honey	484
A Funny Thing Happened on the Way to the Forum	886
Total	1,986

Season's Presentations Last Year

	Attendance
She Stoops to Conquer	412
Who's Afraid of Virginia Woolf?	588
Mary Stuart	226
Irma la Douce	821
Total	2,047

Presentations for Projected Season

	Estimated Attendance
Blues for Mister Charlie	500
The Madwoman of Chaillot	425
Antigone	200
The Skin of Our Teeth	450
Total	1,575

Figure 5-1. Individual-Admission Estimate

In relating these two seasons to the projected season, we can assume that *Blues for Mister Charlie*, a contemporary serious play, should do about as well as *A Taste of Honey*, and almost as well as *Virginia Woolf?*, a play with a "name" and built-in drawing power. *The Madwoman of Chaillot,* a modern comedy, can be compared with *You Can't Take It with You* and *She Stoops to Conquer. Antigone*, a classic serious play, will probably have roughly the same appeal as *Miss Julie* and *Mary Stuart. The Skin of Our Teeth*, the final play, is a modern comedy, and an estimate of individual admissions should be based upon the figures for *You Can't Take It with You.*

The overall individual-admission estimate for our projected season is considerably less than the comparable attendance figures in last two years because, it seems, the projected season does not contain a musical comedy, the most popular individual-admission production during the previous two seasons. It should be obvious, therefore, that (1) theatre managers should examine their projections in great detail in estimating individual-admission figures and not take the total figure, and (2) a conservative estimate is always best.

Group-Rate Admissions. A third source of income for an educational theatre is the money received from selling tickets for individual plays to groups at special reduced rates.

The primary purpose of educational theatre is not to make money but, rather, to expose quality drama and theatre production to as many people as possible. In order to accomplish this, educational theatres usually schedule plays which have not only entertainment value but also educational, cultural, and literary value. It should be incumbent on the theatre to make these plays available to other schools and to English and speech classes.

In our hypothetical seasons in figure 5-1, the theatre had a definite obligation to offer such plays as *Miss Julie*, *Mary Stuart*, *Antigone*, and *She Stoops to Conquer* to as many high school and college English students as possible. These plays are important landmarks in the development of Western dramatic literature, and are read and studied by almost all high school and college students. It is therefore a valuable experience if students see these plays in production, and to make it financially easy for students to attend these plays, it is good educational theatre policy to offer these productions to such groups at a special, reduced rate. A 50 percent reduction in price for educational groups is a reasonable figure to establish as a policy, although each theatre staff will want to discuss this matter and arrive at a decision based upon local situations. In establishing a policy the theatre staff should keep in mind the theatre has a duty to sacrifice box office receipts for the more important obligation of making educationally sound drama available to those to whom this exposure is of greatest benefit.

In addition, there are always a number of adults who form groups to attend "theatre parties." Educational theatres should also make their productions available to these groups, as well as minority ethnic and racial groups that might be interested in particular plays (such as *Blues for Mister Charlie* and *A Taste of Honey*), for a group rate. Usually the special rate offered these groups is not as advantageous as the rate offered to educational groups. The theatre manager, in formulating this policy with his theatre staff, should remember that he has a greater obligation to students and educational groups than he does to the adults in the community. Even if a theatre decides to establish a uniform group rate, the loss of income can be more than compensated for by the "good will" this policy can create. Moreover, if only 2 percent of these people become interested in the theatre and later return individually, this special effort on the part of the theatre will have accomplished an important goal of educational theatre.

An educational theatre manager, therefore, should attempt to estimate the number of special groups he can expect to attract to particular productions and should use this figure in arriving at his estimated income.

Concessions. Many theatres earn extra income by offering their audiences refreshments before the play and during intermissions and by operating a coat check. Moreover, there are several reasons why a theatre manager might want to offer these services.

First, the profit from selling snacks and soft drinks is great. Depending upon the types of drinks offered and the prices charged, the profit can run from 50 to 400 percent. Also, the cost of operating a coat check is nominal and the money taken in is almost all profit.

Second, the availability of refreshments and a coat check are truly appreciated by many members of the audience. For example, hot chocolate and coffee on bitterly cold nights can help put an audience in a much more receptive frame of mind, and a refreshing drink during intermission can improve the audience's receptivity for the next act. Offering theatregoers a place to put their coats and hats during a performance is a great convenience, especially in the winter and during snow and rain. It is extremely uncomfortable to hold a hat and coat on one's lap for two and one-half hours, and doubly so when they are wet.

It takes personnel and time, of course, to prepare and man a refreshment stand and coat check, but if enough students are available and willing to work at it, the advantages far outweigh the disadvantages. Nevertheless, if the educational theatre manager decides to offer these amenities, it would be best to do so as a service to the audience, not for the primary purpose of making money. Again, the audience should come first, not commercial interests. A maximum charge of 15 cents for a soft drink, and a 10 or 15 cent charge for a coat check will help keep audiences, not turn them away.

The policy of the educational theatre should not be to make as much money off each audience member as possible but to provide each theatregoer the best possible drama, production, and services at the most reasonable price. Again, the comfort and well-being of the audience comes first, not the commercial interests of the school theatre. Before deciding upon these services, however, the theatre manager should check with the school officials inasmuch as eating and drinking may not be allowed in certain buildings or areas.

Rentals. Theatres are always being called upon by schools and by members of the community to lend or rent theatrical material: costumes, makeup, lighting equipment, scenery, or even a full set; and thus a possible source of income is for a theatre to rent such items. Unfortunately, however, there are many more disadvantages to going into the rental business than there are advantages.

First, it can start out as a small activity—renting a costume or two for a small fee—but turn into "big business." Once a theatre starts a rental policy, it is difficult to control, short of stopping it altogether. If a theatre manager does not want to get into another time-consuming, record-keeping business, it is best not to start leasing his theatre's equipment and stock.

Second, there is always the problem of broken, damaged, and

even destroyed property, which is difficult to control. The rental fees can't come close to paying for damages to theatre property.

The best policy, therefore, is not to get into the habit of renting theatre items. Lending them only to other theatres, with the understanding that if an item is broken or destroyed the theatre that borrowed it will pay for it, is the best policy. In this way, all theatres that engage in mutual borrowing will benefit. If someone else wants to borrow equipment or stock, a firm no and a polite explanation will usually serve the theatre's best interest.

Program Advertising. Selling advertising space in a theatre program can more than pay for the cost of printing the program. However, as with concessions and rentals, the amount of time required for selling the ads, setting up the copy, designing the layout, etc., might not be worth the income received. Besides, the first business of educational theatre is to put its combined energies and talents into quality theatre productions, not commercial endeavors.

If the theatre staff decides upon a policy of seeking ads for its programs, and school officials approve it, the minimum amount of advertising space for each production's program should be calculated in advance. Knowing this, and the unit price for the smallest ad, an estimated income figure can be found.

Gifts and Contributions. Without specific advance knowledge of an impending gift or gifts to the theatre, this income category should remain blank, at least for purposes of the budget. It is dangerous to "just suppose" that some generous soul will donate money to the theatre during the coming year.

A special type of donation which some theatres (professional, community, and educational) rely upon for supplementary income is the patron list. This is a published list (usually in the first program of the season, and sometimes in each program) of persons who, because they believe in the value of the work done by the theatre and want it to continue, donate various sums of money to the theatre. Usually, in educational theatres, this sum is small: $5 or so. In some community and professional theatres, the sums may be $10, $25, $50, $100, $500, or even $1,000 for the "privilege" of being a theatre patron and benefactor. Most patrons do not receive anything from the theatre for this donation, except the satisfaction of contributing to a worthwhile artistic endeavor and the prestige of having their names on the patron list. Sometimes, however, patrons are entitled to attend a special dress-review performance and an opening night cocktail party, etc. And, it should be remembered, this donation is normally considered tax deductible.

For the educational theatre, this practice can be of significant financial benefit; it can pay for the cost of programs and part of other production expenses. However, it requires a concerted effort early in the school year as parents of the students, friends of the school, and local businesses have to be contacted. If the theatre is selling season subscriptions at the same time, there is a duplication of the persons contacted, and perhaps fewer season subscriptions, which are more important than patrons. In addition, the educational theatre manager should be aware of the fact that athletic programs and the yearbook staff are also contacting those same people to act as patrons to help pay their costs. Thus parents and local businessmen may resent too many contacts for donations, and the image of the school can suffer.

It is best if, early in the season, the educational theatre puts all its time and energy into selling season subscriptions. Attracting audiences is of more value to the theatre than the mere collection of money. Thus it is best to expend the greatest energy in the area of greatest value.

Subsidies

Another potential source of funds for educational theatre is the school subsidy, although, technically speaking, this does not fall in the category of earned income. In requesting a subsidy from the school, the theatre manager is saying that his ordinary production expenses exceed his estimated earned income.

Implicitly, however, the school already subsidizes the theatre program by providing an auditorium, utilities, rehearsal space, scene construction space, and a staff. Thus anything beyond these extraordinary items should be considered a request for a special subsidy.

A subsidy request should not be made until the estimated expense items have been computed and compared with the earned income estimate. Any excess expense over the earned income estimate is considered a subsidy. Again, it is important to stress that the budget policy of an educational theatre should be to bring earned income as close as possible to the total expense figure. If this is done, a school subsidy will not limit the potential growth of the audience.

SUMMARY (A)

The first step in the preparation of a preliminary budget is to make a conservative estimate of earned income, which includes (1) season subscriptions, (2) individual admissions, (3) group rates, (4) concessions, (5) rentals, (6) program advertising, and (7) gifts and contributions. For the educational theatre, whose special interest should be attracting and holding audiences for quality theatre productions and spreading the influence of the theatre, special attention and vigor should be spent on the first three income items, which most directly relate to the aims and purposes of educational theatre.

Another source of income for the theatre is the school subsidy, which should be minimal: only the difference between the estimated expenses and income. The educational theatre should attempt to have a balanced production budget and do without a subsidy, and the former should include all ordinary production expenses.

EXPENSES

The second step in the preparation of the preliminary budget begins with estimating expenses. The best method for arriving at an overall expense estimate is seek bids and obtain rather precise figures in the various expense categories. Thus an expense estimate does not mean guess; the estimate should be calculated, and based upon substantial research and investigation into each expense category of the theatre.

The usual theatre expense categories are (1) general operations, (2) advertising and publicity, (3) scripts and royalties, (4) capital equipment, (5) technical production, (6) salaries, and (7) theatre rental and maintenance.

General Operations

Generally included under the category of general operations are (1) season tickets, (2) reserved-seat tickets, (3) programs, (4) postage and shipping, (5) telephone and telegraph expenses, and (6) supplies. While this is not an exhaustive list, it indicates the general types of items a theatre manager should take into account in estimating the general operating expenses of his theatre.

The cost of purchasing season tickets is directly dependent upon the type of season subscription plan the theatre decides upon, as well as the printing costs. (In chapter 7, "The Box Office," the various types of subscription plans and tickets will be discussed.) After arriving at a specific plan for the theatre, the manager should obtain three bids (cost estimate quotations) from local printers or national ticket companies. He should select the lowest bid for his budget estimate, and inform the company of his acceptance. Individual-admission tickets are handled in the same manner. (Chapter 7 also contains a detailed discussion of the types of tickets available.)

If the tickets are for reserved seats, each ticket must designate a particular seat number and location, and in this case it may be more economical to have them printed by a national ticket company. If they are general admission tickets, which means that the bearers may sit in any seat in the theatre, the most economical method is to obtain three estimates from local printing firms.

The cost of programs can vary greatly, depending upon whether they are simple 8½″ by 11″ mimeographed sheets folded in half or sixteen-page multi-color programs with photographs and ads. Inexpensive program covers with theatre designs can be purchased (from Hermitage Art Company in Chicago, for example) at a cost of about $16 per thousand, and the program information can be mimeographed or printed by a local printer on the inside covers. This inexpensive type of program is not elaborate, but for a theatre which has to be economical it should be satisfactory. Specifically designed program covers for particular plays (which can be purchased from Package Publicity Service in New York) cost about $36 per thousand and $13 for each additional thousand. The front and back inside covers can then be mimeographed or printed by a local printer. Or the theatre can design its own program, for the entire season or for each play.

Whichever type the theatre decides upon and for whatever reasons, the estimated cost should be obtained from local printers. The theatre manager, of course, must tell the printer the number of programs needed for each production and the total number of productions. Again, the lowest estimate should be accepted.

Postage and shipping estimates should include the cost of all bulk mailings the theatre plans to make during the coming year. Will season brochures be sent out? Postcards? Flyers? Also, the theatre manager should estimate the shipping charges which might have to be paid for the rental of costumes and various supplies.

If the school's policy is to charge each department and activity for long-distance telephone calls and telegrams, these charges also should be estimated for budget purposes. Sometimes long-distance calls must be made to secure production rights, to order material, or to check on overdue orders.

There is a vast number of miscellaneous operating supplies which every academic department and theatre must purchase each year, ranging from paper and envelopes to box office forms, scrapbooks, and rehearsal materials. Such items constitute the final estimate in the general operations category.

Advertising and Publicity

The expense items usually included in the category of advertising and publicity are (1) brochures and flyers; (2) newspapers, radio, and television; (3) posters and displays; (4) photography; and (5) miscellaneous.

The season brochure, which lists all the plays to be produced during the season, is normally a costly item if it is printed and meant to be impressive. In addition, many theatre managers print up inexpensive flyers or "throwaways" for each show. If the manager anticipates using these methods to advertise the season and the individual plays, accurate estimates should be obtained in advance from local printers or national publicity agencies.

Another major publicity expense is paid newspaper, radio, and television advertising—although the cost of the latter makes them economically prohibitive for the average educational theatre. However, newspaper ads, especially in the local school newspaper, are feasible and should be carefully planned in advance. The theatre manager must decide upon the number and the size of each ad for each production. Knowing the per column inch rate of the newspaper in which they will be used, he can arrive at a total estimate for advertising expenses (see figure 5-2).

Posters, lobby displays, and signs are also part of the advertising and publicity category, and it is possible to determine in advance the cost of purchasing or designing and printing posters

Dates Of Plays

Blues for Mister Charlie	Oct. 27-Nov. 2
The Lion in Winter	Dec. 9-14
Irma la Douce	Mar. 16-22
Caesar and Cleopatra	May 12-17

Date of Ad	Content of Ad	Size	Col. In.	Cost
9-14	Season coupon sales	3x6"	18	$ 88.20
9-21	Season coupon sales	3x6"	18	88.20
9-28	Season coupon sales	2x5"	10	49.00
10-19	"Blues" mail orders	1x4"	4	19.60
10-26	"Blues" opens tomorrow	2x4"	8	39.20
11-30	"Lion" mail orders	1x4"	4	19.60
12-8	"Lion" opens tomorrow	2x4"	8	39.20
3-8	"Irma" mail orders	1x4"	4	19.60
3-12	"Irma" – coming	2x3"	6	29.40
3-15	"Irma" opens tomorrow	2x4"	8	39.20
5-3	"Caesar" mail orders	1x4"	4	19.60
5-11	"Caesar" opens tomorrow	2x4"	8	39.20
			100	$490.00
			+ 5%	24.50
				$514.50

Budget Estimate	$515.00

Figure 5-2. Estimate Worksheet for Season Newspaper Ad

for each show. And inasmuch as all theatres must take production and publicity pictures, their cost is included in the advertising and publicity category. The price of film, developing, and printing pictures for display, the souvenir scrapbook, newspapers, and the theatre record book can be accurately estimated by the theatre's photographer. In addition, the photographer may have several of the pictures blown up and framed for use in the theatre lobby.

Finally, a number of miscellaneous expenses are usually charged against the advertising and publicity budget. Publicity releases, tryout publicity, ad mats, art services, design materials, and novelty forms of publicity are but a few of the many small expenses the theatre manager should anticipate in rounding out his advertising and publicity estimate.

Scripts and Royalties

Prior to making a final decision on production plans for a particular play, the educational theatre manager would be wise to write to the copyright holder of the play (or his agent) to discover (1) if the play can be performed as an amateur production on the planned dates and (2) what the royalty charge will be.

The United States copyright law allows an author to copyright his work for a 28-year period and to renew the copyright for another 28-year period. Thus if the theatre staff is considering producing a play which was written less than 56 years ago, permission from the copyright holder must be obtained. Almost all dramatists register their plays with one of the several national play publishing companies which act as agents for the authors in granting production rights and collecting royalties. And thus the theatre manager must contact the publisher of the play under consideration, request production rights, and agree to royalty charges. (See the Appendix for a list of the major play publishing companies and their addresses.)

In writing to a publisher, the manager should provide the following information: (1) the name of the theatre which is considering the production, (2) the full name of the play, (3) the name of the author and/or translator, (4) the proposed production dates, (5) the total number of performances, (6) the size of the house, and (7) the admission charges. In receipt of this information, the publisher can tell the manager whether the play may be produced and what the royalty charge will be (see figure 5-3).

In addition to royalty charges, there is the expense of purchasing enough scripts so that each member of the cast has one. Some publishing companies require a theatre to purchase a certain number of scripts, others do not, but it is illegal to purchase a script and make duplicates of it for the cast. Thus the number

January 6, 1969

Tams Witmark Music Library, Inc.
757 Third Avenue
New York, New York 10017

Gentlemen:

We are considering an amateur production of **Irma la Douce** during our 1969-70 Theatre Season. We would like permission to produce this play and a royalty quotation under the following conditions:

Name of Theatre: Bradley University Theatre
Dates of Performances: March 16 through 22, 1970
Number of Performances: Seven
Size of House: 367
Price of Individual Admissions: $2.50
Season Coupon Book: Price, $5.00 for five productions
Coupon Admissions: 75 percent average for musicals

We would appreciate a copy of your contract covering this production if it is available.

Thank you in advance for your cooperation.

Sincerely,

John E. Clifford
Managing Director

Figure 5-3. Sample Letter Requesting Royalty Quotation and Permission to Produce

of scripts needed and their cost should be considered during the preparation of the preliminary budget.

And of course it is also illegal to produce a play without paying royalty fees to the author. This might not, at first glance, seem to be a great crime, but when one considers the energy, creativity, and time a dramatist has poured into his product, one realizes that to produce that play without paying royalties is nothing less than stealing the creative artifact of the dramatist. It is not legal, and it is not ethical.

If the theatre is producing a musical, scripts cannot ordinarily be purchased; the vocal scores, chorus parts, and entire orchestration must be rented. This rental fee, along with the royalty, is also part of the preliminary expense category.

A surprising number of school theatres does not allow the members of the cast to retain their scripts unless they pay the theatre for them, which seems a petty, unreasonable method of making money. Each cast member should be allowed to keep his script without paying for it; it is a fitting souvenir, and it contains many valuable notes which each has made on the production and his part. As an educational tool, the script (which normally costs only $1.25 or $1.50) is of considerable value to the student and by right should belong to him.

Capital Equipment

Whether or not a particular educational theatre requests a subsidy for its capital equipment, the items requested for the next season should be included in the total expense budget. (Capital equipment items are major pieces of equipment which can be used over and over again.) Lighting instruments, for example, are capital equipment but the lamps are not. A power saw is capital equipment but the blades are not. Legs, boarders, and a cyclorama are capital equipment, but the muslin used for constructing flats is not. A set of lenses for the theatre camera is capital equipment but the film is not. The theatre manager should obtain bids for his capital equipment needs, or ask the school purchasing agent to recommend firms.

Technical Production

Included in the category of technical production expenses are the costs for (1) building, constructing, and painting scenery; (2) renting, purchasing, or constructing properties; (3) renting or making costumes; (4) sound; (5) lighting; and (6) makeup supplies.

It is extremely difficult to make an accurate estimate of technical production expenses; in fact, this category is probably the most difficult of all to estimate. For a managing director to expect a designer or technical director to arrive at an accurate estimate of a set which has not yet been designed and for which interpretation and style production meetings have not yet taken place is close to unreasonable. Yet the manager must have an estimate of technical expenses for his budget.

After the plays have been selected, the theatre manager should request an estimate of technical expenses from the designers or technical director, or whoever is responsible for the design and construction of scenery and for the props, lights, and costumes. Usually reasonably accurate figures can be arrived at after the designer has conferred with each of the directors on the overall production style of each play. Will there be a box set? Will there be a costume problem? How many are in the cast? Will there be platforms? How many different sets are needed for each play? Are there any special technical effects envisioned? With the answers to these kinds of basic questions, and an inventory of flats, platforms, lumber, costumes, and set pieces, the designer and technical director can make a reasonable estimate of technical expenses for the season.

After the manager receives the estimated technical budget figures, he should check to make sure that the figure includes a number of miscellaneous items quite often overlooked. The technical expense figure should include replacement of lamps, repairs to sound equipment, lighting instruments and power tools, maintenance of shop equipment and materials used by production and stagecraft classes, and replacement of hardware. In addition to these and costume construction and/or rental costs, the manager should make sure that technical expenses include replacement of make-up, including base, liners, pencils, hair spray, dye, crepe hair, and special effects. Most of these items seem small and are not usually thought of when estimating the cost of constructing a set. They are, however, costly; they can throw a technical budget off by at least 10 percent.

A theatre manager should work closely with the technical personnel when estimating the technical expenses. He should also remember that this is the most difficult expense category to accurately estimate. The best a manager can do is to be certain that he and the technical director have included all possible expenses, repairs, and replacements.

Salaries

In all educational institutions the salaries of the academic theatre staff are part of the school budget and are not included in the theatre's seasonal budget. Some salary items, however, must be included in that budget estimate, depending upon the policies of the school. If the theatre has scheduled a musical and union musicians must be hired for rehearsals or performances, this expense must be considered. Also, some schools expect the theatre to pay for student help out of the theatre budget, in which case an estimate of the number of working hours for each student, along with the hourly rate of pay, must be established. Any other salary items, such as janitor services, police protection, or graduate assistants, should also be included in the estimate.

The theatre manager must therefore check with the school officials about the salary items which should be included in the theatre budget estimate. Even if the theatre is not expected to pay for these items, the school must be informed of these expenses so that they can be covered in the school's budget.

Theatre Rental and Maintenance

The final expense item is one which only a few educational theatres include in their seasonal productional budgets. Although most educational theatres are subsidized to the extent of the use of auditorium facilities and accompanying services without charge, some university theatres whose income is $30,000 or more are expected to share the auditorium/theatre expense with the school. Theatre managers should check this policy with the proper school officials.

SUMMARY (B)

The second step in the preparation of a preliminary budget (after income has been estimated) is to estimate expenses, which include (1) general operations, (2) advertising and publicity, (3) scripts and royalties, (4) capital equipment, (5) technical production, (6) salaries, and (7) theatre rental and maintenance.

Again, an estimate of theatre expenses does not mean a guess; and there is no reason why a theatre manager should not be able to estimate his actual expenses to within 3 percent. However, it takes work, time, and careful thought to get accurate expense estimates; they don't come out of the blue by intuition. Careful advance planning, having bids on hand for all future needs, and complete knowledge of the problems of play production can ensure that the first budget estimate is reasonable and accurately reflects the income potential and expenses for the coming season.

In addition, the wise theatre manager will increase the dollar estimate in each category by 5 percent. For example, if the estimate for programs is $210, he should use $220.50 as his preliminary figure. This practice should ensure his estimate against unforeseen contingencies, such as higher prices.

SUBMISSION OF THE FINAL BUDGET

If in the preparation of the preliminary budget the formula "maximum expense versus minimum income" was used, the theatre manager should be in a good position to arrive at a final budget, which is then submitted to the school administration.

After the preliminary budget is completed, the manager should carefully examine his earned income estimate and his estimated expenses (see figure 5-4). If the theatre has a balanced budget policy, the two totals should be equal (or close to it). But since, in estimating expenses, no attempt was made to keep the figures within a certain range (so that expenses would equal income), it is possible that the preliminary budget is not balanced—as is the case in figure 5-4. If this is true, the theatre manager must make a detailed analysis of his estimated expenses on the basis of priorities.

In other words, in attempting to equalize the expense and the income figures, the former must be adjusted. It would be a mistake to arbitrarily raise the earned income figure if the preliminary figure was arrived at according to the procedures recommended earlier in this chapter. Most probably, it is a reasonable

Preliminary Budget Estimate
1969/70

Income			
Coupon books (1,900)	$ 9,500		
Individual admissions	3,400		
Groups	650		
	13,500		
Expenses			
General Operations			
Coupon books	$ 350		
Tickets	365		
Programs	200		
Postage	400	2,760	14,130
Film Series	625		-13,550
Phone	70		580
Supplies	750		
Publicity			
Brochures	600		
Newspapers	1,900		
Posters	325	3,500	14,130
Photos	475		
Misc.	200		
Other			
Scripts	150	1,250	
Royalty	1,100		
Capital equipment		670	
Technical		4,000	
Costumes		1,200	
Salaries		750	

Figure 5-4. Sample Preliminary Budget

minimum-income figure, and this is what a good theatre manager uses.

In adjusting the expense figure, the theatre manager must trim or cut certain items, and to do this he must establish an order of priorities. In consultation with the rest of the theatre staff, he should review the preliminary expense figures, and the following list of questions might serve as a guide in that review. Can a less expensive type of season ticket be purchased? A less expensive type of reserved seat ticket? Can the program cost be reduced? How was the figure for general supplies arrived at? Is it realistic or could it be reduced? Would a less elaborate season brochure be possible? Can newspaper advertisements be curtailed? Can various capital equipment items be eliminated?

BRADLEY UNIVERSITY THEATRE

Revised Budget for the 1969-70 University Theatre Season

Income Prospectus

5302 – Season coupon books (1,900 @ $5.00 ea.)	$	9,500
5303 – Individual admissions (325 per play @ $1.50 ea.) (325 for musical @ $2.50 ea.)		2,800
5304 – Group rates		655
Total Estimated Income	$	12,955

Expense Prospectus

5401 – General operating	$	2,400
5402 – Advertising & publicity		2,600
5403 – Scripts & royalties		1,250
5404 – Capital equipment		670
5405 – Technical production		5,285
5406 – Salaries		750
Total Estimated Expense	$	12,955

Detailed expense breakdown is on following page.

Bradley University Theatre
July 21, 1969

/s/ John E. Clifford
Managing Director

Figure 5-5. Sample Final Budget

1969-70 University Theatre page 2

Expense Breakdown

	Item	Subtotal
General Operating		
a. Coupon books (2,000)	$ 310	
b. Tickets	370	
c. Programs	125	
d. Postage & mailing	400	
e. Film classic series	625	
f. Telephone	70	
g. Supplies	500	
		$2,400
Advertising & Publicity		
a. Brochures & flyers	$ 450	
b. Newspapers	1,125	
c. Posters & displays	325	
d. Photography	475	
e. Miscellaneous	225	
		2,600
Scripts & Royalties		
a. Royalties & score rental	$1,100	
b. Scripts	150	
		1,250
Capital Equipment		
a. Photographic equipment	$ 120	
b. Lighting instruments	550	
		670
Technical Production		
a. Setting, properties, lights, sound	$3,700	
b. Costumes & makeup	1,350	
c. Shop supplies	235	
		5,285
Salaries for Musical	$ 750	
		750

Figure 5-5. Sample Final Budget (cont.)

After reevaluating the estimated expense figure, the theatre manager should arrive at a final budget that is consistent with the policy of both the theatre and the school. Then, having come as close as possible to a balanced budget for all production expenses, he is ready to submit the budget to the school officials (see figure 5-5 for a sample budget). This budget should itemize the income and the expenses, and indicate the profit or loss. It should be sufficiently detailed that the school administration can clearly see how all the money is to be spent, all the sources of income, and how the manager arrived at these figures. The more completely these items are detailed, the less likely they are to be automatically cut.

When the budget is approved by the school administration (or modified and approved), it becomes the responsibility of the theatre manager to see that it is adhered to—that the theatre staff works to produce the estimated income and to keep expenses within the limits of the final budget. In this way the management staff and the administration can build a solid reputation for fiscal responsibility and a professional attitude toward theatre management. This is desirable not only from an economic viewpoint but also from an educational viewpoint: it is good theatre education to instill a responsible attitude toward theatre management in theatre students. Such attitudes, of course, help strengthen academic, community, and commercial American theatre.

RECORDING EARNED INCOME

For recording earned income during the season, the theatre manager should establish two income records: (1) a master income ledger and (2) an income ledger for each income category.

In keeping income records, it is advisable to label each account with a letter or number code. Selecting an arbitrarily numbered code for income and another for expenses will make it easier to record these amounts in the ledgers. Figure 5-6 shows a sample code system for income and expense categories.

Master Income Ledger

A master income ledger should be kept to record all income during the season. It should be designed so that it can include all of the following information: (1) the date income was received,

Income Categories—5300

5301	Season Subscriptions
5302	Individual Admissions
5303	Group Rates
5304	Concessions
5305	Rentals
5306	Program Advertising
5307	Gifts and Contributions
5308	Subsidies

Expense Categories—5400

5401	General Operating	
	5401-A	Season tickets
	5401-B	Reserved-seat tickets
	5401-C	Programs
	5401-D	Postage and shipping
	5401-E	Telephone and telegraph
	5401-F	Memberships
	5401-G	Film classic series
	5401-H	Supplies
5402	Advertising and Publicity	
	5402-A	Brochures and flyers
	5402-B	Newspapers, radio, and television
	5402-C	Posters and displays
	5402-D	Photography
	5402-E	Miscellaneous
5403	Scripts and Royalties	
	5403-A	Scripts and rentals
	5403-B	Royalties
5404	Capital Equipment	
5405	Technical Production	
	5405-A	Settings
	5405-B	Costumes and makeup
5406	Salaries	

Figure 5-6. Budget Categories and Code Numbers

(2) the sources of income, (3) the amounts of income, (4) total income received to date, and (5) the balance.

Figure 5-7, a sample page of a master income ledger, shows that on November 3, 1969, the theatre received $55 from season ticket sales (5301 is the code for season ticket income, as shown in figure 5-6). On November 4 the theatre received $15 from individual ticket sales. And on November 5 the theatre received $54 from individual admissions and group-rate sales (5302 stands

Date	Code	Amount		Total		Balance	
11/3/69	5301	55	00	9,425	00	3,575	00
11/4/69	5302	15	00	9,440	00	3,560	00
11/5/69	5302 & 3	54	00	9,494	00	3,506	00
11/6/69	5302 & 3	135	00	9,692	00	3,371	00
11/7/69	5302	45	00	9,674	00	3,326	00

Figure 5-7. Sample Page of Master Income Ledger

for individual admission income and 5303 for group-rate income). The total income received from all sources as of November 7 was $9,674, which left a balance of $3,326.00.

Individual Income Ledger

In addition to a master income ledger, which records the income received from all sources, it is necessary to keep ledger accounts for each income category. When income is posted to the master income ledger, it should also be posted to the specific-income ledger.

Figure 5-8 shows a sample page from an individual admission income ledger and figure 5-9 shows a sample page from a group-rate income ledger. Their entries correspond to the same time periods recorded on the master income ledger (figure 5-7). Thus it is clear that, on November 5, $45 of the $54 received that day came from individual admission ticket sales and the other $9 came from group-rate ticket sales. As of November 7, the theatre had received $234 in individual admission income, leaving a balance of $1,866 (which was based upon an estimated individual admission income of $2,100 for the season). From group rates as of November 7, the theatre had earned $24 of a total estimated group-rate income of $200.

Recording Expenses: Purchasing

In keeping records of expenses, the educational theatre manager should keep a separate ledger for each expense category in the

Date	Amount		Total		Balance	
11/4/69	15	00	15	00	2,085	00
11/5/69	45	00	60	00	2,040	00
11/6/69	120	00	180	00	1,920	00
11/7/69	45	00	225	00	1,875	00

Figure 5-8. Sample Page of Individual Admission Income Ledger

Date	Amount		Total		Balance	
11/5/69	9	00	9	00	191	00
11/6/69	15	00	24	00	176	00

Figure 5-9. Sample Page of Group-Rate Income Ledger

final budget. Each of these ledgers should record the following information for each purchase: (1) the date of purchase, (2) requisition number, (3) purchase order number, (4) amount of the purchase request, (5) total amount of purchase requests to date, (6) amount of payment, (7) total amount of payments to date, and (8) the budget balance. Figure 5-10 is an example of an expense ledger for settings.

Requisition Number. In educational theatre the manager usually does not have authority to make purchases without first obtaining permission from the school purchasing agent. In effect, then, all school purchasing is done through the school's purchasing director or the purchasing office. The reason for this is obvious: if every faculty and staff member were able to spend school funds, it would be impossible for the school administration to control expenditures. Thus, because the administration is responsible for controlling its funds, it is the only agency that can spend those funds.

			Requisitioned		Payments		
Date	Req. No.	P.O. No.	Amount	Total	Amount	Total	Balance
9/26/69	8043	36490	123 00	123 00	121 16	121 16	2,378 84
9/30	8044	36518	42 00	165 00	42 50	166 36	2,336 34
10/4	8045	36604	100 00	265 00	94 25	260 61	2,242 09
10/12	8051	36690	12 80	277 80	12 80	273 41	2,229 29
10/20	8055	37082	94 00	371 80			
10/28	8081	37109	68 00	439 80			

Figure 5-10. Sample Expense Ledger for Settings

The usual procedure in making purchases for an educational theatre is for a staff member to fill out a request for the needed materials and forward it to the theatre manager (see figure 5-11). This request should specify (1) the quantity and description of the needed items, (2) the firm from which the purchase is to be made, (3) the estimated cost, (4) the date by which the items are needed, and (5) the theatre's expense category which should be charged.

When the theatre manager receives a purchase request, he sends an official school purchase requisition to the school's purchasing director (see figure 5-12). This requisition is usually prepared in quadruplicate, and the theatre manager keeps a file copy and sends the others to the purchasing director. The theatre manager should include the following information on each requisition: (1) the complete name and address of the firm, (2) the estimated cost, (3) the date when the materials are needed, (4) a complete description of each item, including part number, model number, color, size, and quantity, and (5) any shipping and/or delivery instructions.

After the requisition is sent to the purchasing director, the purchase can be entered in the proper expense ledger and charged against one of the theatre's expense categories (see figure 5-10 for the entry of the sample requisitions in figures 5-11 and 5-12).

Bradley University Theatre

REQUISITION REQUEST

Firm Name Claus Lauterbach Lumber Co.

Firm Address Bartonville

Date Wanted 5/2 Date Requested 5/1

Charge Theatre Account Tech. Prod.

Deliver To Shop Requested By J. Ludwig

QUANTITY	ITEM	COST
4	1" x 12" x 8' pine	
16	1/4" ply sheets, 4' x 8'	$132.00

DO NOT WRITE IN THIS SPACE

Req. No. 216709 P. O. No. 114771

Sent to Pur. Off. 5/1 Rec. ______

Acct. No. 5405A By ______

Figure 5-11. Theatre Internal Purchase Request

RETAIN YELLOW COPY.
SEND REMAINDER TO-
PLANT OPERATION
OR
PURCHASING DEPT.

BRADLEY UNIVERSITY
PEORIA, ILLINOIS

REQUISITION NO. 198188

PURCHASE	DEL. FROM STORES	MAKE	REPAIR	REPLACE	WHEN NEEDED	ESTIMATED COST	DATE OF REQUISITION
X					at once	$46.00	March 27, 1970

IF PURCHASE-FIRMS RECOMMENDED:
Walters Paint Company 1624 E. Washington City 61606

QUANTITY	DESCRIPTION
10 gals.	White Paint (Stock #21406)
8	3" Paint Brushes (#16a)

CHARGE TO 72230.3 (Theatre) ORIGINATOR John E. Clifford APPROVED BY L. E. Norton
PURCHASING DEPT. USE ONLY

ORDER PLACED WITH ____ PRICE $ ____ BY ____
PURCHASE ORDER NO. ____ DELIVERY ESTIMATED ____ DUP. RET. TO DEPT. ____

PLANT OPERATING USE ONLY-

MATERIAL REQUIRED		DEBIT	$
SUPPLIER		CREDIT	$
DELIVERY DATE		DEBIT	$
MATERIAL COST	COMPLETION DATE	CREDIT	$
IF ON HAND CHECK	DUP. RET. TO DEPT.	CREDIT	$
CONTRACTOR	HOURS		

Figure 5-12. Purchase Requisition

The date of the purchase and the requisition number are entered in the proper columns. The estimated cost of the purchase and the total amount of purchases to date can also be recorded on the ledger, as orders outstanding (encumbered).

Purchase Orders. When the purchasing director receives a requisition from the theatre manager, he prepares a purchase order, an official order form for materials or services, which he sends to the firm in question (see figure 5-13). After the purchase order is sent, the purchasing director usually informs the theatre manager that the order has been executed and gives him the order number assigned to that transaction. The manager then records the number on his file copy of the requisition and in the correct space on the proper expense ledger.

Invoices. After materials have been delivered, the firms will send an invoice, sometimes to the theatre and sometimes to the purchasing office. An invoice should always contain the relevant purchase number and a complete list of the materials which were sent, their cost, shipping and packing charges (if any), and the

PURCHASE ORDER

BRADLEY UNIVERSITY

1501 WEST BRADLEY AVE. PEORIA, ILLINOIS 61606 No. 114771

DATE OF ORDER	DEPT.	ORIGINATOR	TERMS: 2% 10 DAYS, NET 30 DAYS UNLESS OTHERWISE STATED.
5-1-71	72230.3	J. Clifford	
REQ. NO.	DELIVERY DATE	SHIP VIA	F.O.B.
216709			

TO

Claus Lauterbach Lumber Co.
914 W. Garfield
Bartonville, Illinois 61607

SHIP TO -
RECEIVING DEPT.
1308 W. BRADLEY
BRADLEY UNIVERSITY
PEORIA, ILLINOIS 61606

QUANTITY	ARTICLES	PRICE
8	1" x 12" x 8' white pine	
16 shts.	4' x 8' ½" plywood	
	$132.00	

THE ABOVE PURCHASE ORDER NO. MUST APPEAR ON ALL INVOICES, B/L, CASES, BUNDLES, PACKING LISTS, AND CORRESPONDENCE.

MAIL INVOICES IN TRIPLICATE & ORIGINAL BILL/LADING TO THE ABOVE ADDRESS

By Thomas H. Taylor
PURCHASING AGENT

— IMPORTANT CONDITIONS —

1. Mail acceptance of this order immediately.
2. No charges allowed for boxing, packing or crating.
3. If prices are higher than specified, do not ship. Advise us.
4. If price is omitted on order, it is agreed that your price will be lowest prevailing market price.
5. Goods subject to our inspection on arrival, notwithstanding prior payment to obtain cash discount.
6. If these conditions are not acceptable, please advise us on receipt of the order, and before you make any shipment.

Figure 5-13. Purchase Order

total amount due. If the theatre manager receives an invoice, he should send it at once to the school's purchasing director, who will then approve it for payment by the school's business manager or treasurer.

When payment is made, the amount and the check (or voucher) number is posted against the theatre's account in the business office. If the school does not inform the theatre manager of the amount of each payment, he should periodically (at least once a month) check his account in the business office so that he can record the payments in his expense ledgers.

The example in 5-10 shows that our lumber order, requested on September 26 for $123, was invoiced and paid at $121.16. The ledger shows that the expense category of settings had encumbered $439.80 as of October 28; however, the payments of $273.41 as of October 12 (the last day for which payments have been posted) is $4.39 less than the estimated (encumbered) total. Therefore the total payments as of October 28 are $4.39 less than the $439.80. By checking the difference between the last payment total and the last estimated (requested or encumbered) total, it is possible to find the balance at any time.

The process of a single purchase is now complete: from the initial request by the theatre staff member to the theatre manager, and through the requisition form, the purchase order, the delivery of materials, the invoice, the voucher, and the payment (see figure 5-14).

Confirmed Orders. Sometimes a staff member will have to make emergency orders or purchases, in which case the order must be placed by telephone at once. The theatre manager should

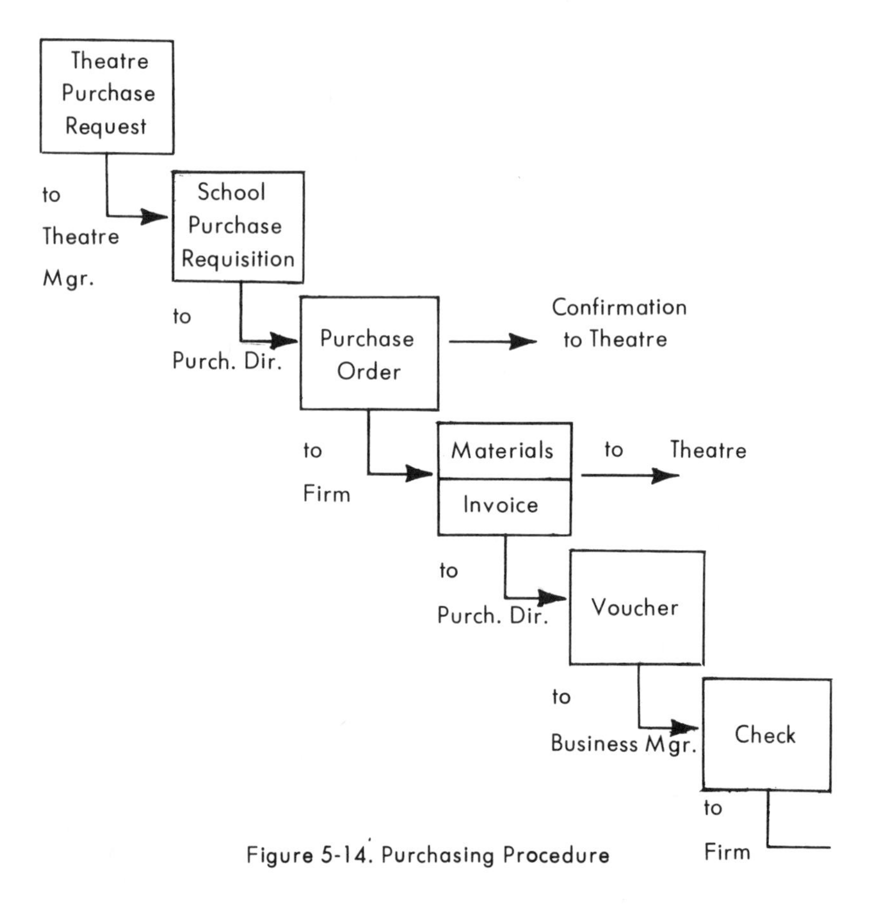

Figure 5-14. Purchasing Procedure

then explain the situation to the purchasing director and tell him what must be purchased, from whom, and for how much. The purchasing director will then assign a number to that order (on the phone), and the theatre manager should mention this number to the firm when he calls in his order.

After an order is placed in this manner, the theatre manager should fill out a purchase request in the usual way, but he should write *Confirmation* and the purchase number on the requisition. When the purchasing director receives this requisition, he will send a purchase order to the firm as an official confirmation of the verbal order the theatre manager made on the phone.

Standing Orders. A few schools permit the theatre manager to set up a standing order with certain firms with which the theatre does a great deal of business. This means that a permanent order number is assigned to all purchases from that firm (a credit or charge privilege), and the theatre manager does not have to prepare a requisition form for each purchase from that firm. Instead, he mentions this number when making purchases, and the firm bills the school under that number.

This procedure, if not carefully controlled, can be very dangerous since anyone who knows that number could use it and the school and theatre would be accountable for those debts. Also, it is very important for a theatre manager to know of a purchase *before* it is made, not after. Otherwise, the management loses control of the budget.

If this system is used, there should be a limit on the amount which can be purchased under that number. This will help to ensure that the privilege is not abused and that the budget is adhered to. The disadvantages and dangers of this system far outweigh any advantages and a theatre manager would do well to consider this policy very carefully before deciding in favor of adopting it.

The Financial Report

It is a good policy for everyone who has responsibility for receiving and spending money to periodically take stock of that money—to discover and report the financial condition of the concern. Similarly, the educational theatre manager should from time to time compile a financial statement of the theatre and send it to the school officials,

Also, a financial report should be made at the close of each play. It should contain accurate to-date expense and income figures, as well as the estimated figures of the final budget. Figure 5-15 is a typical financial report for an educational theatre.

SUMMARY

As stated in chapter 1, one of the functions of the educational theatre management staff is to coordinate, under a

BRADLEY UNIVERSITY THEATRE
FINANCIAL REPORT

INCOME

Season Coupon Books...$ 9,725.00
1944 @ $5.00 ea.

Individual Admissions... 1,044.00
"Blues" - $714.00
"Lion" - 330.00

Group Rates... 123.00
"Blues" - $58.50
"Lion" - 64.50

TOTAL INCOME $10,892.00

EXPENSES

Category	Budgeted	Expended	Balance
General Operating			
Coupon Books	$ 310.00	$ 306.50	$ 3.50
Tickets	370.00	367.05	2.95
Programs	125.00	180.15	(55.15)
Postage & Mailing	400.00	73.85	326.15
Film Classic Series	625.00	398.20	226.80
Telephone	70.00	9.55	60.45
Supplies	500.00	521.65	(21.65)
Advertising & Publicity			
Brochures & Flyers	450.00	443.00	7.00
Newspapers & Magazines	1,125.00	510.65	614.35
Posters & Displays	325.00	133.29	191.71
Photography	475.00	105.69	369.31
Misc.	225.00	169.20	55.80

Figure 5-15. An Educational Theatre Financial Report

Books & Royalties			
Royalties & Rental of Score	$1,100.00	$1,123.00	$ (23.00)
Books & Scripts	150.00	82.71	67.29
Capital Equipment	670.00	101.45	568.55
Technical Production			
Settings	3,700.00	1,621.69	2,078.31
Costumes & Makeup	1,350.00	1,322.11	27.89
Shop Supplies	235.00	234.16	.84
Salaries for Music	750.00	0	750.00

SUMMARY

INCOME

Category	Budget Est.	Income	Balance
Season Coupon Sales	9,500.00	9,725.00	225.00+
Individual Admissions	2,800.00	1,044.00	(1,756.00)
Group Rates	655.00	123.00	(532.00)
TOTALS	$12,955.00	$10,892.00	($2,063.00)

EXPENSES

Category	Budget Est.	Expended	Balance
General Operating	$ 2,400.00	$ 1,856.95	$ 543.05
Advertising & Publicity	2,600.00	1,361.83	1,238.17
Books & Royalties	1,250.00	1,205.71	44.29
Capital Equipment	670.00	101.45	568.55
Technical Production	5,285.00	3,177.96	2,107.04
Salaries	750.00	0	750.00
TOTALS	$12,955.00	$7,703.90	$5,251.10

Bradley University Theatre
December 16, 1969

/s/ John E. Clifford
Managing Director

Figure 5-15. An Educational Theatre Financial Report (cont.)

central director, all of the theatre's business, purchasing, and sales activities and to act as a liaison between the theatre staff and the business officers of the school. This chapter has attempted to indicate a responsible manner of approaching the problems of budget preparation and control, purchasing procedures, and financial record keeping.

Successful and organized educational theatre does not hinge only upon good play direction, design, and acting but also upon good commercial management. Even though the commercial or non-artistic aspects of educational theatre are not as glamorous or aesthetically rewarding as the acting and directing areas of play production, they require fully as much devotion and energy. All are part of a successful educational theatre production and training program, and should not be regarded as a "hit or miss" operation. Sound principles apply to the commercial activities of play production, just as they apply to the artistic activities.

6 Advertising and Publicity

AN EDUCATIONAL theatre cannot fulfill all its major aims and purposes if it cannot attract an audience. In chapter 4 it was mentioned that an attractive, well-planned season of plays can serve as one method of attracting an audience, but it is always a difficult task to inform potential audience members and theatre patrons about the season and the individual plays.

Theatre promotion, though one of the most important aspects of educational theatre's play production process, is often taken for granted and, even more often, totally neglected in theatre education. The vast majority of play production textbooks do not have discussions of publicizing and promoting plays. In fact, one of the most widely used play production texts doesn't even mention the word "publicity" in all its 500 pages. What is the use of producing excellent plays if no one in the organization takes the time, effort, and interest to get an audience? And what is the use of taking the time, effort, and interest to obtain an audience if all this is misdirected and inefficient? Just as the artistic aspects of a play take thought, planning, and study, the same are required for the "art" of publicity.

DEFINITIONS

Publicity

In general, publicity is that activity whose aim is the promulgation of information to the public with the intention of influencing opinion and conduct. Specifically, in educational theatre and the play production process, publicity seeks to inform and persuade the general public to purchase tickets and attend productions.

It is true that, by providing an audience, publicity also helps finance the theatre; however, financing the theatre should be treated as only a secondary purpose of publicity. To say that financial profit is the ultimate aim of publicity may be perfectly acceptable in the context of commercial theatre, but it is glaringly inconsistent with the aims and objectives of educational theatre, which wishes to attract audiences in order to accomplish these other aims and objectives, not to make money. If all activity in educational theatre is directed toward the audience, what greater function could publicity serve than providing that audience?

Advertising

The terms "advertising" and "publicity" are often used interchangeably, even though it is possible to distinguish between the two. Advertising is a specific form of publicity, whereas publicity refers to all forms of theatre activity, whether free or paid for, which seek to inform and persuade the general public to attend productions. Advertising refers to the paid forms of public notice, and specifically to those in newspapers and magazines and on radio and television. An article in the local newspaper about an opening of a play is "free publicity." An announcement of the play on the theatre page, which is paid for by the theatre, is "paid publicity," or advertising.

This distinction, which is somewhat academic and has no great significance, is made only to clarify the terms as they will be used in this chapter. Also, this distinction is made simply because it is the one which most people use, who understand that advertising is expensive while publicity need not be.

Public Relations

A second distinction in terminology is that between "publicity" and "public relations." Publicity seeks to promote interest in the plays of an educational theatre and thereby persuade the general public to attend those plays. Public relations seeks to enhance the image of the theatre as a cultural center which makes a valuable contribution to the educational institution and to the community.

While the aim of publicity is participation as a direct result of its activity, the aim of public relations is awareness by the members of the community (academic and/or town) of the theatre, its activities and procedures, and the cultural role it plays in the area. Selecting a good season of plays year after year serves to enhance the image of the theatre, as do good productions. Faculty members who speak to school clubs and community organization also serve to enhance the image of the theatre. All of these activities that get people to come to the theatre are normally considered "PR" activities.

Although these two activities, publicity and public relations, often overlap, this chapter is primarily concerned with publicity—informing the public about a season of plays and the individual plays in order to build an audience. It is through good publicity and intelligent management and administration of the commercial aspects of play production which affect the general public that the aims of public relations are fulfilled. The motivation for many administrative and managerial policy decisions in educational theatre is often of a public relations nature.

PERSONNEL

As this chapter will indicate, the field of publicity for educational theatre is much wider and more complicated than most people imagine. For this reason, therefore, it is unrealistic for one person to attempt to do all the work connected with a publicity program. Working under the jurisdiction of the managing director of the theatre, the publicity director should recruit a group of qualified students to carry out specific publicity assignments. He should appoint one student as a kind of director of each of the various areas of publicity—radio and television, posters, newspapers, and direct mail—to oversee and direct that activity under the director of publicity. The exact chain of command will of necessity vary from school to school, but it should suit the nature of the specific program, the number of available and qualified students, and the size of the staff.

The student who is in charge of radio and television should be responsible for furnishing local radio and TV stations with the necessary information about the upcoming productions. The director of newspaper publicity has a twofold job: to plan, write, and submit news and feature stories, as well as paid ads. The poster chairman is in charge of designing, printing, and distributing posters. And the student who is chairman of the direct mail aspects of publicity supervises the printing, addressing, and mailing of direct mail pieces.

All of these student chairmen work under the direct supervision of the publicity director, who should be a faculty member or a highly qualified student who can work responsibly under the supervision of the managing director. He should be energetic, creative, and imaginative; willing to work with deadlines; able to write well; likeable; able to meet people as equals and make a favorable impression; and tactful and considerate of other people's time and problems. This is a tall order, and the student or staff member who comes even close to fulfilling the ideal publicity director's shoes is a "tall man" indeed.

The theatre manager (a member of the faculty) should exercise rigid control and supervision over the publicity workers. He should delegate responsibilities but not the right of final decision. Periodic publicity meetings, at which schedules are set, decisions made, and the chairmen report their progress, should be mandatory. The chain of command, control, and responsibility in publicity must be tightly knit, well organized, and unified; the image of both the theatre and the school is at stake.

A strong educational theatre manager should attempt to accomplish all this and at the same time provide meaningful educational responsibilities and experiences for his students

RADIO AND TELEVISION PUBLICITY

Probably no development has stimulated advertising more than the electronic mass media of information and entertainment: radio and television. In fact, advertising became one of the most dominant economic and motivating forces in American life largely as a direct result of radio and later television. Unfortunately, however, air time on radio and TV is very costly, which again reflects the great importance and influence of those media on advertising. Because the cost of ads is so high that it is almost impossible for educational theatre to purchase broadcast time, radio and TV advertising are impractical or impossible for the average educational theatre.

Nevertheless, although an educational theatre publicity director cannot afford to purchase advertisements on radio and TV, there are many excellent opportunities for free publicity for educational theatres. In 1934 the Communications Act created a seven-member Federal Communications Commission that is charged with regulating broadcasting stations so that they operate in "the public interest, convenience and necessity." The definition of "public interest" has been broadly defined throughout the years, and to many has come to mean "public service." Included in this definition is the idea of free spot-announcements for agencies and organizations that are dedicated to advancing the health, welfare, and happiness of the community. Most of the organizations which fall into this category are the so-called nonprofit or charitable organizations (the March of Dimes, the public library, the Girl Scouts, Civil Defense, the Heart Fund), but educational theatres also operate in the public interest and welfare.

Thus radio and television stations often devote some of their public service time to informing the public about the activities and events of various "public service" groups. This action helps broadcasters satisfy part of the broad scope of operating in the "public interest, convenience, and necessity." It also offers educational theatre an opportunity to reach a large group of people at no cost. It should be remembered, however, that such free publicity is more or less a gift from the stations to the theatre; they are not required by law to donate time to such announcements. Because they can fulfill their service obligation in other ways, the educational theatre publicity director cannot demand this privilege, and therefore he should cooperate fully with the requirements, schedules, and other commitments of a station. There is no better way to turn this most potent ally into an enemy than by demanding free time or by complaining that a message wasn't aired.

Radio Announcements

Most educational theatres can expect local radio stations to make periodic announcements of their productions, usually in the form of a "community bulletin board" or "around the town" program. This type of program, sometimes on tape and sometimes live, is usually one minute in length and is usually repeated some ten times daily; it features straight, factual announcements of upcoming meetings and events. An educational theatre however, should not expect much more than ten- or fifteen-second announcements—which does not permit the theatre publicity director a great deal of freedom in the type of announcement or the information he can expect to be aired.

Before submitting information to a radio station for use on such a program, it is best that the publicity director contact the station personally to talk with the public service or public affairs director about the station's policy, format, and requirements. This initial contact should not be made from the point of view of a demand but as a request for information. Reminding the station manager or public affairs director of his obligation to serve the public could result in a very poor working relationship. At this initial meeting the theatre representative should learn (1) the station's policy for public service announcements, (2) the form in which the station wants the information submitted, (3) the deadlines for submitting material, and (4) the name of the person to whom material should be sent.

Most radio stations prefer that organizations send in only the essential facts, without flowery phrases and unnecessary details. If the radio station requires such a "fact sheet," these data should be typed tripled spaced and in capital letters on one sheet of paper. The page should be headed with the name of the organization (such as Willard High School Drama Club), the name of the person responsible for publicity, and the date. The fact sheet should also answer the traditional journalistic queries of who, what, where, when, and how much (figure 6-1 is a typical fact sheet for the play *Antigone*). Using this simple, one-page sheet, the radio station personnel can write a fifteen-second announcement which will adequately present the essential information, or they can write a thirty-second announcement with more details about the play.

If a radio station prefers not to write the copy from the theatre's fact sheet, the publicity director must prepare a fully scripted announcement, and in this case it is best to submit several announcements of different length. These announcements should be written so that they can be read easily in the allotted time. In general, a

Public Service Announcement
WILLARD HIGH SCHOOL DRAMA CLUB
Thomas Watson, Dir. of Publicity
March 3, 1969

WHO: Willard High School Drama Club
WHAT: A Play: ANTIGONE by Jean Anouilh
WHEN: March 14 through 16, 8:00 P.M.
WHERE: Willard Auditorium, 1600 Wilson Avenue
TICKETS: Adults, $1.50; Students, $1.00
For reserved seats phone 287-4100, or purchase at door

ABOUT
THE PLAY: Jean Anouilh's tragedy ANTIGONE, written in 1944, follows the emotional, dedicated Antigone and pits her beliefs in human dignity and decency against the all-powerful, politically expedient nature of the State as she attempts to bury the body of her brother against the command of the dictator. It is a modern-dress version of Sophocles' famous tragedy.

Figure 6-1. Sample Radio Fact Sheet

person can read between 140 and 160 words per minute, or about 35 to 40 words in a fifteen-second announcement. This, of course, can vary with individuals, but these figures should suffice as a rule of thumb.

Announcements should begin with an interesting general idea that will catch the attention of the audience. Sentence structure should be simple, with easy-to-comprehend words and ideas. Announcements should not contain clever tongue twisters or hard-to-read alliterations. Figure 6-2 is an example of a fifteen-second announcement for a radio station.

For a thirty-second announcement, the ideas can be expanded and more details can be added. The time of the performances and the phone number can be mentioned twice and the nature of the play can be given more emphasis. Figure 6-3 is an example of a thirty-second announcement as submitted to a radio station.

For Use Week of March 9
Public Service Announcement
WILLARD HIGH SCHOOL DRAMA CLUB
Thomas Watson, Dir. of Publicity
March 3, 1969

THE STATE VERSUS THE INDIVIDUAL—THAT'S **ANTIGONE**, WILLARD HIGH SCHOOL'S NEXT PRODUCTION, EVENINGS, MARCH 14 THROUGH 16 IN THE SCHOOL AUDITORIUM. FOR RESERVED SEATS FOR THIS TRAGEDY AT $1.50 AND $1.00, PHONE THE SCHOOL BETWEEN 10:00 AND 4:00 DAILY.

Figure 6-2. Sample Fifteen-Second Radio Announcement

Whether the radio station suggests a fact sheet or a scripted announcement is not important; what is important is that the theatre publicity director, or the student in charge of radio and television publicity, complies with the wishes and requirements of the station. This compliance should not be only in the area of format but also in deadlines and the occasions for announcements; for example,

For Use Week of March 9
Public Service Announcement
WILLARD HIGH SCHOOL DRAMA CLUB
Thomas Watson, Dir. of Publicity
March 3, 1969

THE TRAGIC STORY OF A YOUNG GIRL WHO DEFIES THE STATE BY BURYING HER REBEL BROTHER'S BODY – THAT'S **ANTIGONE**, WILLARD HIGH SCHOOL'S NEXT PLAY, MARCH 14 THROUGH 16 AT 8:00 P.M. IN THE SCHOOL AUDITORIUM. TICKETS FOR THIS MODERN-DRESS VERSION OF THE CLASSIC GREEK TRAGEDY CAN BE RESERVED BY CALLING THE SCHOOL AT 287-4100, DAILY FROM 10:00 TO 4:00. THAT'S **ANTIGONE**, AT WILLARD HIGH AUDITORIUM. . . $1.50 FOR ADULTS, $1.00 FOR STUDENTS . . . PHONE 287-4100.

Figure 6-3. Sample Thirty-Second Announcement for Radio

an educational theatre should request free time only to announce major plays, not films, tryouts, meetings, studio theatre plays, etc. It is much better to approach a radio (or TV) station infrequently —three or four times a year—than for every minor event which the theatre sponsors. A station might soon get tired of too many requests and invoke the gift-horse-in-the-mouth adage.

Radio Interviews

Another possibility for using local radio is interview and talk shows. If a local radio station has such a program, the publicity director should contact the program's host and/or producer to see if he might be interested in talking to someone from the theatre about an upcoming production. Many talk, interview, and telephone programs are willing to do this if properly approached.

If such a show is arranged, the publicity director should suggest sending the director and one or two of the lead actors to appear on the program. He should make sure that the host and the producer are furnished with background information on the play, on the director, and on the actors. He should also make sure that the actors who are selected are personable, are well briefed on the play and the production, are proficient in discussion, and are able to bring up interesting, unusual, or exciting aspects of the play and the production.

Television Announcements

Purchasing television time is much more difficult than purchasing radio time for an educational theatre. Like radio, though, many television stations devote a portion of their public service commitment to announcements in the public interest. Unlike radio, however, the amount of such time available on TV is extremely limited, and an educational theatre should not expect thirty-second announcements several times a day for a week or so to announce a play. Once or twice prior to a production run, and possibly once during the run of the play, would be a generous commitment from a local television station to an educational theatre. The publicity director who receives that much time should count himself indeed fortunate.

Again, before he submits information to a television station, the publicity director should personally contact the public service or public affairs director of the station. He should discuss the station's policy on free announcements, visual and audio requirements, deadlines, and the form for submitting copy.

Television stations, like radio stations, usually request a fact sheet, which they can rewrite to suit their own requirements. This can be similar to the one sent to radio stations unless the material is to accompany a specific visual image. In that case the script should be written for the visual, complementing it with the sound. This type of "voice over" is the most common form for the educational theatre.

If the TV station will accept visuals, it is the duty of the theatre to prepare them according to the station's requirements; the theatre director should not expect the TV station to prepare visual material at its own expense. Of the numerous types of visuals or graphics which a TV station can use—charts, photos, slides, Balop cards, flip cards, etc.—the most practical type for a short (ten second) public service announcement for an educational theatre is the slide. When a TV station uses slides, it does not have to use a live camera, personnel, or lights, and the slides are easy to handle and store. Most TV stations, therefore, will probably want slides if they accept visuals.

It is a time-consuming job for a non-professional to make an acceptable slide for use on television. Some of the numerous problems which the artist and photographer must keep in mind when preparing a slide for TV projection are the 3″ by 4″ aspect ratio, the size of the lettering, tonal contrasts, the gray scale, glare, and many more. The best advice to the educational theatre publicity director is to purchase ready-made slides or have a local advertising agency prepare the slides for him (at a cost, of course).

The type of slides which TV stations use are 2″ by 2″ on glass-mounted 35 mm film. The "critical area" which TV can reproduce is roughly ¾″ by 1″. Slides that are made to these specifications can be purchased or rented for specific plays (from Package Publicity Service in New York). They illustrate the play in an interesting manner, and voice-over messages work well with them. This is the most practical and economical method of obtaining slides for TV. However, the publicity director should check with the TV representative to determine if slides can be used.

Another use of visual TV material, besides the voice-over announcement, is the "call letter" or "ID slide." Every television station must identify itself periodically during each hour of broadcasting, and quite often the station takes ten seconds for the entire "station ID" even though the verbal identification takes only three seconds ("This is WMBD, Channel 31, Peoria"). In the remaining seven seconds the station usually broadcasts a "time check," a weather or temperature check, or a "promo" for a later program. Also, a great many TV stations use those seven seconds for public service messages, and this is where the educational theatre can make use of the ID slide, which contains two messages: the call letters of the station and a public service message. The call letters and the public service message are seen for the entire ten seconds, but the call letters are given only three seconds of audio and the public service message is given seven seconds.

In *Television in the Public Interest*, the authors explain the make-up of the ID slide and how it can be used by a public service organization.

> In preparing the ID slide, remember that the upper right hand 1/4 of the screen is used for call letters, and the remaining 3/4 for visual message. Stations will generally have their own logo or type-face for call-letters, and will have copies available for use by agencies or groups who prepare slides. If they prefer to add their own call letters, artwork as prepared for an ordinary slide can be submitted, so long as the upper right hand quarter is general background only and does not have design or lettering. The station will simply place a clear acetate overlay over the artwork, with its call letters added in this area. Both are photographed together for the slide.
>
> The ID slide can be a wonderful promotion device for public service agencies who take the initial risk of investment in a large group of slides. The Navy Recruiting Office once created a slide carrying the picture of a cartoon sailor peering through a telescope at the call letters. By the overlay method, it then added call letters for various stations and sent the final product out for free use. There is no hard sell or demand to "give," but there is a subtle and constant reminder that sailors, and the U.S. Navy, are still in action. Many budget-conscious stations welcomed the free slide, and used it!

Television Interviews

There is not as much opportunity for members of an educational

A. William Bluem, John F. Cox, and Gene McPherson, *Television in the Public Interest*, New York: Hastings House, 1961, p. 95.

theatre production to appear on a TV interview program as in similar programs on radio. Unless the production is highly unusual (an original script, a premiere, a special guest actor, etc.), there is little likelihood of getting any of the valuable, costly time on a local TV talk show. However, if there is such a show, the publicity director of the theatre might feel no harm would be done in trying; there is everything to gain and nothing to lose.

In making the initial contact with the program's producer, the publicity director should emphasize the benefits which will accrue to the program from this interview, not the benefits the theatre can receive. The obvious benefits for the program are (1) an interesting interview, which many people will appreciate, and (2) news value. If the producer thinks that the interview can enhance the program and appeal to a large audience, he will be more willing to consider it than if he thinks it would be just another "free plug" type of discussion.

Broadcasting offers educational theatre the opportunity to reach a large group of people, many of whom are potential theatregoers, at little or no cost. If it is used properly, and if the publicity director cooperates with the stations, this opportunity can be most valuable.

Posters

The poster, a well-defined form of graphic communication, plays a very important part in the daily lives of a great many people, and especially students, who regularly receive information from posters and from notices on bulletin boards. Posters are used for specific purposes: to inform, to persuade, to sell, and to stimulate. They can be most useful in publicizing an educational theatre production or an entire season of plays.

Sources. The first question the publicity director faces is Where do I get posters? He can either (1) purchase them, already designed and printed, or (2) have them designed and printed.

A very simple and economical way of obtaining posters is to purchase professionally designed ones from commercial theatrical or advertising firms. A number of play publishing companies furnish posters for the plays they license and Package Publicity offers the widest selection of plays for which specifically designed posters are available. This service company can provide specifically designed cardboard posters for over 700 plays. These can be imprinted with the name of the theatre, dates of production, price of tickets, and other information. They can be purchased in two sizes for most plays: 11″ by 14″ or 14″ by 22″. Or if the theatre publicity director wishes to imprint special information, the posters can be ordered with only the specific designs. One hundred 11″ by 14″ posters for *The Odd Couple*, for example, would cost about $32 fully printed. For plays for which they do not have specific designs, there is a choice of two stock designs. In addition to Package Publicity Service, the theatre publicity director has a number of local advertising, printing, and poster firms at his disposal, plus the art department of the school. He should check all of these sources to determine the best source of posters.

Commercially designed posters, which are adequate for use by educational theatres, are slick, colorful, and well organized. They are not, however, "personal," or overly creative and imaginative. If a publicity director wants posters with a more personal touch and a closer relationship to a specific production, he should rely upon the second source of posters: have it done himself. Home-made posters can add a great deal to the charm and quality of the overall advertising campaign, as well as a certain amount of unity.

Poster Design. Designing posters is not an easy task; that is, designing *effective* posters is not easy. The publicity director should seek out a theatre student who has a good background in art—commercial art, design, and lettering. If he cannot find a theatre student who has an adequate art background, he should go to the art faculty and ask the members to recommend a student who is able to design an effective poster. This is much better than to attempt the job with no experience, background or talent, in which case it would be better to purchase professionally designed and printed posters.

To be effective and meaningful, a poster should be (1) simple, (2) attractive and well proportioned, (3) appropriate for the play, (4) suitable for display, (5) economical, and (6) informative. The usual purpose of a poster is to convey information about a production, and information is best conveyed if it is simple and easy to see, read, and comprehend. Just as a simple, straightforward, declarative sentence can be understood more easily than a complex sentence with adverbial phrases, dependent clauses, and prepositional phrases, a simple declarative poster can be understood more easily than a complex one. And it is understanding and comprehension that are needed before persuasion can take place.

The essential and minimum information which a poster should carry is (1) the name of the producing organization, (2) the name of the play and author, (3) the dates and time of performances, and (4) ticket information (prices, where to buy them and when, etc.).

A poster should also be attractive, and compositionally effective; in other words, a competent art student is needed. The elements of makeup or composition which determine the effectiveness of a poster are (1) illustration, (2) lettering, and (3) color.

Illustration. Illustrations are the designs, artwork, or pictures that are used as the central visual feature of poster design. An illustration, to be effective, should be bold and dynamic in order to attract attention and more or less compel understanding. While it might be considered arty and clever to use an abstract design which people have to study and study before they can decipher it, it is best if the design is evident at the first look. In addition, the design should reflect or illustrate the play in some manner: by a central character or by the theme, setting, mood, or story line of the play. *Of Thee I Sing*, for example, might use the capitol building, or red, white and blue bunting for its main illustration. *Death of a Salesman* featured a man's figure, bent forward and carrying two sample cases. *The Miracle Worker* could use dark glasses, a water pump, or a young girl using sign language as its central illustration. In short, there should be a valid reason for the selection of illustrative material for a poster.

Lettering. Lettering, along with illustration, is a most important element of poster composition, and practically all advertising requires some hand lettering. The student who designs the posters should know a variety of lettering styles and be able to use them consistently.

It would not be possible to point out here all of the many styles and types of lettering, since there are literally hundreds, and the possibility for variations with variations are almost infinite. The publicity director can find any number of valuable books in his school library or by consulting with the art faculty. Books on lettering and the history of lettering contain numerous illustrations of the various styles and types as well as how to write them.

The important principle is to select a lettering style which will provide the necessary variety and emphasis. In addition, of course, it should be appropriate to the play. A comedy, for instance, may be suggested by light, frilly lettering—unlike a tragedy, which might be suggested by the use of bold, heavy lettering.

Color. The third important element in determining the appropriateness and effectiveness of a poster is color. Every student of art knows that color attracts attention, and many times influences people in their choice of a product in a store. Selection of the appropriate color and its qualities of hue, value, and intensity are very important in the overall effectiveness of a poster, as is also true in the effectiveness of a setting.

Also, color should reflect the type of play that is being publicized inasmuch as they can evoke certain feelings and impressions. If the play is a tragedy, dark and heavy hues, such as black, red, gray, or navy blue, might be used. If it is a comedy, bright pastel colors, such as pink, blue, yellow, or green, might be most appropriate.

Poster design can be a time-consuming task for one who does not have an adequate artistic background. If no one is available with the ability to design clear, effective, attractive, and appropriate posters, the publicity director would be wise to purchase them from a professional company. But if the talent is available, designing an original poster for a play can be a most creative and educational experience, and the result can be immensely superior to that of commercially or professionally designed posters.

Reproducing the Poster. If the theatre's publicity director sees that he has student talent and sufficient time and therefore decides to design an original poster for a play, he must select a method for reproducing that design in quantity. If the school is small and there is no need to make more than ten or twelve posters, it might be cheaper and easier to make them by hand. Using good quality cardboard, poster stock, and tempera, students can turn out a dozen 14″ by 22″, 28″ by 44″, or 42″ by 66″ standard-size posters in a very short time after the design is completed. If, however, larger quantities are needed, three reproduction methods are available to the publicity director: (1) letterpress printing, (2) offset printing, and (3) the silk-screen process.

Letterpress. In the letterpress (typeset) process, the oldest method of relief printing, the copy is printed from raised surfaces.

Letters are cast in metal, inked, and pressed directly on the paper. The stereotyped picture of the printer with his green eyeshade, bent low over a table under a bare bulb and carefully picking up type with a tweezers, is largely outmoded. The art of typesetting for the letterpress process in a local print shop is a dying art. There are now much quicker, less expensive, and more mechanical (and chemical) ways of printing.

If a printer uses letterpress, he probably has a good stock of type sizes and styles available, so that it is important to work with him on selecting the typefaces which are most appropriate for the design of a poster. In letterpress printing, moreover, there is a limit to the art work which can be used economically. If a two-color design is used along with printing, the printer has to have an engraved plate for each color of the artwork before he can reproduce it on his press. When one uses letterpress, it is cheaper to use only letters and simple designs.

The publicity director should check with the printer he selects (after receiving bids from at least three printers) to see what type of process is to be used to make the posters so that he can submit his copy in the proper form.

Offset. The most common printing process, and usually the cheapest, is the offset lithograph method. In this process—called planeographic—the inked impression is made first on a rubber roller and then on the paper, rather than directly on the paper from type. A gelatin roller picks up the image from a plate into which the artwork has been burned by a special photographic method.

A photograph of the artwork is made for each color which is to be used on the poster. If there is to be a three-color poster design, the printer should be given three overlays—one for each color. He will then make a plate of each color and run the poster through his press three times, using a different plate and a different color ink for each run. It should be remembered that the printer photographs the artwork and the design *exactly;* so they should be as perfect as possible. Imperfections in the drawing and the lettering will show up on the plates and consequently on the finished poster.

Offset printing is inexpensive if the publicity director gives the printer "camera ready" copy; that is, all the printer has to do is photograph the copy and run the press. If he does not have to set any type, use a Linotype, or do any artwork, the cost is reasonable.

Press-type letters, which can be purchased in any art store in a number of different styles and sizes, can be used for preparing professional-looking printing and lettering on a piece of copy which will be run on an offset press.

The printer should also be given an exact idea of the ink color to be used and the color of the stock. Most printers will have color samples of ink and stock, and in various combinations, to show when discussing color. If he is truly interested in the finished product and the customer, he will make sure that he has the proper color combinations for the run.

Silk-Screen Printing. Letterpress and offset work must be done by a commercial printer on special equipment; it cannot be done at home or by amateurs. The silk-screen process is also done by many local firms which specialize in printing and advertising; however, it can also be done by a theatre staff if two or three interested students know a little about silk-screening. (Or they can learn it quickly from books or from someone in the art department.) Of all three methods, do-it-yourself silk-screen posters are probably the cheapest, most creative, and most representative of the energies and abilities of the educational theatre staff. Besides, they can be a great source of pride.

Basically, the silk-screen method is a stenciling procedure in which liquid colors are squeezed through silk, gauze, or wire screen that is stretched on a wooden frame. The design is blocked out on the screen by the application of stencils or tusche and glue.

Commercially made silk-screen sets may be purchased, and this is an excellent way for a novice to get started. If they are strong and properly constructed, they will last a long time. Each outfit comes with a squeegee, pieces of silk, a frame, and the other necessary elements. For educational theatre publicity directors who wish to make their own silk-screen set, the following materials are needed: (1) assorted lengths of 2″ by 2″ oven-dried pine, spruce, hemlock, or boxwood; (2) pieces of number 10xx or 12xx silk mesh; (3) plywood to support the frame; (4) two loose-pin flap hinges; (5) turpentine, kerosene, or benzine; (6) a squeegee; (7) tusche; (8) film; (9) ink and extender; and (10) a mat knife and tacks and hammer, or a stapler.

To make the screening outfit, the frame should first be made out of the 2″ by 2″ lumber. The size of the frame is determined by the

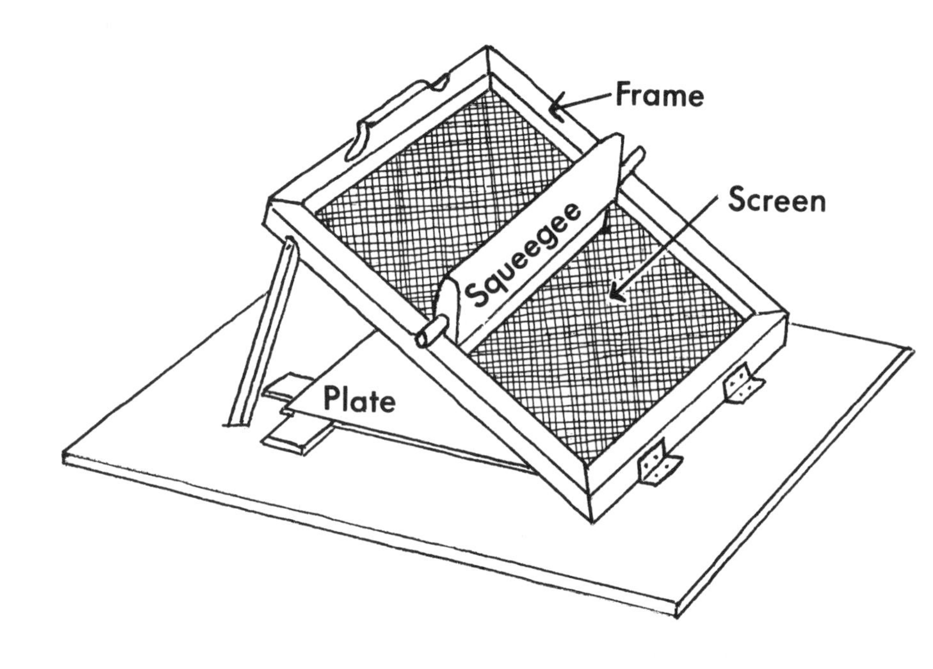

Figure 6-4. A Typical Silk-Screen Set

size of the largest poster which will be made. The silk is then stretched over the frame so that the threads are parallel to the sides of the frame. It should be affixed at the center with tacks or staples and then stretched outward. The screen is then hinged to the plywood base (as shown in figure 6-4). Stops, made of plywood or cardboard, should be added to register the correct placing of the poster and colors. For convenience, a handle should be placed on the screen for raising it and a bar should be added to hold it away from the poster.

After a design has been drawn on a special film and cut out with a mat knife or razor blade so that the cut-out parts are arranged where the ink will flow through them, the film is attached to the screen. The poster paper is then placed on the plate with the screen over it. Special silk-screen ink, or pait (which can be purchased at all art stores and most hardware stores), is then diluted with an equal amount of silk-screen color extender to liquefy the color. After the ink is diluted, some of it is poured along the top of the screen. With one stroke of the squeegee (a rubber blade about 1 inch shorter than the frame), the color is pulled from the top of the screen to the opposite end. The screen is then raised, the poster is taken out and set to dry, and a new one is put in. This process is repeated for each poster.

After all the posters have been printed with one color, the remaining ink is scraped off the screen and the screen is washed with turpentine or some other solvent. A new film, containing the design for the second color, is then placed on the screen, and the second color is printed in the same manner as the first. The result is usually a very professional and creative piece of work.

This discussion does not cover all the details for setting up a silk screen and operating it; it is only an outline of the general procedure. For more details, the publicity director should consult some of the books listed in the Appendix. These books contain much more specific information and diagrams which should enable any novice to set up and operate a silk screen. In the long run, it can be well worth the time and effort put into it.

Displaying the Poster. Once the posters are completed, they must be displayed in important, well-traveled locations. Some of the best places to display theatre posters on campus are the student union building, the hallways and entrances of academic

Figure 6-5. Sample of Poster

and administrative buildings, dormitories, fraternity and sorority houses, the auditorium, and all bulletin boards. The theatre should also have its own easels to place in entrances to buildings.

To reach the community, it would be wise to place posters in the large stores in town and in the stores in various shopping centers around the town. They should be placed in all stores near the campus which are frequented by the students. Of course, the poster chairman must first obtain permission from the store managers to display the posters.

No matter how striking a poster is, if it is not placed in a good, heavily frequented location it will not serve its purpose, and much of the time, energy, and money will have been spent in vain. Therefore careful attention should be given the locations in which posters should be placed to be most effective.

After the production run, the poster chairman must take down all posters. They do no good after the play closes, and may even do harm because people get used to seeing them. Then, when the posters for the next play are put up, they are not likely to be noticed. Also, store managers will be prone to allow the theatre to continue to use his store window if he knows the posters will be taken down after each play has ended. Figure 6-5 shows a poster.

NEWSPAPER PUBLICITY

"How can I get a story on our play in the newspaper?" "I sent them an article and they never printed it." "They cut my four-page article down to two paragraphs." These are some of the typical questions and laments of many educational theatre directors, managers, and publicity directors. But such is the life of the educational theatre publicist: educational theatre events are not the most newsworthy event in town.

No educational theatre director ever feels that his play has received enough newspaper space. The local high school or college play—no matter what its title or how well it is directed, or how long and hard the cast rehearsed, or how badly it needs publicity—is not terribly newsworthy. A newspaper prints *news*, and if a play is not important news there is no reason why it should receive much space in a newspaper.

Although this may seem to be a bitter attitude, it is better to be realistic than idealistic about the public attitude toward educational theatre. The ideal attitude and relationship between the newspaper on the one hand and the educational theatre on the other hand will come through hard work and dedicated service. This, also may be a bitter pill for the educational theatre to swallow, but it is very close to fact. When I direct a play, and especially a difficult one, which turns out well, I feel that its production is an important event, but I know that if I get a six-inch news item in the Sunday newspaper just prior to opening I have done very well in this category.

An educational theatre publicity director should not expect much more. One article, brief and factual, and one picture for each play is about all any educational theatre can expect in the way of free coverage from a local newspaper. In addition, it is sometimes possible to get a feature story on one of the plays during the season. To expect a feature story on each play, a news story or two, pictures, and a review is expecting too much for most theatres and newspapers. Although a few local newspapers might give this much space to an educational theatre, the majority will not.

Thus an educational theatre can expect (1) a news story about the play just prior to opening night, (2) a picture prior to the opening, and (3) one feature story. Much of this, however, depends upon the publicity director's contacting the newspaper in the proper manner, knowing what a news story and a feature story should contain, and conforming with the proper newspaper writing style.

Contacting the Newspaper. It is important to establish personal contact with the proper person at the newspaper. Therefore a new publicity director or manager should read the paper carefully to see if theatre, art, movie, and music news and features are consistently written by the same person. If so, the paper has probably assigned a special staff writer to cover the arts, and he is the logical person with whom to hold the initial meeting. If there is no feature writer who covers entertainment and cultural affairs, the publicity director should consult the city editor, who will tell him whom to contact.

At their first meeting, the publicity director should introduce himself to the newspaper man as the person who is directly responsible for all publicity for the theatre. He should also find out the newspaper's policy for stories about school plays. He should also try to show that a local play is important to a good many people and that the newspaper serves a significant segment of its readers by informing them about the various theatrical productions done by local groups. He should also find out about pictures—should he submit them or will a photographer from the paper take them? If the theatre is expected to submit photos for publication, they should be 8″ by 10″ glossy prints. Other important items of information which the publicity director should obtain include deadlines, the number of articles he might reasonably expect would be printed for each play, and the style and format of the paper.

With this information and personal contact, the publicity director is in a good position to make profitable use of the local paper—and vice versa.

News Stories (Readers). The type of story which an educational theatre publicity director most often wants to have a newspaper publish is the simple news story (sometimes called a "reader") which is, in essence, an announcement of an upcoming play. The essential purpose of this type of news release is to inform the public (1) that a play is about to open, (2) what kind of a play it is, (3) when it opens, and (4) essential ticket and box office information. Most city newspapers will be happy to carry one such reader for each of an educational theatre's plays. Other information which a publicity director likes to have played up in the press includes the cast, the production staff, the background of the play, quotes from the director, etc. Not many news editors, however, will permit that much "persuasive material" to be printed under the guise of news copy. Some of it, they contend, belongs in a paid ad.

The news release should be written in the style of the newspaper, and be written so well that the editor does not have to do a great deal of rewriting. The less work on a news release that an editor has to do, the more favorably he will look upon the release and the organization which submitted it. But no matter how well a release is written, it is bound to be changed slightly by the editor, especially in length.

The first paragraph of the news release should contain the most important information, and subsequent paragraphs add more and more detail. This "pyramid" style of writing allows the editor to shorten story lengths by merely cutting the terminal paragraph(s).

The lead paragraph should be no more than two sentences, and preferably only one, and getting all the essentials into one sentence is really not as difficult as it might seem. Avoiding the usual "Bradley University Theatre will present *Hamlet* by William Shakespeare Tuesday through Friday in. . . ," one can make the opening more interesting, more readable, and even more informative with very little effort. The following examples show how a lead paragraph for the same play might be rewritten.

> The box office opens Monday for reservations to *Hamlet,* William Shakespeare's celebrated tragedy of revenge, insanity, and murder which opens Tuesday for a six-performance run at Bradley University Theatre.
>
> *Hamlet*, William Shakespeare's most remarkable play and the most produced play in the English language, opens a six-night run Tuesday at Bradley University Theatre.
>
> The curtain rises Tuesday night at Bradley University Theatre for a six-night run of *Hamlet*, William Shakespeare's violent play which is the most widely read, produced, and talked about play in the English language.

Each of these lead sentences, which also are lead paragraphs, tells what, where, and when. The following paragraphs can expand upon these leads.

The publicity director should make each sentence interesting and colorful and yet convey essentially factual news material. He should keep colorful adjectives and flowery phrases to a reasonable, minimum level. Such overused "theatrical" words and phrases as "a sexational, side-splittingly hilarious comedy of love, romance, sentiment, and pathos which will leave you rolling in the aisles with laughter" or "the powerful, poetic, compelling tragedy of a proud, vain, arrogant tyrant who lashes out at the cosmic forces of the universe in an attempt to master his own destiny, which will leave you limp and drained of all emotion" should be eliminated. Such blurbs might be suitable for a brochure, flyer, or ad, but they are not suitable for a news release for a city paper. An

"A THURBER CARNIVAL" is Limestone Community High School's spring play scheduled Friday and Saturday nights at 8 p.m. Shown are Crystal Anderson as Red Riding Hood and Ron Sweetin as the wolf in one of the 11 short sketches. Also taking parts will be Greb Schwab, Dean Albritton, Mike Schermer, Rich Garmers, Steve Selman, Gail Schindler, Barbara Bergman, Chris Jacoby, Vickie Bledsoe, Kristy Quinn, Sandy Kirkwood, Chris Franz, Donna Kessinger, Dianne Brown, Barbara A. Brown, Janis Peters, Sue Bozarth and Irene Bunner. The student director is Tom DeMarini and the stage manager is Bill Murphy.

"BECKET," A PLAY based on the friendship of King Henry II of England and Thomas Becket, archbishop of Canterbury, is the final play of the season to be staged by the Peoria High School Thespians. David Lush (left) as King Henry and Ron Everts as Becket rehearse a scene from the drama which will be presented at 8 o'clock tonight and tomorrow night in the school auditorium. Miss Ann Caveny is the director.

Figure 6-6. Two examples of Pictures and Captions for a Play in a City Newspaper

occasional "lively" adjective will get by the editor, but not a string of them. Be truthful, interesting, and brief.

If there is more than one newspaper in the city, it is a good idea to vary the news releases slightly. Each, of course, must contain the same essential information, but the style, construction, and emphasis can be varied. An editor who reads the same news article in the competing paper will treat the publicity director's next request with reservation.

Finally, the news release should be delivered personally to the newspaper and on time. This means a special trip to the paper at least two full days prior to the date of insertion. An article which is scheduled for publication in a Sunday edition (which is most desirable) should probably be delivered Thursday morning.

Feature Stories. A story which singles out a special aspect of a production in an informative, interesting manner is called a feature story. It does not deal with straight news, and is not an announcement, but highlights human interest. It might center, for example, on the unique manner of rehearsals imposed on the director of *Marat/Sade* because of its asylum atmosphere. To get the actors to convey the proper feeling of insanity in all they do, the director has "patient rehearsals" for thirty minutes prior to each regular rehearsal. Or a feature story could center on the chairman of makeup who designs and builds the masks for *The Blacks.* Or it can be an interview with a scene designer on the problems of designing a multi-set show for a stage with no wing space and no fly area.

None of these is a news story about the play as such, but each deals with a special or unique aspect of the play production process and informs the readers. Nor should the publicity director neglect the business staff. Feature articles can also be written on box office operations and various theatre problems, such as silk-screening two hundred posters, or even on play selection problems. Very few people know of the many problems which confront the theatre staff of a college or university when it attempts to select the plays for a season.

Feature stories, which generally are longer than news releases, should be prepared or written in conjunction with a representative of the newspaper because very few editors will read through six or seven pages of copy if they have no advance knowledge of the idea. If the publicity director has a unique idea for a feature story, he should talk it over with his contact at the newspaper, explaining the idea and why it would be of interest to the paper's readers. Many newspaper people are wary (and understandably so) of publicity agents' "features." They are constantly bombarded with "features" which are untrue, faked, and exaggerated. The old story of the "mysterious disappearance of the female star . . .perhaps kidnaped. . ." still haunts newspaper editors.

Some publicity agents are more subtle today but nevertheless indulge in pure fictions. If the newspaper contact believes the theatre has a genuine feature story, and believes in the honesty and integrity of the theatre publicist, he will probably take charge of the story and write it. After all, a newspaper looks for good features as hard as a theatre looks for free publicity. If the newspaper man doesn't think an idea has any possibilities, the publicity director probably should not go ahead with it on his own.

A final note of caution about feature stories: a publicity director will dig his own grave if he gives the same feature to different newspapers. An important aspect of a feature story is that it is exclusive. To allow two competing newspapers to feature the makeup man for *The Blacks* on the same Sunday means grievous trouble.

The publicity director should take a careful look at the play, the production, and the personnel to find a story which might be interesting to people who are not closely associated with theatre and the play production process. He should also, once a year, look at the entire theatre and production process to find an interesting theatrical story. Moreover, he has a jump on many other businesses because people are generally interested in theatre people and activities; for many, it has a magic allure. They don't necessarily want news but *inside interest*, so that their response to a feature story is something like: Isn't that interesting? I never knew *that*. Accordingly, the publicity director should ask himself if he has any stories which will provoke such reaction.

The Mechanics. When news releases and feature stories are written by the theatre staff they should be typed with double or triple spacing on one side of white, 8½″ by 11″ paper. There should be a margin of at least 1″ on both the right- and the left-hand side. At the bottom of each page the word "more" should by typed, and "End" or "###" or "-30-" should be typed below the final paragraph.

The upper left-hand corner of the first page should have the name of the theatre, the name of the person responsible for the release and his phone number, and the date. The upper right-hand corner should contain the name of the newspaper and the release date (the date on which the article should appear in the newspaper). See figure 6-7 for a typical sample of the proper form.

In addition, it might be helpful to include a heading in each news release, such as "Bradley Theatre to Open *Hamlet*" or "*Hamlet* Opens Tuesday at Bradley." Few newspapers will print the heading suggested by a publicity director or press agent since each has its own style and special requirements for headlines, but there is no harm in letting the editor know immediately what the release is all about.

Submitting articles for the school newspaper is somewhat easier than for the city paper because the theatre's productions are much more important events for the school newspaper. The school paper, therefore, can be expected to run a lengthy feature article on each play, as well as several news articles. These articles should include (1) an announcement of the entire season at the start of the year, (2) an announcement of auditions in the issue prior to each audition, (3) a story announcing the cast after the auditions, (4) an article on the progress of rehearsals and the technical production process, (5) a story announcing the opening of the box office, and (6) a long news story just prior to the openings. Add to this a feature story and pictures, and the school newspaper can be a focal point of campus publicity.

The news releases given to the school paper can point up much more local color and interest than the ones that are given to the city paper. Cast members can be identified according to class and their various extracurricular activities. School personalities, events, activities, and color should be given greater stress in the school paper. Mentioning items of special interest to students and class members makes the stories more readable and appropriate for a school paper.

Advertisements. Every newspaper operates on the income it receives from its advertisements, not on the 10 cents that each reader or subscriber pays for the paper. News releases and fea-

Bradley University Theatre
John E. Clifford
676-7611, Ext. 410
9/1/69

Peoria Journal Star

FOR IMMEDIATE RELEASE

FIVE PLAYS SELECTED FOR BRADLEY THEATRE SEASON

Bradley University Theatre will present five major plays, four film classics, one children's play, and one experimental play during its 1969-70 season. All eleven events will be included in the theatre's 1969-70 season coupon book which goes on sale to the public tomorrow.

The five major productions of the season are "Blues for Mister Charlie" by James Baldwin, "The Lion in Winter" by James

... show both sides of black and white

... of the murder and the trial. It

...tober 27 through November 2 with

...ty comedy about the conflict between

..., will open on December 9th for a

...ins J. Bell, the play will feature

BU Theater Opens Season Ticket Sale

Bradley University Theatre will present five plays, four film classics, one children's play, and one experimental theatre production during the 1969-70 season. All theatrical events will be included in the theatre's 1969-70 season coupon book, available beginning tomorrow.

The five major productions of the season are "Blues for Mr. Charlie" by James Baldwin, "The Lion in Winter" by James Golden, Alexandre Breffort's musical "Irma La Douce," a Readers Theatre production entitled "Expressions of Love", and George Bernard Shaw's "Caesar and Cleopatra."

THE OPENING play will be black author James Baldwin's only attempt at writing for the theatre, "Blues for Mr. Charlie," deals with the "black-white problem in America with honesty and dedication. Baldwin takes his plot from the Emmett Till murder in Mississippi in 1955, and attempts to show the divergent views of black and white Americans caught up in the aftermath of the killing and the trial. It will run October 27-November 2 with Dr. John E. Clifford directing.

"The Lion in Winter," a witty comedy about the conflict between King Henry and Eleanor of Aquitaine, will open December 9 for a six night run. It will be directed by Dr. Collins J. Bell. The play, which was made into a movie recently, will feature costumes designed by the University Theatre's new Costumer, Gwendolyn I. Anderson.

Thomas J. Joyce will direct the "adult" musical comedy "Irma la Douce" which will run from March 16-22 and Dr. Kent Campbell of the School of Music will serve as musical director. "Irma" is the sophisticated musical which originated in Paris, was transported to London for a long run and has set box office records here in the United States.

"Expressions of Love" is an original Readers Theatre script written by Dr. Ronald J. Koperski of the theatre staff and will feature poems and writings accompanied by music throughout the ages. This unique production, never before presented to the public, will run for five performances only begining on April 22.

George Bernard Shaw's portrait of the elderly Caesar coaching the girlish queen of Egypt in the etiquette of ruling, "Caesar and Cleopatra" will close the season May 12-17. This first attempt at producing in the Peoria area Shaw's wittiest play will be directed by Dr. Bell.

THE UNIVERSITY Theatre's Film Classic Series, available only to Season Subscribers, will feature John Ford's Academy Award film "The Quiet Man" October 13 - 14, the mystery "The League of Gentlemen" November 17-18, the Japanese film classic "Ugetsu" Feb. 23-24, and "The Pawnbroker" April 27-28.

In addition to the major plays and films Coupon Book Holders will be entitled to see the "Experimental Theatre" Jan. 15-17, and children of coupon book holders will be admitted free to the Children's Theatre production of "Winnie the Pooh" which will be produced in cooperation with the Children's Theatre League of Peoria October 11-12 at Manual High School.

Season coupon books are available until Oct. 3, or until sold out.

Figure 6-7. Sample News Release, as Sent to the Paper and as It Appeared in Print

ture stories are published free, but advertising costs money. Nevertheless, the educational theatre should take advantage of newspaper ads to contact a wide variety of people.

When first submitting an ad to a city newspaper, the publicity director should contact the display advertising department and find out who will be in charge of handling the school's account. This way the display advertising representative will know whom to contact for more personal service, and vice versa. The publicity director should find out at this meeting (1) if space must be reserved in advance, (2) the deadline for the submission of ads, and (3) the rate for the school's theatre.

Newspapers usually have a special "charity" rate for educational institutions and non-profit organizations, for which educational theatre can qualify. This rate is approximately one-third the regular rate.

Advertising rates are usually given in terms of column inches: $4.95 per column inch, for example. This means that it costs $4.95 for an ad which measures one column wide by 1 inch deep. An ad that measures two columns by 4 inches (see figure 6-8) would occupy 8 column inches and cost $39.60. If newspapers do not charge by the column inch, they charge by the line. Because there are 14 agate lines to an inch, an ad which measures two columns by 4 inches is equal to 112 column lines, and at 35 cents per column line the cost would be $39.20.

It is difficult to state the average cost per column inch in newspapers, but the charity rate for educational theatres runs from $4 to $7 per column inch, depending upon the size of the newspaper and the size of the town. Otherwise, theatre ads can cost as much as $50 per column inch. The *New York Times*, for example, charges $3.80 per line for a Broadway theatre ad in the Sunday edition (which is always higher than their weekday rates). This is $53.20 per column inch. The ad in figure 6-8 which measures two columns by 4 inches and costs $39.60 at $4.95 per column inch in the *Peoria Journal Star* would cost $425.60 in the Sunday *Times*. If there were a special rate for educational theatre, that ad could cost around $140 in the *Times*.

Obviously, an educational theatre cannot spend $140 for an ad, but $5 per column inch in a local newspaper is not unreasonable, and can be well worth the money. An easy way to check this cost

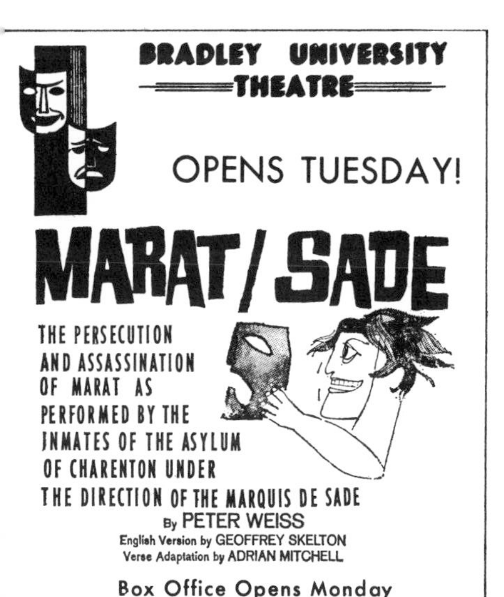

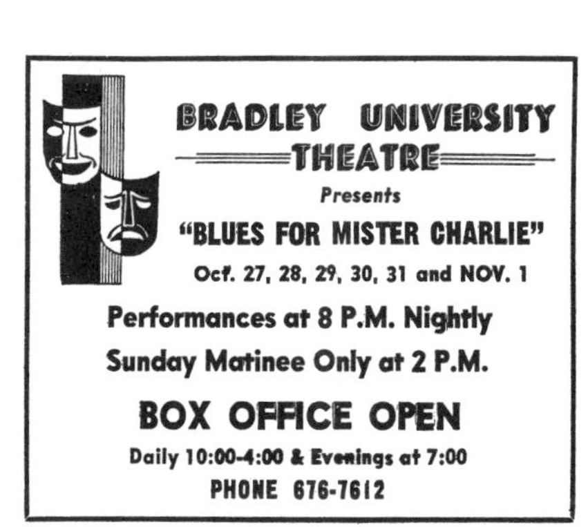

Figure 6-8. Newspaper Ads of Various Sizes

against sales is to place a coupon in the ad and see how many patrons return that coupon with their ticket order. The income far exceeds the cost of the ad in most cases.

In designing ads it is important to keep them simple, easy to read, well spaced, and interesting. They should contain all the important facts and information, and also a certain amount of persuasive material. Most theatre ads are built around an illustration that is called a logotype, which contains the title of the play, the author's name, and a simple drawing that is representative of the theme, mood, or plot of the play. If the theatre has a talented artist who can create a unique and interesting illustration, the publicity director can give it to the newspaper along with the copy. Then, for the additional cost of engraving the design and making a "cut," the ad will have a much more meaningful and interesting character. For theatres that do not have talented artists, Package Publicity Service can supply logotypes around which an ad can be designed. These come in the form of mats which can be given to newspapers.

It is always best to sketch an ad as the publicity director wants it, indicating the important items, the size of type to be used, etc., rather than leaving it to the newspaper to design. Figure 6-9 shows an educational theatre ad and the original design that was sent to the newspaper.

In planning the dates for the ads it is a good idea to try to use Sundays and Thursdays, which are usually the days with the largest circulation. An ad in the Sunday edition just prior to the opening of the box office (or mail order period), followed by a large ad on the Sunday just prior to the opening of the play, would be a good minimum. Depending upon the budget and the cost of the ads, this can be expanded or reduced.

Advertising in the school newspaper should be used, too. This is much less expensive (usually between $1 and $2 per column inch), and so should be an integral part of the advertising campaign. Most school newspapers are published once a week, and a theatre ad should appear in each issue for three weeks prior to the opening. But again, it is important to check with the school newspaper to determine the method of printing used—letterpress or offset. Because most school newspapers are printed by offset

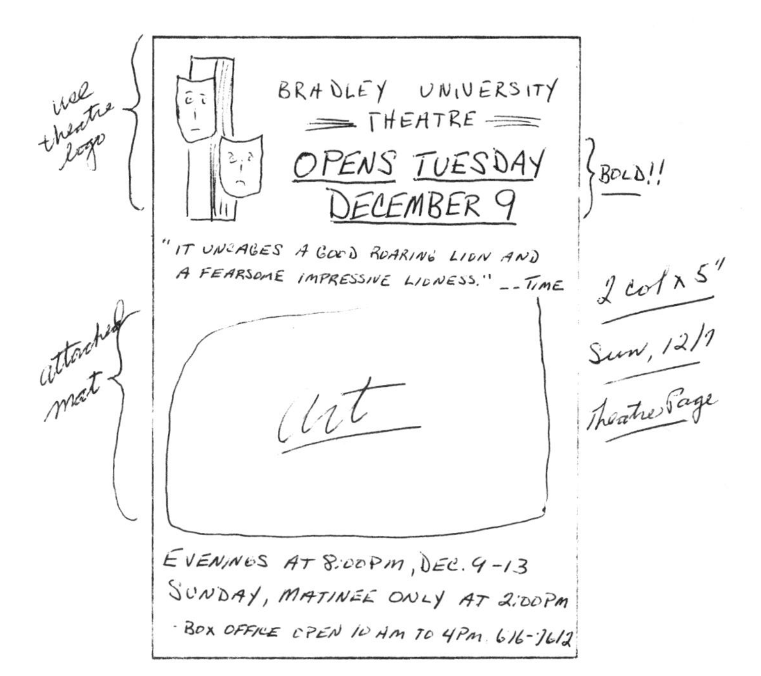

Figure 6-9. A Newspaper Ad and the Original Design

rather than letterpress, it is usually possible to submit artwork and an ad layout *exactly* as they will be printed.

DIRECT MAIL PUBLICITY

Another type of publicity which many educational theatres use is direct mail advertising, which consists of any publicity material sent by mail to specific prospects on a large scale. It includes a number of forms, such as postcards, letters, brochures, folders, and flyers, that are sent out for the purpose of obtaining orders, following up on inquiries received from other advertising media, or keeping patrons aware of productions as the time for ordering tickets approaches.

Direct mail is probably the most flexible of all advertising media. After a selection of recipients is made, the theatre follows up with some form of direct correspondence. Obviously, the most important and time-consuming project in utilizing direct mail is compiling a list of those from whom the theatre publicity director seeks acknowledgment. This is the core of the direct mail process.

The Mailing List. Every educational theatre will want to compile, insofar as possible, a complete list of prospective theatregoers. The best prospects, of course, are those who have subscribed to a theatre season or attended plays in the past, and they should most certainly become part of the list. If there are other theatres in the area, every effort should be made to secure the names and addresses of those who attended their plays.

In compiling the list, the theatre manager should begin with his own theatre patrons. Keeping the stubs from season ticket sales and transferring those names to a mailing list is a start. In addition, he should keep a complete record of the names and addresses of all patrons who call the box office to make reservations for individual admissions, as well as maintaining a sign-up desk or sheet in the lobby during production runs for those who wish to be added to the theatre's mailing list.

To gain a greater audience, the educational theatre manager might also seek out other prospects. As a survey of non-student educational theatre subscribers by O. Franklin Kenworthy* indi-

*O. Franklin Kenworthy, "A Study of Non-Student University Theatre Attenders." (Ph.D. dissertation, Michigan State University, 1967).

cates, they are primarily middle- and upper-middle income families, college graduates, and professional people, and they might be contacted through the use of alumni and zip code lists. However, it is often advantageous to use the names and addresses compiled by a mailing list broker or advertising specialist, who serves in the capacity of a consultant, on a rental basis.

Experienced advertising specialists say that persons on a magazine subscription list are good prospects for a record club; and if they subscribe to the *New York Times* or the *Saturday Review*, surveys show that they are good prospects for the theatre. With such further qualifiers as income, profession, special interests, education, etc., the direct mail advertising campaign can be directed toward select groups and thus will be more effective, as well as much more economical, than if mailings were sent to names picked at random from telephone listings or similar directories. The cost of such lists is not prohibitive; it usually runs from $15 to $25 per thousand names. Because they provide the theatre with the best prospects, they are well worth the investment. With only a 5 percent return, which is about average for general mailings, the theatre should benefit.

But the best list, of course, is the theatre's list of patrons from past seasons. A good theatre manager will always keep such a list and use it for his basic mailings—and keep it up to date. Research shows that the average mailing list, if not constantly updated, can be as much as 50 percent obsolete in a period as short as two years. Experts also say that the factor most damaging to the effectiveness of direct mail advertising is inaccurate addressing of the mailing forms. Besides revising the list each year (based upon season subscriptions), another effective and inexpensive solution is the periodic mailing of reply cards that ask the recipients for correction of their listing or changes of address.

Under the present postal regulations, brochures and postcards in large bulk quantities must be mailed in units that are labeled by zip codes. For this reason, a great many mailing lists are arranged alphabetically and according to zip codes. In the long run, the educational theatre manager will find this the most convenient method for organizing his mailing list.

Forms of Direct Mail. The particular form of direct mailing to be used is determined by the purpose of the advertisement and, of course, reasonable budgetary considerations. Three forms seem to lend themselves to successful advertising for the educational theatre: brochures, postcards, and letters.

Season Brochures. An attractive, neat, and well-organized season brochure can help in getting a good response to a theatre's offerings. Season brochures are usually mailed to past subscribers seveal weeks prior to the official opening of the seasonal sales period (see chapter 7). Later they can be sent to others on the mailing list, when the official sales period begins.

There is a great variety of season brochures which an educational theatre can design, print, and mail, and figure 6-10 shows several types and sizes which accomplish the essential purposes. Most of these brochures are designed as announcements and order forms; that is, they list the plays for the season and provide an order form which patrons can return to the theatre.

The important information in such a brochure is (1) a list of all of the plays and their dates of production, (2) a paragraph or sentence or two that characterizes each play by type, theme, or plot, (3) a list of all "bonus" or "extra" attractions and their dates, (4) the prices for individual plays and the cost of a season ticket, and (5) a form for ordering season tickets. In addition to this basic information, some theatres list their past productions and staffs, reproduce pictures of last season's plays, etc.

The brochure can be designed by either the theatre staff and students or by professional artists. For best results, many college and university theatres hire a commercial artist to design the brochure. This is costly, because commercial art firms and advertising agencies are expensive, but the results are always excellent and very professional. For the educational theatre manager who does not have a large budget, or wants to give theatre and art students the experience of designing a brochure, there is always the "home made" option. The task is difficult and time consuming, but it can be rewarding and well worth the effort.

In either case, the design should be submitted to several printers for estimates, and the brochure should be printed on high-grade stock. Designing a season brochure is much more involved than designing a poster, and care should be taken in selecting the stu-

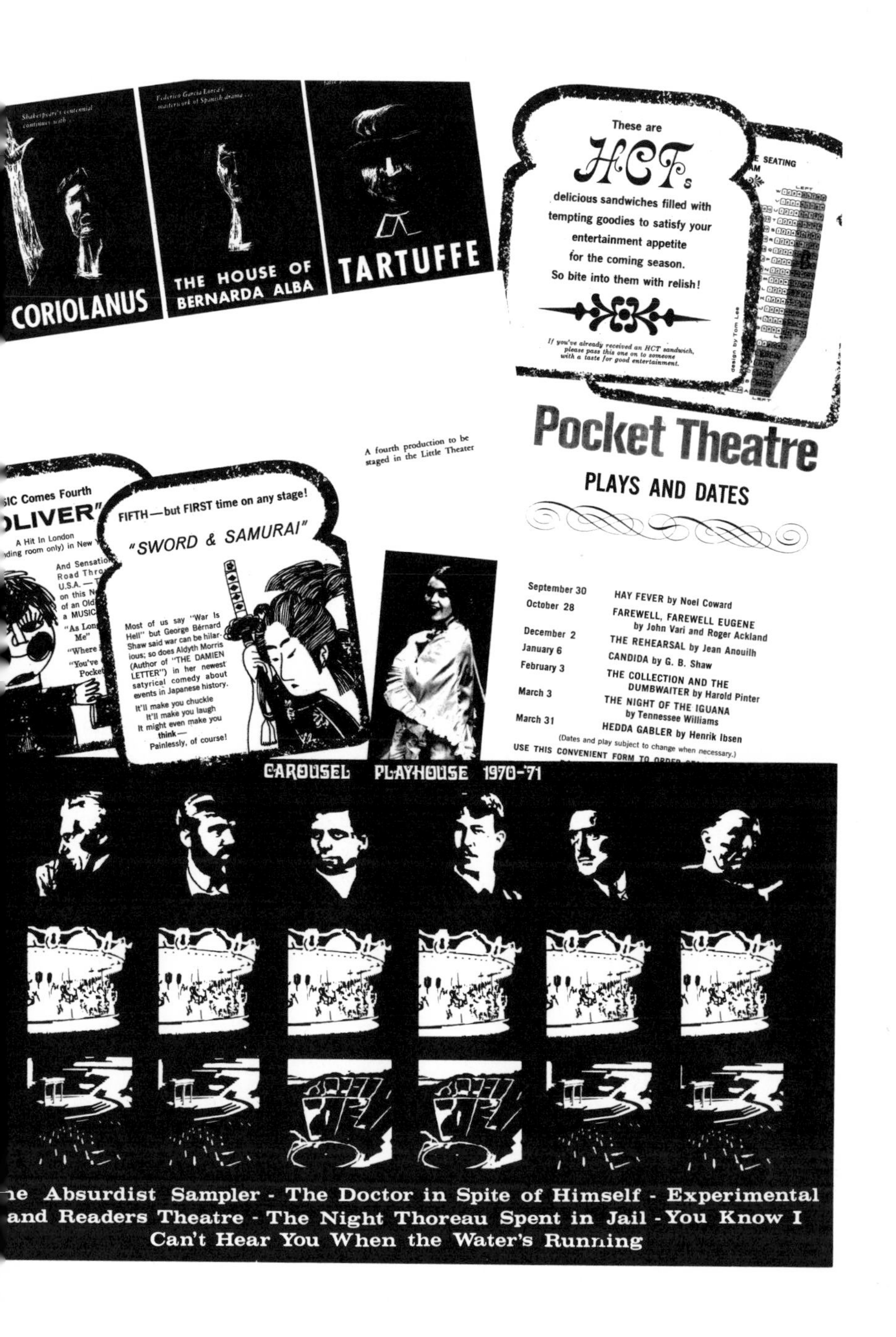

Figure 6-10. Samples of Season Brochures

dents and supervising the execution of the design. For a theatre in which the personal education of the students has prime importance, student-designed and -executed brochures are much more rewarding and fitting than farming them out to a professional art firm.

Postcards. Postcards, the simplest form of direct mail, are best utilized in advertising attractive offerings, such as a reduced rate on a particular play or an upcoming "extra" production, or as a reminder of a "hit" production. In general, the postcard is most effective when an offering is especially attractive and almost self-explanatory. Figure 6-11 is a postcard announcement that was sent to 2,000 people to supplement the regular newspaper and radio or television publicity.

Letters. The season brochure, which is more attractive and impressive than the postcard, is used when a great deal of information must be presented in a persuasive manner. The letter, on the other hand, is a more personal form of contact than either the brochure or the postcard, and is normally used in advertising that is directed to selected prospects on a mailing list or as a follow-up to season subscribers. This latter use can thank patrons for their support, explain the season-ticket reservation procedures, and serve as a good public relations tool.

Some small high school and college theatres send a letter to all the parents of the students explaining the nature of the theatre activity and requesting support. In addition, such a letter is usually sent to each member of the school's faculty and staff.

Mailing Procedures. Depending upon the number of persons on the mailing list, there are several methods for mailing brochures, postcards, and letters. With enough volunteers, if the mailing list is small, it may be possible to address all the mailings by hand. If this is not possible, the theatre manager can look into various label-making devices or inexpensive addressing machines, or merely the typing of names and addresses on sheets of gummed labels (with from one to five carbon sheets). A check with the school purchasing director and of various business catalogues should yield a number of other mailing techniques.

Also, there are many companies which can take over all the mechanical, procedural problems in a direct mail program, and some of them utilize the latest computer techniques for creating and maintaining mailing lists. If the educational theatre manager

BRADLEY UNIVERSITY
THEATRE

BRADLEY HALL
PEORIA, ILLINOIS 61606

Non-Profit Organization
U.S. Postage
PAID
Peoria, Illinois
Permit No. 688

Figure 6-11. Sample Postcard for Direct Mail

decides he needs to go to a large direct mail operation (if his budget and program allow it), he might look into some of these services. But for most educational theatres, high school or college or university, it should be possible—with much hard work and a small expenditure of money—to maintain a mailing list of at least season patrons and others who are interested in local educational theatre.

The educational theatre manager should also investigate the bulk rate mailing cost for direct mail, and especially for brochures and postcards. Most schools have bulk rate, non-profit permits which permit the theatre, as a function of the school, to mail its items at the special rate. The educational theatre manager should consult the school business manager for the proper form of the mailings in order to use the bulk rate. In addition, he should contact the local post office for a list of the regulations and instructions for bulk mail.

NOVELTY PUBLICITY

Besides radio, television, posters, newspapers, and direct mail, there are a number of miscellaneous methods by which the theatre publicist can bring a theatrical event to the attention of the public. These other forms of publicity are broadly listed here under the all-encompassing heading "novelty publicity."

Novelty forms of publicizing theatre events can "get away" from the theatre publicist if they are not carefully controlled— they can become "freak shows" or partake too much of a carnival atmosphere. For example, dressing up cast members and parading around the campus, or having them pulled in a wagon or float, is usually inappropriate for a play. For this reason, most theatre publicists try to keep all publicity and advertising (1) in good taste, (2) honest, and (3) in keeping with the nature of the play.

John Bos, director of Philadelphia's Theatre of the Living Arts, recommends that theatres use "selective honesty." "Press agentry in resident theatres," Bos says, "is the exercise of selective honesty." This means that theatre publicists should resist every form of *publicity;* he should select, with care, only those means of *communication* which will best sell not only the production but also the image of the theatre. Theatre publicists have an obligation to be honest with the public and present a true picture of the theatre. Perhaps the term "selective honesty" should be tacked up on the wall of every theatre publicist's office.

The theatre publicist must also remember his budget. He should not get so carried away with novelty or gimmick forms of publicity that they seriously deplete the budget—the forms of publicity listed here should merely *supplement* the usual forms of publicity. Novelty publicity can be expensive, and there is no guarantee that they will obtain satisfactory results. They should, however, be tried occasionally for they can help a publicity campaign.

Matches. Theatre match books, printed with the name of the theatre and the season's titles, can be purchased at the start of the season and dispensed around town.

Balloons. For advertising children's plays or some musicals, balloons imprinted with the name of the theatre and the dates of the play can be given away at fairs, shopping centers, downtown, etc.

Pins. Printing large pins with the name of a play and having the cast members wear them on campus and to class should promote interest in a production. The pins, similar to campaign buttons, can be purchased for a reasonable sum.

Napkins and Placemats. Many restaurants will accept and use paper napkins and placemats bearing the name of a theatre's play, its dates, and a tasteful artwork. It saves the restaurants money, and they look at the device as a good public service. If this form is used, the publicity director shouldn't forget the campus cafeteria.

Shopping Bags. Many of the shopping bags sold in department stores and supermarkets have a printed advertising message, and inquiry at such stores might lead to using this publicity outlet.

Calendars. Many theatres use some form of a theatre calendar as a promotional device. Many people like to have such calendars in their homes, especially if they remind them of an activity in which they have a special interest. The theatre calendar can take many forms, some of which are not prohibitive in terms of cost.

Flyers and Throwaways. Another inexpensive yet effective method of getting the name of an upcoming production before the public and the student population is the use of flyers or throwaways. These can be mimeographed 8 ½″ by 11″ sheets of paper announcing the play, dates, ticket information, and a short blurb

Figure 6-12. Samples of Various Types of Flyers and a Theatre Calendar

about the production. Or if a more elaborate form is desired (and can be afforded), the flyer can be prepared with artwork and lettering and be given to a printer to run off on an offset press.

After they have been prepared, the flyers can be placed in all faculty mailboxes, student dormitories and mail boxes, and handed out to students as they enter buildings, classrooms, the lunchroom, library, gym, etc. They can also be tacked up on bulletin boards and taken to neighborhood stores with a request that they be placed near the exit so they can be taken by customers.

This type of advertising can be much more effective than posters because of the more informal or personal nature of the flyer. It can be placed directly in the hands of prospective theatregoers. Figure 6-12 shows several types of flyers.

Costume Displays. It might be possible, when the theatre is producing a period play, to set up a costume display in one of the large windows of a downtown department store or in a clothing store in a large shopping center.

Billing Inserts. Many department stores and public utility companies put advertising inserts in the monthly statements of their customers. For a nominal charge (the cost of printing), department stores have included such announcements for a local theatre in their monthly billing. Contact should be made with such firms at least six months in advance.

In addition to the above-mentioned publicity ideas, which if used in a controlled manner can help provide excitement and comment for a production, the publicity director should remember such other items as bookmarks, athletic programs, lobby displays, announcements in class and on the school's public address system, and announcements in theatre programs. He should also, when the theatre is producing a musical, provide all local disc jockeys (or perhaps the music programmer) with recorded music from the show. An inventive and imaginative publicity director can utilize these and other publicity outlets to enhance the total publicity for any play.

THE PUBLICITY CAMPAIGN

The function of the theatre manager is to control all aspects of publicity both for a production and for the season's ticket sales. As an administrator of the theatre, he should plan the entire campaign carefully, so that it is a unified effort (*really* a campaign) and not a hodgepodge of various (however serious) independent efforts. Each play should have a unified and all-encompassing approach. Also, the manager should be aware of the best publicity methods for a play vis-à-vis the appropriate publicity methods used for other plays. Only careful advance planning can accomplish a unified yet interesting publicity approach for a season of plays.

Since it is so important to prepare and plan the advertising campaign in great detail for each play and for the entire season, the theatre manager should complete a publicity calendar or schedule before the season opens. This schedule should designate all the deadlines by which the various publicity activities must be accomplished—the dates and deadlines for ordering posters, submitting news releases, reserving advertising space, placing and removing posters, etc. Figure 6-13 is a typical publicity schedule.

SUMMARY

Lest the contents of this chapter be inadvertently misleading, it should again be pointed out that a theatre's greatest publicity is consistently good, high-quality theatrical productions. No matter how well posters are designed, no matter the number of mail orders, and no matter how many interview programs feature the theatre's cast members, if the play is not good the seats will not be consistently sold out. Nevertheless, a good production needs to have its name and merit publicized. No one will come to even a good production if he doesn't know when it opens.

Very possibly, the combination of the artistic and the commercial or business aspects of the theatre comes to a head in publicity. The business manager must rely upon the artistic director; the artistic director must rely upon the business manager. In any event, that is the point of this book: the commercial and managerial aspects of the play production process are as important as the artistic aspects. Equal attention should be given to both for successful educational theatre and for successful education.

Publicity Schedule

YOU KNOW I CAN'T HEAR YOU WHEN THE WATER'S RUNNING

April 16	—Article to Scout for 4/23 issue (on cast)
April 19	—Order posters
April 23	—Article to Scout for 4/30 issue —Ad to Scout for 4/30 issue
April 26	—Contact Ann Lane
April 29	—Ad to Journal Star for 5/2 issue (1 x 4)
April 30	—News release to B.U. publicity office —Article to Journal Star for 5/2 issue —Design and write up flyers (4/30 to 5/2) —Ad to Scout for 5/7 issue —Article to Scout for 5/7 issue
May 3	—Mail fact sheet to local radio and television stations —Contact Scout pic ed for picture appointment —Take flyer copy to BU print shop (early A.M.)
May 4	—Contact Peoria Savings & Loan for moving sign use.
May 5	—Distribute posters on campus and in town
May 6	—Paint sign on front of building —Ad to Journal Star for 5/9 issue (2 x 5) —Ad to Journal Star for 5/13 issue (2 x 4) —Ad to Journal Star for 5/16 issue (1 x 4)
May 7	—Article to Scout for 5/14 issue —Article to Journal Star for 5/9 issue —Contact Jerry Klein about pic on Sat. —Distribute flyers to dorms, mail boxes, faculty, etc. —Ad to Scout for 5/14 issue
May 8	—Make carts for WCBU
May 10-13	—Go to Street Scene (possibly next week, too)
May 14	—Take sign to Bradley Hall entrance
May 24	—Remove all posters, signs, etc.

NOTES:

—Cary Libkin to check w/Ritter on sign on Stud Center

Figure 6-13. A Sample Publicity Schedule

7 The Box Office

Usually a theatre patron has only three contacts with the personnel of a theatre—three sources for receiving a good impression of the theatre: (1) the actors who entertain him on the stage, (2) the usher who seats him, and (3) the box office personnel who sell the tickets. But as the actors do not meet the patron personally, his only direct personal contact with a theatre is through the box office. It is important, then, that box office procedures, policies, and personnel reflect the theatre's interest and concern for the convenience and comfort of the theatre patron.

BOX OFFICE PERSONNEL

The students who work in the box office deal directly, either on the phone or in person, with the theatre's public. These workers should be selected with great care. They should be personable, well groomed, intelligent, efficient, and capable of working well under pressure—without getting frustrated or careless. There are many times when the phone rings while a difficult person is at the window and there is a long line behind him, when it takes a cool head to keep all concerned in a good mood. The box office manager will soon discover that the fewer workers he has, the more experienced each will become and the greater will be the efficiency of the box office operations.

This is not a job for any student who happens to come along. Just sitting in the box office and selling tickets might seem to be a very simple job. But an efficient operation requires trained personnel. Efficient, personable, and diplomatic box office personnel can do much to keep theatre patrons satisfied. Therefore, great care should be exercised in the selection and training of box office personnel. They should be thoroughly familiar with all the procedures and policies of the theatre as they relate to tickets and reservations.

Specific suggestions and recommendations for educational theatre box office personnel of necessity depend upon the procedures and policies of each theatre. The following suggestions, from the instructions given each box office worker at Bradley University, indicate the general advice that is most helpful for theatre box office workers.

1. Give the patrons the best possible seat location(s) which are available, regardless of the price he is to pay. If he pays the $1.50 regular price, or receives one from a season coupon, or gets a special children's rate, he should get the best seat available.

2. Always show the patron his seat location on the chart and ask if it is satisfactory. Show him where he will sit in reference to aisles, the stage, and the rear doors. Make sure he knows the location.

3. Inform the patron of the best location for each night if he has no preference. Try to sell him the night for which the least number of tickets have been sold. But don't force him!

4. After the patron has paid his money and before you put the tickets in an envelope for him, make sure that the seats he bought together ARE together. There is nothing worse than for the patron to get home and find that his seats are not together but are in different rows or sections.

5. Check the date and performance day on each ticket before tearing off the audit stub. Read the date and performance day aloud to the patron. Make sure that you give him tickets for the night he wants to attend. Again, there is nothing more frustrating than for the patron to get home and find out that you gave him tickets for the Friday performance when he asked for Saturday.

6. Listen to every patron who has a special problem. To him that problem is important. It should be to you, too, as a representative of the theatre. Care!

7. *Be courteous!* You are the only contact our patrons have with the University Theatre outside the productions themselves. The impression they receive of us through you is IMPORTANT, and must be a good one.

8. Always explain our telephone reservation policy carefully. We will NOT hold unpaid reservations after 7:50 P.M. on the night of the performance. Make sure that every person understands that clearly. It will save us trouble later.

9. Always repeat the name, address, and phone number of each person for whom you make a reservation. And don't forget to tell him the location of his ticket(s).

10. The box office telephone is for incoming calls only! Don't tie it up.

BOX OFFICE PROCEDURES AND POLICIES

Racking Tickets

The first task of the box office manager is to rack his tickets for each performance (which assumes that the theatre is using reserved-seat tickets). This means that he places all the tickets for a given production in a ticket rack, a shelf-like rack with slots or compartments. It may have a separate slot for each seat in the house, but more often it has a slot for each row in each section. Either way, a ticket rack holds all the tickets for each performance of a production. Figure 7-1 is a rack which holds tickets for six performances; each slot represents two rows, and the rack is arranged according to the three sections of the house: right, center, and left.

Displaying the tickets in this manner enables the box office manager to tell at a glance the number and kinds of tickets that have been sold. It also makes it easy for box office personnel to find seats for patrons, and because the rack is clearly visible through the box office window, patrons are less likely to argue about the availability of tickets and seating locations. Theatre patrons, therefore, tend to look upon ticket sellers with less suspicion. Nevertheless, many patrons will not believe a ticket seller who says he has nothing better than row S seats—that, for some reason, he is holding better seats for someone else.

Unfortunately, box office workers have a reputation for unfair treat-

Figure 7-1. A Ticket Rack

ment of the patron at the window, and the notion of the ticket seller who keeps a stack of better or cheaper seats under the counter for "special" people is not entirely unfounded. Although somewhat justified by the practice of New York box office agents, this image can and should be countered by the educational theatre.

Pulling Tickets

All good theatre managers "pull" the tickets for what are called house seats prior to the opening of the box office. These are the tickets a manager holds in reserve for use in emergencies. What does a manager do, for example, when a couple arrives at the box office ten minutes before curtain time on a sold-out night to pick up their reserved tickets and finds that the tickets are not there? When the patron insists that he called four days ago and made the reservations, there is no point in arguing or in finding out what happened to his reservations or who is at fault. Selling him two house seats saves time and trouble, and keeps a satisfied patron. Or what if the reservations are there but they are for tomorrow night? Rather than arguing who said what and who misunderstood whom, the theatre should assume it made the mistake and should sell the patron a pair of house seats.

There are many such emergencies every night in a theatre: lost reservations, lost tickets, tickets for the wrong night, separated seating—and the little old lady whose hearing aid batteries don't work and wants a seat closer to the stage. The theatre manager who has seats available for such cases can greatly enhance the reputation and image of the theatre. If, instead, he says "I'm sorry; we have no more seats," he might as well be saying "Go away and don't come back; we aren't interested in you." It is far better to turn a few people away on a sell-out night and keep three or four pair of house seats than to sell every ticket and not be able to take care of emergencies. In simple terms, it's better to have empty seats than angry patrons.

Emergencies, moreover, are not the only reason why experienced theatre managers keep back a few house seats. There are always "VIPs" who call at the last minute and ask for seats—out-of-town guests or parents of cast members, the principal, the dean, or faculty members. A good theatre manager will anticipate these problems and plan accordingly.

The question of how many house seats to pull is difficult to answer, and the best teacher is experience. After several shows, the theatre manager will have a pretty good idea of how many house seats he will need in the future. A new manager would do well to hold out ten or twelve pair of tickets until experience tells him the precise number he is likely to need.

The locations of the house seats also are important. The best policy is to scatter them throughout the house—a few good ones (front center) and a few in poorer locations (right and left rear). This is better than pulling one or two rows, which, if they remain empty, look strange and incriminating.

Dressing the House

Sometimes, with a large theatre and a small anticipated audience, the theatre manager will want to spread the latter around so as to make it appear that the house is fuller than it really is. The technique of making a small audience appear larger is called "dressing the house," which is accomplished by leaving a number of vacant seats and scattering the audience throughout.

A well-spaced or well-dressed house has definite psychological advantages for both the actors and the audience. Inasmuch as all actors like to play to full houses, a small audience, grouped together down center, does not help create the optimum excitement in the actors. Similarly, audiences tend to react more strongly and more often when they are assembled in large groups.

The technique for dressing the house, when it seems obvious that it will be small, is to remove scattered blocks of tickets from the rack and to sell an equal number of seats in all sections. The effect of a well-distributed, well-balanced house can be obtained when seats are sold from the center to the sides, and from the front to the back.

Mail Orders

Some theatres, mostly commercial theatres, which have a no-reservation policy take ticket orders through the mail. For large commercial theatres in cities where theatregoers most often come from a great distance, this system is advantageous, provided the patrons send the proper remittance and a self-addressed and stamped envelope for the forwarding of his tickets. For the educational theatre, however, large-volume use of mail orders for individual admission sales is not as advantageous. In the first place, the vast majority of the educational theatre audience comes from the immediate academic community and there is no real problem of getting to the box office. Most members of the audience who come from the town also are able to purchase tickets with little difficulty, and so the convenience of mail orders is not a great advantage. A good "policy" for an educational theatre manager to adopt vis-à-vis mail orders is to neither encourage nor discourage them. Accept mail orders routinely but don't go out of the way to advertise or promote them. It is always best to have the personal, box office contact with theatre patrons, and the only exception to this general policy is in selling season tickets.

If an educational theatre sells season tickets, a real advantage that the theatre can offer is the opportunity to purchase tickets by mail prior to the general public sale and thereby get the best seats. In this case, patrons should be asked to state their choice of performances and send a self-addressed, stamped envelope for the return of their tickets. The box office manager, who fills the orders, should keep a record of the seats which are issued to each season ticket holder in case of loss in the mail or other problems.

Telephone Reservations

Very few large commercial theatres make reservations by telephone. Obviously, many people, with good intentions, will reserve seats but be unable to honor this commitment and pay for their tickets, and thus the theatre has a number of tickets which people promised they would use but did not. If only from a commercial point of view, this is bad business.

A reservation is a request from a patron asking a theatre to hold a ticket (or tickets) at the box office without immediate payment. For the educational theatre, it is advisable to accept reservations over the telephone, but with certain limitations. First, reservations should be taken on a special phone and only during regular box office hours. Second, orders should be filled at the time of the phone calls and placed in envelopes that show the names, addresses, and phone number of the patrons, the number of tickets reserved, the performance date, and the amount due. Third, a policy should establish the time after which all unpaid reservations will not be kept but will be sold as needed.

Some theatres require that phone reservations be paid for on the day prior to the performance (or twenty-four hours in advance); others hold phone reservations for only one day; and others hold them until one hour (or perhaps fifteen minutes) prior to curtain time. Depending upon the individual theatre, some workable policy should be set. The educational theatre manager should remember that holding reservations for townspeople until fifteen minutes or so prior to curtain time is a real convenience, and probably should be followed if this policy is not abused. But if too many people fail to pick up tickets which could have been sold, a change of policy is indicated.

Group Plans

The purpose of group rates in educational theatre is twofold. First, it encourages large groups to see theatre performances at substantially reduced rates. This also aids the theatre by providing larger audiences. And if the theatre experience is pleasant, several members of these groups are likely to return to see other productions, again enlarging the theatre's audience.

Second, and more important, it can provide a genuine, educationally enriching experience for high school and college groups. By offering English and speech classes special incentives to see certain plays which have an educational value, the theatre can supplement the classroom study of plays. Therefore, every production needn't be offered to schools at reduced rates but only plays which can truly supplement classroom study. These are usually the classics, which students read and study in their academic courses.

If the theatre has a production it wishes to offer to groups, special publicity (usually a letter) should be sent no later than six weeks prior to the opening performance. Included in that mailing should be an order form and a deadline for making group reservations. This deadline should be at least one week prior to the opening of the play so that the theatre manager can plan his individual admission ticket sales and advertising and keep his commitments to the other ticket holders. Season patrons should still get their choice of seats, but this does not mean that those who pay a reduced rate must of necessity be given poor seats. They should get the best tickets available after season patrons have selected their seats.

Exchanges and Refunds

Every box office and theatre manager is confronted by patrons who wish either to exchange their tickets or receive a refund for tickets purchased but not used. Firm but reasonable policies and procedures in this area can save the box office personnel a great deal of trouble and the patrons a great deal of embarrassment.

Theatres should allow patrons the privilege of exchanging tickets for a different performance as long as the one for which the original ticket was purchased has not been performed. In other words, a patron should not be allowed to exchange a Friday night ticket for a Saturday night ticket on Saturday night. After all, the Friday ticket is no longer valid; it has no cash or intrinsic value after the performance time has passed.

The procedure for taking care of exchanges is simple. If the box office uses coupon tickets with an audit stub, the box office worker merely collects the patron's ticket, takes a new ticket from the rack, tears the audit stub from the new ticket and clips it to the old ticket, and returns the old ticket and the new audit stub to the rack for resale.

The biggest problem is the patron who wants a refund on his ticket—who cannot use the ticket and therefore expects the theatre to take it back and return his money. The theatre manager's safest course is a policy which does not permit refunds, which is easy to establish but somewhat difficult to follow—even when "No Refund" is printed on the ticket.

A way to temper this policy (which many patrons think is unreasonable) is to allow refunds up to one day prior to a performance. This twenty-four-hour limit should take care of most reasonable requests, but same-day refunds should not be allowed. The theatre manager should remember that once he gives in and makes an exception to this policy, the floodgates have been opened. The problem of refunds is important, and the educational theatre manager should prepare himself for it.

The Daily Audit

At the close of each box office business day the box office manager should make an audit of the day's business and the total business of the box office to date. This audit should include the total number of tickets handled that day according to the categories of season ticket exchanges, individual admissions, group rate tickets, and complimentary tickets. It should also include the cash receipts for the day. Figure 7-2 is a typical daily box office report.

BRADLEY UNIVERSITY THEATRE
DAILY BOX OFFICE REPORT

PRODUCTION Irma la Douce DATE 3/16/70

MAIL ORDER DAY — CASH SALE DAY /

Description	Price	No. Sold	Receipts
Individual Admission	$2.50 2.00	136 117	$ 340.00 234.00
Group Rates	$ 1.50	0	$ —0—
Coupon Exchange	- 0 -	233	- 0 -
Complimentary	- 0 -	10	- 0 -
TOTALS	—	496	$ 574.00

Amount Deposited $ 574.00 Over/Under $ —0—

Discrepency Explanation

Prepared CN Approved By JC

Figure 7-2. A Daily Box Office Report

Box Office Sales Breakdown

A second box office report, which also is compiled daily, is the sales breakdown, which is essentially a compilation of the daily audits so as to bring the total sales up to date. It shows the daily and the total season ticket exchanges, individual admission sales, group rate sales, and complimentary tickets. Figure 7-3 is a typical box office sales breakdown form.

The Daily Barometer

In addition to recording sales on the daily box office report and the box office breakdown, the box office manager should keep an up-to-date record of the sales for each performance. The box office manager merely breaks down the daily sales by performance and enters the totals on a "performance barometer." This tells the theatre staff how the various performances are selling, and thereby enables the box office personnel to attempt to channel patrons into performances which are "down" and to start to dress the house. Figure 7-4 is a performance barometer for one performance.

Final Box Office Report

At the conclusion of a production run the box office manager, along with the business manager, compiles a final box office report. This report is essentially a summary of the individual reports. It shows (1) the total number of season ticket exchanges, (2) the total number of individual admission sales and their receipts, (3) the total number of group sales and receipts, (4) the total number of complimentary tickets, (5) the total number of tickets issued for each performance, including exchanges, and (6) the number of unused tickets for each night ("deadwood").

After this final report is prepared the audit stubs and season ticket exchanges should be filed in envelopes by sales day, and the deadwood should be stored in a safe place. These items should be kept for at least one year, in the event the school wishes to audit the theatre's sales. Figure 7-5 is a typical final box office report.

SEASON TICKETS

The practice of offering the public a season ticket plan was

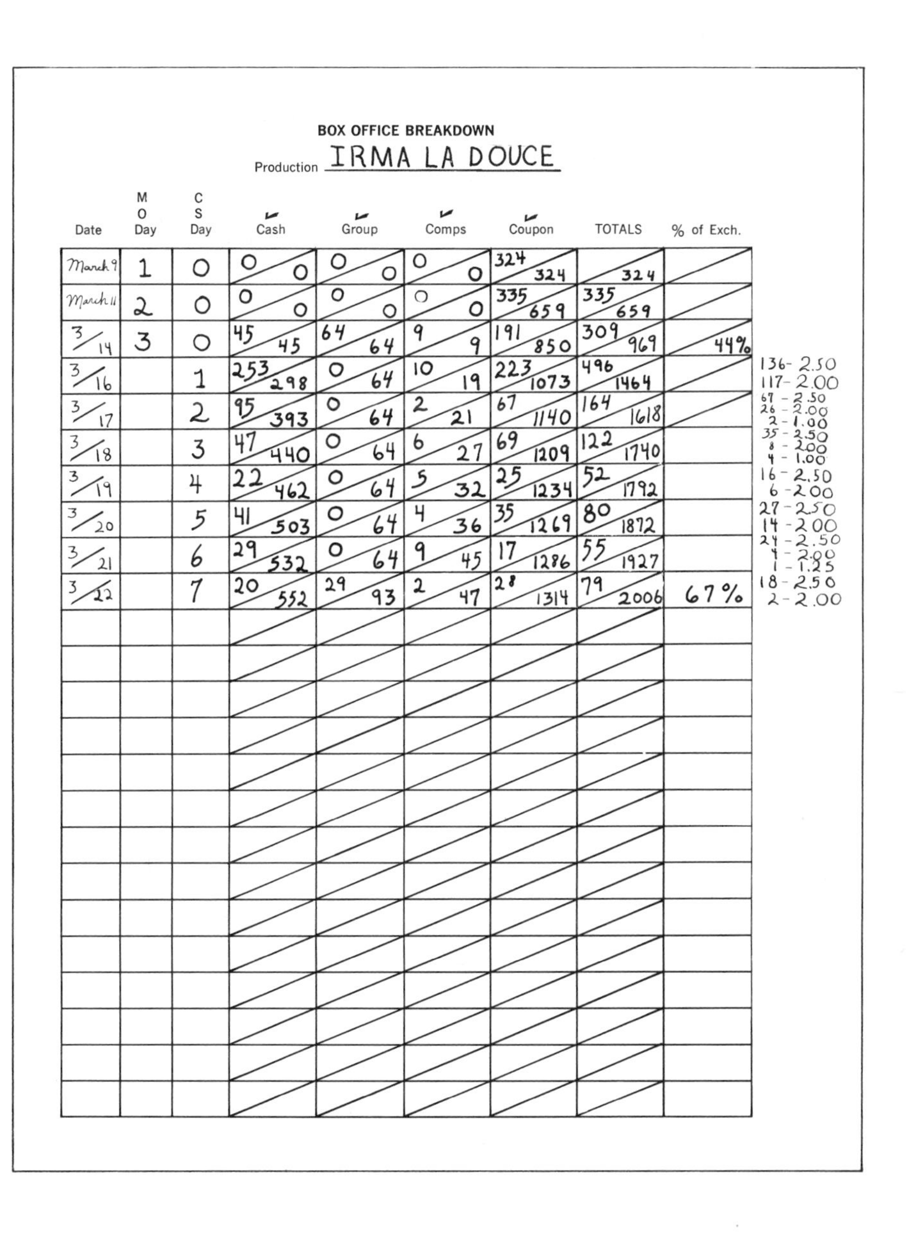

BOX OFFICE BREAKDOWN

Production IRMA LA DOUCE

Date	MO Day	CS Day	Cash	Group	Comps	Coupon	TOTALS	% of Exch.
March 9	1	0	0 / 0	0 / 0	0 / 0	324 / 324	324	
March 11	2	0	0 / 0	0 / 0	0 / 0	335 / 659	335 / 659	
3/14	3	0	45 / 45	64 / 64	9 / 9	191 / 850	309 / 969	44%
3/16		1	253 / 298	0 / 64	10 / 19	223 / 1073	496 / 1464	
3/17		2	95 / 393	0 / 64	2 / 21	67 / 1140	164 / 1618	
3/18		3	47 / 440	0 / 64	6 / 27	69 / 1209	122 / 1740	
3/19		4	22 / 462	0 / 64	5 / 32	25 / 1234	52 / 1792	
3/20		5	41 / 503	0 / 64	4 / 36	35 / 1269	80 / 1872	
3/21		6	29 / 532	0 / 64	9 / 45	17 / 1286	55 / 1927	
3/22		7	20 / 552	29 / 93	2 / 47	28 / 1314	79 / 2006	67%

136- 2.50
117- 2.00
67 - 2.50
26 - 2.00
2 - 1.00
35 - 2.50
8 - 2.00
4 - 1.00
16 - 2.50
6 - 2.00
27 - 2.50
14 - 2.00
24 - 2.50
4 - 2.00
1 - 1.25
18 - 2.50
2 - 2.00

Figure 7-3. Box Office Sales Breakdown

BRADLEY UNIVERSITY THEATRE

Sales Barometer

Production ____________ Performance ____________

Day	Date	No. Sold	Prev. Total	Grand Total
1	3/9	99	0	99
2	3/11	43	99	142
3	3/14	44	142	186
4	3/16	39	186	225
5	3/17	6	225	231
6	3/18	7	231	238
7	3/19	3	238	241
8	3/20	30	241	271
9	3/21	51	271	322
10	3/22	2	322	324
				323
				—4
				319

Exchanges ____________

Figure 7-4. Sample Performance Barometer

BRADLEY UNIVERSTY THEATRE

Final Box Office Report

IRMA LA DOUCE

Description	Price	No. Sold	Receipts
Individual Admissions	$2.50 $2.00 $1.25 $1.00	323 222 1 6	$ 807.50 $ 444.00---$1,258.75 Total $ 1.25 $ 6.00
Group Rates	$1.00	93	$ 93.00
Coupon Exchange	—0—	1,320	—0—
Complimentary	—0—	47	—0—
Totals	———	2,012	$1,351.75

Day	Sold	Exch.	Total	Unsold	Total
Mon.	277	−4	273	98	371
Tue.	198	−8	190	181	371
Wed.	300	−3	297	74	371
Thu.	306	+10	316	55	371
Fri.	310	0	310	61	371
Sat.	320	−1	319	52	371
Sun.	301	+6	307	64	371
			2,012		

Figure 7-5. A Final Box Office Report

discussed and recommended for the educational theatre in chapters 1 and 2. Once the general policy of establishing a season plan is agreed upon, the managerial and administrative problems of the specific plan to be adopted by the theatre must be faced. In general, the type of plan the educational theatre manager adopts will depend upon the purposes and functions he believes a season ticket plan should fulfill.

There are many valid reasons for having a season ticket policy for the educational theatre. First, it ensures the theatre a large sum of pre-season operating capital. It also provides the theatre a guaranteed income for each play. Second, it ensures a minimum audience for each play—for popular or hit plays as well as the classics.

Because one of the aims of educational theatre is to provide a variety of meaningful theatrical experiences for each member of the audience, selecting a well-balanced season and selling the entire season as a package is a practical method of implementing this most important aim. Thus the theatre patron who buys a season ticket will tend to see all the plays on the bill rather than just one or two. In addition, a season subscription gets a person to the theatre on a regular basis; it gets him into the *habit* of seeing plays. This third purpose of offering a season program and season ticket is the most important one for an educational theatre because it is the means of implementing one of the theatre's fundamental aims.

A fourth benefit of season tickets is that they increase the individual admission sales. By putting a number of "free" tickets in the hands of a large group of people prior to the general sales period, the theatre has, in a sense, acquired a number of publicity agents. Here is a group of people who are going to the theatre, who have a "commitment," and it is likely that they will publicize the season to their friends, and if not bring someone with them at least influence others to attend. Indeed, the number of season ticket holders who bring dates, other couples, and guests is surprising. Instead of impinging on individual admission sales, season ticket holders can expand individual admission sales and bring more people to the theatre.

Finally, season subscriptions assist the growth and enhancement of the theatre. Provided the artistic aspects of the theatre are high, season ticket holders continue to be the backbone of the theatre's audience. Thus they render an important service to educational theatre, and they are especially benefited in return.

Incentives

After the theatre staff reviews the advantages of offering the public a season ticket plan and decides that this is a sound policy, the theatre manager must begin to implement that decision. The first question he should ask himself is What type of plan should we offer and how will it work? Any of several good plans might be selected, each of which is used by different educational theatres for various reasons. Before one decides upon the plan for a particular theatre, it should be resolved that it will (1) offer the patron an incentive to buy, (2) be inexpensive and easy to handle, and (3) fulfill the advantages and purposes of a season ticket plan (as previously discussed).

There are a number of inducements a theatre can use in selling season tickets. First, there is no better incentive for purchasing a season ticket than an attractive, well-planned season of plays. Whatever else the theatre offers its patrons, the first and most important consideration should be to provide a fascinating season.

A second incentive is lower cost. A season ticket should be priced substantially lower than the cost of purchasing each play individually. For example, if a theatre season consists of five plays and each play sells for $1.50, the season ticket should sell for about $5. In this case the patron saves $2.50, which is a substantial savings.

Besides the season offerings and a financial savings, a theatre can offer season patrons several "bonuses" or "extras." Such bonus attractions as movies (a "film classics" series), experimental plays and productions, or special lectures are offered by many educational theatres as incentives for purchasing a season ticket.

Season ticket holders should also have an easier method of obtaining tickets, and a mail order privilege might be one method of accomplishing this.

Preferential seating is another benefit for season ticket holders, who obtain their tickets prior to the general public. Thus they have an advantage over non-subscribers by having an earlier selection of seats. This can be accomplished during a mail order period a week prior to the opening of the box office, or by opening the box office several days in advance for season ticket holders only.

Another advantage might be the privilege of purchasing extra tickets for a play at a reduced rate. Quite often people who have season tickets like to invite guests for a performance, and it might be possible to let them purchase these extra tickets at a somewhat lower price. (This means, however, that tickets are sold for various prices, which can cause auditing problems if the procedure is not well planned in advance by the theatre manager.)

Other special privileges which theatres offer their season subscribers are invitations to opening-night backstage parties; a special monthly publication which contains theatre news, articles, etc.; special parking privileges; and free refreshments or a free souvenir program.

An educational theatre need not offer all of these extras to its season subscribers. The theatre staff should discuss their relative values, the problems they would create, and the best means of implementing the selected incentives. The process of selecting incentives and advantages should never lose sight of the aims and purposes of the educational theatre.

Types of Season Plans

Basically, there are only two types of theatre season subscription plans, although each has several aspects. In the first type the patron is entitled to one ticket for each play in the season. In the second type, the patron is entitled to a prescribed number of tickets during the season.

Plan 1. Probably the most common type of season ticket plan allows the patron to attend each play in the season. In effect, the subscriber purchases a ticket to each play in advance. The particular form which this plan takes may be a single ticket or coupon or a strip or booklet of tickets or coupons.

The Single Ticket or Coupon. When a theatre uses only one ticket or coupon as the season ticket, the design should show the titles and dates of all the plays for which the ticket is valid, a statement of policy and procedures for obtaining extra tickets to each play, a numbered audit stub that corresponds with the coupon number, and space for the patron's name and address. (see figure 7-6).

To audit season ticket sales, the box office manager records the patron's name on the audit stub and on a master list of season tickets (arranged in numerical order), tears off the audit stub, and files it alphabetically. The alphabetical file can be used both for next season's mailing list and to assist the manager in case season tickets are lost.

When a patron reports a lost season ticket, the box office manager looks up the patron's name in the alphabetical file to find the audit stub and ticket number. He then voids that number on his numerical list and gives the patron a new season ticket. He should staple the new stub to the voided one and put it back in the file, making sure that he also records the patron's name on the numerical list under the new number. He should then post the voided number in the box office so that the lost ticket cannot be used.

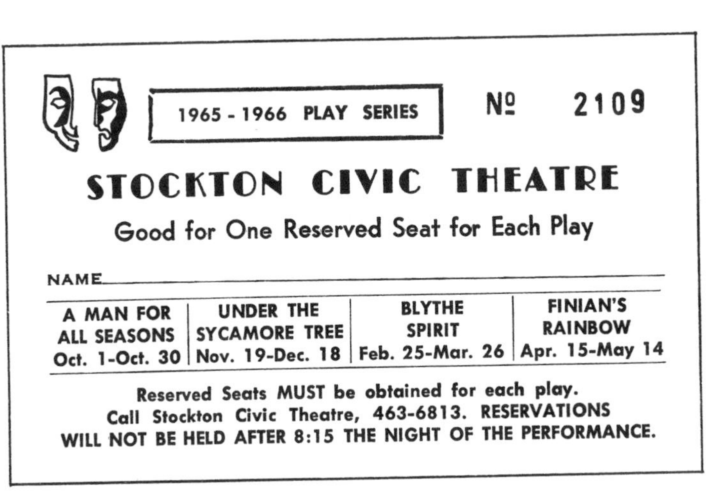

Figure 7-6. Single Ticket for a Season Ticket Plan

The only practical manner in which a single season ticket or coupon can be used to obtain a reserved-seat ticket for each production is for the patron to present it in person at the box office. It can then be punched each time the patron uses it (once for each play).

The chief advantage of a single season ticket or coupon is that it is simple to use and inexpensive for the theatre to have printed. The disadvantages, however, outnumber the advantages. First, the ticket must be brought to the box office personally; there is no convenient method to mail it in. Second, it is difficult to audit the number of season tickets for each play. Since the patron does not give the theatre anything to keep (except the punched-out hole), the theatre manager has no record of how each season ticket was used.

The Strip or Booklet of Tickets. Another system a theatre manager may use to accomplish the aims of plan 1 is that of the strip or booklet of tickets or coupons. In this case the patron does not receive a single ticket but a number of tickets, each one entitling him to a reserved seat for a particular performance. The design should include (1) an audit stub, similar to the one described for the single ticket, (2) a coupon which contains the same information as the single ticket, and (3) a strip of tickets, one for each play, which can be exchanged for a reserved-seat ticket for each of the season productions.

The audit procedure and the method for handling lost season tickets are the same as for the single ticket or coupon. The audit stub, the coupon, and each ticket on the strip contain the same identification or audit number.

There are two ways in which the strip ticket may be exchanged for reserved-seat tickets for each play: by mail or in person at the box office. The patron may mail in one of the tickets and receive a reserved-seat ticket by return mail. If this exchange procedure is allowed by the theatre, each ticket on the strip should contain space for the patron to indicate the performance he wishes to attend.

The main advantage of the strip ticket is that it offers the patron a variety of exchange procedures and thus is more convenient. However, the patron's convenience might be outweighed by the more costly nature of the strip tickets—although this system offers an easier method of auditing and keeping track of season ticket exchanges.

A variation of the strip tickets is the season coupon book (see figure 7-7), which is a booklet that contains a number of coupons which can be exchanged for a reserved-seat ticket to each play. The coupon book in figure 7-7 is simple in form, quite inexpensive, and readily available from most national ticket houses. The coupons are usually numbered to correspond to the productions and can be easily exchanged at the box office.

The coupon book in figure 7-8, on the other hand, is more detailed and costly. Each coupon indicates the play or performance for which it is valid, and has a form for ordering tickets by mail. The difference in the cost of these two types is considerable. While the cost of the simple coupon book in figure 7-7 is $135 for 2,000, the cost of the book in figure 7-8 is about $300 for 2,000.

THE PEORIA PLAYERS COMMUNITY THEATRE

1969 - 50th ANNIVERSARY - 1970

This book is issued subject to conditions stated on inside cover.
It is not valid unless signed by the person to whom issued.

Issued to ______________________________

Address ______________________________

NOT TRANSFERABLE Book No. 1599

WELDON, WILLIAMS & LICK, FT.SMITH, ARK.

This booklet contains your admission to each production for this season. Present it at the box office when calling for reserved seats. Make reservations by mail, telephone or in person. Tickets not picked up 15 minutes before curtain time on the day of performance will be sold

Curtain times: Friday and Saturday - 8:15

Sunday - 7:30

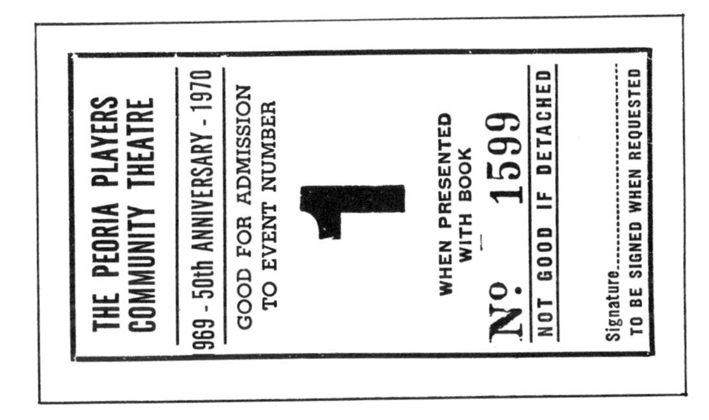

THE PEORIA PLAYERS
COMMUNITY THEATRE
969 - 50th ANNIVERSARY - 1970
GOOD FOR ADMISSION
TO EVENT NUMBER
1
WHEN PRESENTED
WITH BOOK
No. 1599
NOT GOOD IF DETACHED
Signature..........................
TO BE SIGNED WHEN REQUESTED

Figure 7-7. Standard Season Coupon Book (Plan 1)

UNIVERSITY THEATRE SEASON COUPON POLICIES

1. Each coupon guarantees the patron a reserved seat ticket for ONE of the performances listed on the coupon.
2. Coupons are guaranteed only until 5:00 p.m. of the night of the first performance. (Coupon for **Take Me Along** guaranteed only until March 25 at 5:00 p.m.) However, if there are tickets available, the coupon is exchangeable as late as the last performance of any production.
3. Mail orders will be filled in order of their receipt in the Box Office. Coupons sent in during the mail order period will receive preferential seating. See COUPON EXCHANGE PROCEDURE for details.
4. This Coupon Book is transferable; anyone may use it if you cannot attend.
5. No refund will be made for this Coupon Book, either in whole or in part.
6. Tickets for **Reynard the Fox** and "Showcase" productions General Admission **ONLY.**

Western Michigan University—Department of Speech
University Theatre   No. 1367

Season Coupon Book Insurance Record

NAME ....
ADDRESS ....
PHONE .... CHECK ONE ....Student
...........University Staff
Did you own a Season Book last year? ....Non-University

This certifies that the above-named person has purchased a season coupon book for the 1965-66 University Theatre Productions.
Returning this Record guarantees admission if the season ticket is lost.
Mail to: UNIVERSITY THEATRE, Department of Speech, Western Michigan University, Kalamazoo, Michigan. 1 2

COUPON EXCHANGE PROCEDURE

1. Coupons must be exchanged for a reserved seat for each of the SIX regular productions by Mail Order or at the Box Office. See reverse side for mail order acceptance dates. DO NOT SEND THE ENTIRE BOOK. If mailing, fill out the back of the coupon, and be sure to enclose a stamped, self-addressed envelope. Mail to: UNIVERSITY THEATRE, Department of Speech, Western Michigan University, Kalamazoo, Michigan. Coupons will be RETURNED if they arrive prior to acceptance dates.
2. Additional tickets may be purchased by enclosing proper amount.
3. Patrons wishing to sit together should send coupons in one envelope.
4. This book includes a special "reduced price bonus" coupon which will save you $1.00 on the purchase of two tickets for *Hamlet*. (See page 19 for details.)
5. Telephone reservations will be held 'til 7:45 the night of performance.

BOX OFFICE

PHONE: 383-1760; HOURS: Monday through Saturday 1:00-5:00 p.m. The Box Office is open starting on Monday one week prior to each performance. It is located in The Theatre lobby. On performance nights the Box Office is at The Theater and opens at 7:00 p.m.

BE SURE TO READ OTHER SIDE

Figure 7-8. Season Coupon Book

THIS IS NOT A TICKET

Production	Mail Orders Accepted	Box Office Sale Opens	Performances
Rashomon	**Sept. 20**	**Sept. 27**	**Oct. 5, 6, 7, 8, 9**
The Cave Dwellers	**Oct. 25**	**Nov. 1**	**Nov. 9, 10, 11, 12, 13**
Earnest	**Jan. 17**	**Jan. 31**	**Feb. 8, 10, 12, 16, 18, 22, 24, 26**
The Crucible	**Jan. 17**	**Jan. 31**	**Feb. 9, 11, 15, 17, 19, 23, 25**
***Take Me Along**	**Mar. 14**	**Mar. 21**	**Mar. 28, 29, 30, 31; Apr. 1, 2**
Bernarda Alba	**May 9**	**May 16**	**May 24, 25, 26, 27, 28**

ALL EVENING PLAY PERFORMANCES BEGIN AT 8:00 P.M.

Curtain times for **Reynard the Fox** listed on inside back cover.

*The musical **Take Me Along** will also play a matinee at 2 p.m. on April 2.

This coupon will be exchanged for a reserved seat ticket for the 1965-66 University Theatre Production

Rashomon

by Fay and Michael Kanin №. 1367

at

THE THEATRE

OCTOBER 5, 6, 7, 8, 9

Mail Order Accepted (Coupon or Cash) . . . . Sept. 20
Box Office Sale (Coupon or Cash) . . . . Sept. 27

Guaranteed until 5 p.m. night the production opens.

(over)

P l e a s e ! !

NUMBER AT LEAST THREE NIGHTS IN ORDER OF PREFERENCE

( ) Tuesday, Oct. 5 ( ) Friday, Oct. 8

( ) Wednesday, Oct. 6 ( ) Saturday, Oct. 9

( ) Thursday, Oct. 7 ( ) Any Night, Best Location

NAME ....

ADDRESS .... PHONE ....

Please enclose a stamped, addressed envelope for return of tickets.

This coupon will be exchanged for a reserved seat ticket for the 1965-66 University Theatre Production

The Cave Dwellers

by William Saroyan №. 1367

at

THE THEATRE

NOVEMBER 9, 10, 11, 12, 13

Mail Order Accepted (Coupon or Cash) . . . . October 25
Box Office Sale (Coupon or Cash) . . . . November 1

Guaranteed until 5 p.m. night the production opens.

(over)

Thus the disadvantage in using the coupon book is that it is more expensive than the single ticket. It has advantages, however, in that the method of exchange is flexible and therefore of greater convenience for the patron (which at the same time means more work for the business and box office staff). In addition, the second type of book allows the theatre to include a great deal of information which can be helpful to patrons throughout the season.

Season Tickets and Reserved Seats. The plan which offers the patron one ticket for each play in the season can take another form: the seasonal reserved-seat ticket. In this case the patron purchases a specific seat for each play prior to the opening of the season. The major difference between this system and those discussed earlier is that, in the other systems, the season patron purchases a coupon or ticket which entitles him to a reserved-seat ticket for each production, and he must exercise that right a number of times during the season, as each play comes along. With the seasonal reserved seat, however, the patron purchases reserved-seat tickets for all the plays without going through the exchange procedure for each play. Figure 7-9 shows a pad of reserved-seat tickets for a season.

Basically, the system is similar to that of the strip of tickets or coupons, which must be exchanged. During the season-ticket campaign the tickets are sold on what might be called a nightly basis: the patron purchases a ticket for each play, for the same night of the week, and for the same location. When a strip or pad of reserved-seat tickets is sold, the audit stub is detached and filled out with the name and address of the patron. The audit stub automatically records the night and the seat location since this information is printed on each ticket and stub. When the season-ticket campaign is over, the audit stubs are detached from the unsold tickets and the strips or pads are broken up and sold as individual admission tickets, using the individual admission audit (see figure 7-9).

There are two additional advantages in having a seasonal reserved-seat policy, besides those mentioned earlier for the "one ticket per play" plan. First, there is a distinct advantage for the patron who knows in advance which evening he will attend the theatre on four, five, or six nights during the year. If he knows this, he can obtain his tickets without bothering about the exchange procedure. Second, if the theatre can sell all its reserved-seat tickets in this manner, it will be guaranteed a full house for each performance, the theatre

A.

B.

C.

D.

Figure 7-9. **B** is a pad of season reserved-seat tickets for a Friday evening series; **A** shows one of the tickets removed. Note that the patron purchases the same seat for each play.

C and **D** show a variation of the season reserved-seat ticket. Note that after removing the audit stubs the theatre can sell the tickets as season tickets. After the season campaign, the tickets may be sold as individual admission tickets.

manager will have an accurate idea of the season's income, and the business manager will not have to operate a box office and sell individual tickets for each performance.

The obvious disadvantage is that many people cannot commit themselves to five or six nights a year so far in advance. The theatre which adopts this system should, therefore, make provisions for exchanging reserved-seat tickets. Another disadvantage is empty seats. When a patron does not attend a particular play, his seat cannot be sold again, and must remain empty. This means, of course, that individual admission tickets cannot be sold, and it cuts down on the possibility of selling large numbers of group-rate tickets. If, however, the theatre does not sell all of its reserved seat tickets on a season basis, a limited number of individual admission and group-rate sales is possible.

Thus the major disadvantage seems to be that this system limits rather than encourages individual admissions and in a sense makes the theatre a closed, private, or subscription theatre. This does not promote the best image of public theatre, or theatregoing by students and the community, or the full aims and purposes of educational theatre. The theatre manager and staff should make a careful, detailed analysis of the problems, advantages, and disadvantages of this type of season plan before embarking upon it.

Plan 2. The second general type of season plan entitles the patron to a prescribed number of tickets during the season that he can use in any manner he wishes—all of them for one play, one for each play, or in any other combination. For example, if the theatre offers a season of five plays, under plan 1 the patron is entitled to five tickets—that is, one for each of the five plays. In plan 2 he also receives five tickets, but he may use one for each play, or two for the first play, etc., or all of them for one play.

The advantage of this plan is that it saves the patron money and gives him great flexibility. If, in a season of plays, there is one play to which he would like to take his entire family, he can purchase a season ticket and receive five tickets for this play at a great discount. In effect, then, he purchases tickets at a discount, which is the main advantage of this system. In some cases, of course, the season ticket isn't really a *season* ticket since it need not be used for the entire season of plays. Plan 2, then, is essentially a discount plan. (see figure 7-10)

There are, also, a number of important disadvantages to this type

DENISON UNIVERSITY THEATRE
Subscription Ticket
1965-1966

This coupon is good for one reserved ticket to any production presented by the Denison University Theatre. Reservations may be made by writing Box 131, Granville, or by calling the University Theatre Box Office, 582-9181, Extension 231, from 1:30-4:30, Monday through Friday.

Production Dates

Oct. 26-30 "Ring Round the Moon"
Dec. 7-12 "The Physicists"
March 8-12 "Desire Under the Elms"
May 3-7 "Romeo and Juliet"
and
November 16 "Iphigenia in Tauris"

Two Experimental Theatre Productions. Dates to be announced.

Figure 7-10. A Season Coupon Book for Plan 2

of season ticket plan, and all of them are disadvantageous to the theatre. First, the theatre manager has little control over the size of his audience for each production. To illustrate: what would happen if all (or most) season ticket patrons (under this system) exchanged their tickets for reserved seats for one production? The theatre could not possibly take care of this demand, and it would also mean small houses for the less popular plays. For a five-play season of five performances per play in a 300-seat house with a season ticket sale of 500, the theatre manager has, theoretically, oversold by 1,000 tickets if all the patrons exchange their tickets for one play. This will never happen (every theatre manager hopes), but it illustrates the problem of allowing patrons the privilege of using their five tickets for any play. It can create large-attendance plays on the one hand and low-attendance plays on the other.

Second, this plan does not fulfill some of the important aims and purposes of educational theatre, or of season tickets. It does not encourage the season ticket holder to attend all of the theatre's plays, thus becoming exposed to a great variety of dramas and production styles. Indeed, it might even be said that this system encourages patrons to attend the most popular plays at the expense of some of the less popular offerings.

Because of the lack of control over the size of potential audiences for each play and the fact that a minimum audience for each play is not guaranteed, and the fact that this plan does not fulfill the aim of educational theatre and frustrates an otherwise well-planned season, it should be considered carefully before a theatre staff adopts it. If it is adopted, a safeguard for the theatre is to inform the patron that his season ticket does not guarantee him a ticket for a particular play; it will merely be honored for the exchange of reserved-seat tickets as long as they are available.

There are a number of specific methods of implementing this plan should a theatre decide to adopt it, and the simple coupon book is a popular method (see figure 7-10). Each coupon in the booklet may be exchanged by mail or at the box office for a reserved-seat ticket as long as they are available. The strip of coupons or tickets is also popular with many college and university theatres, especially for summer operations. The tickets (or coupons) may be exchanged for reserved seats by mail or at the box office. The single coupon or ticket can also be used for this plan. In this case, only a box office exchange is possible, and the ticket should be punched each time it is presented for exchange.

SUMMARY (A).

Two basic types of season ticket plans are available to the educational theatre manager. Under the first plan the patron is entitled to one reserved-seat ticket for each production. This can be accomplished by (1) a season ticket which is presented at the box office for each exchange, (2) a strip of tickets which can be exchanged by mail or at the box office for an individual admission ticket to each play, or (3) a booklet of coupons which can be exchanged by mail or at the box office.

The advantages of plan 1 are that the patron sees the *entire* season of plays; he receives each ticket for each play individually; and he has his choice of seat and performance (provided the season's reserved-seat ticket is not used). This plan distributes the season's audience equally for each play, and comes closest to fulfilling the aims and objectives of educational theatre and a bona fide season ticket plan.

The second plan entitles the season subscriber to a prescribed number of reserved-seat tickets to use in any manner he desires. This essentially means a savings in money for the patron, but it does not give the theatre adequate predictive power and control over the size of the audience for each play. Nor does the plan contribute to several of the aims and objectives of educational theatre.

Before deciding upon a season plan and a specific method of implementing that plan, the educational theatre manager and staff need to have a clear idea of the aims and objectives of their theatre. What are they trying to accomplish? Also, they must have a clear idea of the aims and objectives of a season ticket plan. What should it accomplish? After these questions are answered, the theatre manager should examine in detail each of the possibilities for implementing those aims and objectives. A well-thought-out and well-implemented theatre season ticket policy can be a great aid in accomplishing the aims and objectives of educational theatre.

Whatever system is selected, it should (1) accomplish the purposes and functions which the educational theatre manager believes a seasonal system should have (based upon the purposes of his theatre); (2) be understood and fair to the patron; (3) offer the patron advantages and benefits; (4) have a guarantee limit (date and time) after which seasonal privileges are void in order to protect the theatre; and (5) encourage, rather than limit, individual admission sales and the growth and influence of the theatre.

Season Ticket Sales Methods

After selecting a season ticket plan and a specific method of implementing that plan, the theatre manager is again faced with a number of practical, administrative problems. When should the season tickets be sold? Where should they be sold? By whom should they be sold?

The Sales Period. There are a number of times when it is best to sell season tickets for an educational theatre, depending upon the intended buyers. In the general sales campaign, the first group of people to whom the theatre ought to direct its attention is the theatre's past patrons. If the theatre manager has kept a file of last year's season ticket patrons, he should check it against his mailing list and add the new season patrons from last season to his list. (This job of bringing the mailing list up to date can be undertaken by the management staff during the preceding season—any time after the end of the season's sales campaign.) Then, at least three weeks prior to the general public sales period, previous-season patrons should be given an opportunity to purchase season tickets for the coming season. This contact with past patrons (usually by mail) should be in the form of either a personal letter or a season brochure with an order form attached.

Some theatres offer additional benefits to past patrons during this early sales period: either a further financial discount, a guarantee of tickets, or the choice of reserved-seat locations (if the theatre has a reserved-seat plan for the season). In addition, this early sales period allows the management staff to get some paperwork out of the way prior to the busy general sales period.

In educational theatre, the general sales period for season tickets should begin during the school's registration week or during the first week of classes. It probably shouldn't last longer than one month. During that period the theatre staff should saturate the campus and the town with their campaign. It is better to have a short period of highly saturated information than a long-drawn-out period. It might also be advisable to offer an early event to close the season sales period, or at least to set a firm deadline for the sale of season tickets.

Another good time to sell season tickets, in addition to the two periods mentioned above, is during preregistration or the freshman orientation period. Many colleges and universities (and a number of high schools) conduct a preregistration, testing, and general orientation period for incoming freshmen students some time prior to the official, general registration schedule. In some schools this takes place during the summer months; in others it is a week or so before the first day of the official registration.

In any event, this is a very good time for the theatre to involve the incoming students in theatre activity, both as participants and as audience members. The educational theatre manager should make a concerted effort at this time to introduce the new students to the general theatre program. They should be given a schedule of the plays, along with the tryout dates and some specific information on the theatre program. They should be told that they are welcome, and indeed encouraged, to participate in all plays in any capacity. They should also be encouraged to buy a season ticket, for if the theatre can instill the theatre-going habit in freshmen it will begin to build an audience not only for the particular educational theatre but for theatre in general. Theatregoing, after all, is a habit, and should be instilled in people at an early age.

Sales Locations. A central location in a school is important for theatre sales, but the theatre manager should attempt to locate his season ticket headquarters in the same place as his box office. In addition to opening the box office for season ticket sales, it might be advantageous to establish several other sales booths for this purpose about the campus. These booths, manned by students, could be placed near the registration area, where all the students must present themselves, and in the student union building, bookstore, and other important and frequently used buildings. The sales at these booths should be audited at the end of each day.

The booths need not be complicated affairs—a table, chair, and sign are enough to establish their identity. But the student salesmen should be charming, polite, and interested.

Sometimes various merchants and store managers will allow educational and cultural organizations to use their store facilities to sell tickets. This might take the form of a booth that is operated by the organization, or an arrangement might be made whereby the merchant or his employees sell tickets at their cash window or sales desk. Drug stores, large downtown department stores, and variety stores are the usual business places which might consent to such a plan. The educational theatre also might contact other cultural and entertainment organizations in the area to see if they will assist in selling season tickets. Other theatres (community or professional) and the local civic center, art museum, library and branches, and chamber of commerce might be willing to handle season tickets.

The theatre manager should remind the organizations that they will receive a certain amount of free publicity each time the theatre announces and advertises its season and the locations of its "ticket centers." However, community sales centers mean more work for the theatre staff since someone from the management should make the rounds each day to pick up the receipts and see that each location has enough tickets. Also, if the theatre has a reserved-seat plan for the season, the theatre manager must be sure that he distributes the seat locations equitably among all ticket centers. Before selecting these locations to supplement the campus sales booths, the theatre manager should consider all the advantages and disadvantages.

Another successful method of selling season tickets is through the mail. An attractive brochure which lists the season's plays and dates, tells a little about each play, gives the price of a season ticket (along with its advantages and benefits), and a coupon order form is a valuable sales method when it is sent to all past-season patrons. Moreover, brochures can be placed in all student and faculty mail boxes, around the campus (in the library, bookstore, student union, lounges, dorms, fraternity houses, and cafeteria), and around the town (art centers, libraries, theatres, museums, fairs, exhibits, stores, etc.). It is surprising how many people pick up a brochure, read it, and become interested enough in the theatre's season to send in the order form.

Finally, the theatre manager should utilize both the school and the town newspapers. Part of each paid ad for the season should be an order form which can be clipped out and mailed to the theatre (along with the proper amount of money). If the season's sales campaign lasts for a month, an ad—with an order form—should be placed on the theatre or amusement page in each of the four Sunday issues of the town paper preceding each play and in the four preceding issues of the school newspaper. This is a most effective manner of getting new season subscribers, and has proved to be well worth the effort and cost.

The Sales Force. Theatre students make the most effective season ticket salesmen. It should therefore be the duty of the theatre manager to instill in theatre students the crucial importance of a successful season ticket campaign. Besides the financial benefits that accrue to the theatre, the students should be made aware of the importance of getting a large group of people to commit themselves to the entire season of plays. The students should realize that the theatre is, in part, accomplishing its reason for existing by providing larger audiences for the plays. Working for the good of the theatre program and contributing to the success of theatre at the school should be the most important and meaningful incentives for the theatre student to do his best selling season tickets and talking up the theatre on campus and in town. These pursuits are much more meaningful incentives (and more valuable in the development of the students' character) than pay or commissions.

Individual Admission

One of the responsibilities of the theatre manager and his staff is selling tickets to the individual plays. This, necessarily, involves a knowledge of the purposes and types of tickets and the general policies of ticket procedures in an educational theatre.

Purpose of Tickets. A ticket, though only a piece of printed material, allows the holder to attend a particular event subject to the conditions listed on the ticket. These conditions might specify the seat the holder must occupy, the date he can attend the event, etc. But in addition to allowing the holder entrance to an event, it should perform several other functions.

It should allow a theatre to audit the number and type of sales and to know at any given time how many tickets to each performance have been sold. The audit means that the theatre manager is able to keep an accurate record of the number of tickets sold, the type of sale (full price, group rate, or season ticket exchange), and the type of ticket sold (seat location and performance). A theatre ticket should also facilitate the handling and seating of an audience. Finally, two general types of theatre tickets are available to the theatre

Pekin Community High School Drama Department

presents

Edgar Lee Masters'

Spoon River Anthology

adapted by Charles Aidman

F. M. PETERSON THEATRE, EAST CAMPUS

Friday, May 1, 1970

Curtain 8 p. m. Sharp

No 607 Admission $1.00

Figure 7-11. Sample General Admission Ticket

manager: (1) the general admission ticket and (2) the reserved-seat ticket.

General Admission Tickets. A general admission ticket allows the holder to attend an event but does not specify the seat he will occupy; in other words, he can sit in any seat which is empty. General admission tickets can be printed with the day, date, and time of the performances for which they are valid, or they can be color-coded (blue for Tuesday, red for Wednesday, etc.), with only the dates of the full production run printed on them. Another option is to have the ticket fully dated *and* color-coded. A final possibility is the use of roll-type tickets, which are usually color-coded and undated. Figure 7-11 shows a general admission ticket.

With general admission tickets, both an advance sale and sale at the door are possible. The theatre's major advantage in using general admission tickets is that they are much more inexpensive than the other type. A local shop can print them—color-coded, fully dated, and consecutively numbered—for a fraction of the cost of having reserved-seat tickets prepared by a regular ticket printing company. Also, general admission tickets are easy to administer and keep track of for record-keeping purposes. The problems of ushers' seating patrons, as well as box office operations, are alleviated by the less complicated procedures of general admission tickets.

However, there are a number of disadvantages to using general admission tickets. Unless they have stubs, an accurate audit is difficult, and especially if there is more than one price. (The simplest audit procedure is to have the tickets consecutively numbered and *then* subtract the "deadwood" or unsold tickets from the total number.) A second disadvantage is the inconvenience to patrons in not having reserved seats: most theatres have reserved seats and many patrons *expect* this convenience.

General admission, then, does not have a "professional air." It seems to imply that such a theatre is substandard both in management and quality of productions. Inasmuch as part of management policy in educational theatre is to raise the image and status of the theatre, having patrons search out and "save" good seats, rather than being shown to their seats by an usher, does not raise the image of educational theatre in their eyes.

Reserved-Seat Tickets. Reserved-seat tickets are commonly re-

A.

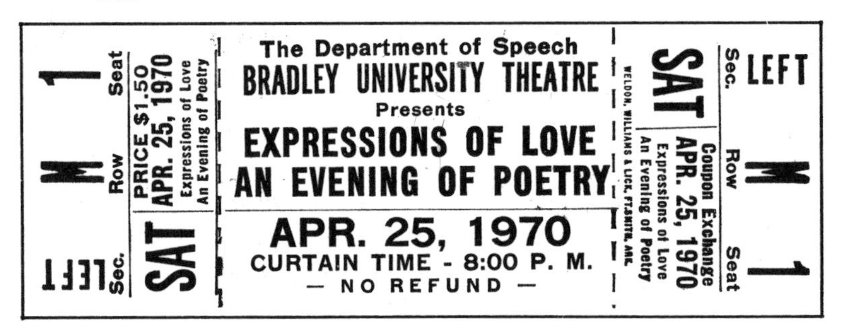

B.

C.

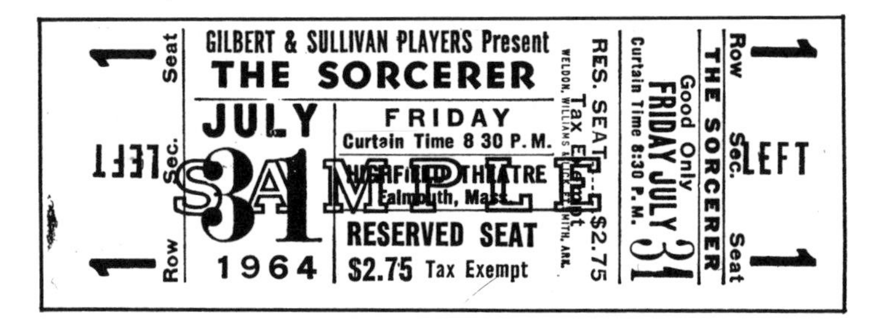

Figure 7-12. Sample Reserved-Seat Tickets. (**A** and **B** have an audit stub at both ends; **C** has an audit stub at one end)

ferred to as "coupon tickets" because they bear a coupon and an audit stub. Both the coupon and the stub designate the performance for which the ticket is valid and the particular seat to which a patron is entitled. Moreover, the audit stub enables the theatre to keep a record of all the tickets sold and unsold.

Sample A in figure 7-12 is a reserved-seat ticket with an audit stub at one end. When this ticket is sold, the stub will be torn off and retained by the theatre. At the end of the business day the theatre or box office manager need only count all the stubs to arrive at the number of tickets sold that day and the amount of money he should have.

Sample B has an audit stub at both ends of the coupon, and when a patron pays for the ticket the box office worker will tear off the stub which says "Coupon Exchange." At the end of the day the box office manager merely counts these stubs to determine the number of tickets which were sold. The patron, if he is a season ticket holder, exchanges one of his season coupons for a ticket and the box office worker tears off the stub which says "$1.50" and clips it to the patron's season ticket. At the end of the day the box office manager should have a season coupon for each $1.50 stub.

All of these stubs should be saved for at least one year in case the school auditors wish to examine the theatre account to verify sales and receipts. The unsold tickets also should be filed away for a year.

Reserved-seat tickets, with coupon and audit stub (like any of those in figure 7-12), can be purchased by theatres from any number of ticket printers in units called "sets." A set of tickets comprises one ticket for each seat in the house for one performance, and according to section, row, and seat number. If, for example, a theatre which seats 377 people offers five productions of six performances each, the manager would order thirty sets of 377 tickets.

If theatres purchase individual admission reserved-seat tickets, seat locations would not be printed; instead, blank spaces would be provided in which the theatre manager would have to write all that information by hand. The reason for this is that very few local printers have the equipment necessary to print the row, section, and seat location, which changes for each ticket. A thirty-set order for a 377-seat house from a ticket printer is a great deal more expensive than ordering unnumbered tickets from a local printer, but the theatre manager should realize that the latter means the theatre staff must number 11,310 tickets for the season. And if seat locations are noted on both ends, that means writing 22,620 sections, rows, and seats. At ten seconds a ticket, that is more than sixty-five hours of extra work. In addition, there is always the possibility or likelihood of making mistakes, whereas an order from a ticket printer is guaranteed against error.

The standard size of most reserved-seat tickets is 1¼″ by 4″, 1½″ by 3″, or 1¼″ by 3½″. Standard size and design reserved-seat tickets are usually less expensive than specially designed sizes and styles; however, if a theatre has a particular size and design requirement, it can order its tickets at a slightly higher price.

Reserved-seat tickets can be color-coded in a number of ways. Some theatres use a different color for each section in the house (blue for the balcony, red for the orchestra, yellow for the right section, etc.); other theatres use a different color for each play (red tickets for the first play, blue tickets for the second play, etc.). A much widely used and advantageous system is to use a different color for each performance within a production run; for example: red for Thursday, blue for Friday, yellow for Saturday. This means that all Thursday tickets would be red, whether for the first play, the second play, or the third play. This system aids the box office workers in keeping track of the tickets in the rack, in pulling the correct ticket for a patron, and in helping the ushers validate a person's ticket when he enters the theatre. It is much easier to identify a ticket by color than by its printed date.

Before ordering reserved-seat tickets from a printer, the theatre manager should send letters to at least three reliable printers requesting a price quotation. The letter, written on official school stationery, should state (1) the number of productions, (2) the number of performances for each production, (3) the size of the house, (4) the size and type of ticket desired, (5) the number of colors and type of color code desired, and (6) any changes in price within a set (see figure 7-13). The type of stock should also be specified; but most tickets are printed on "safety stock," which is laminated and very difficult to forge. The extra charge for safety stock is small and its use is highly recommended. Having all this information, any of the

June 19, 1970

Weldon, Williams & Lick, Co.
Fort Smith, Arkansas 72901

Dear Sir:

Our theatre is interested in purchasing reserved seat tickets for our 1970-71 theatre season, and would like you to bid on our specifications.

We will need 16 sets of 1-1/2" X 3-3/4" safety stock tickets, fully dated, for a 400 seat house (four plays, four performances each play). We will supply our own design and would like them color coded -- each set within a production a different color -- four colors only.

We would appreciate your estimate as soon as possible. We will place our order during the first week in July with the firm submitting the lowest estimate.

Sincerely,

Wm. Jones

William Jones, Drama Director
Washington High School
Princeton, Ohio

WJ:vs

Figure 7-13. Letter to Ticket Printer Requesting Cost Estimate

ticket printing companies listed in the Appendix will be glad to send their estimate.

After selecting the lowest bid, the manager can order the tickets for the season (a letter of appreciation should be sent to the companies that submitted higher bids). But in order to print the tickets accurately, the company must have a seating plan of the theatre, which can be handwritten or typed on a plain sheet of paper (see figure 7-14). In addition, it must know the style of ticket desired—that is, single audit stub, double audit stub, season audit stub, etc. If the theatre manager wants a special design, the artwork for the tickets should also be included (otherwise the ticket company will use a standard design). If the theatre has a season coupon exchange procedure and an individual admission purchase price, the double audit stub ticket should be used. The specific information for each stub should also be given to the ticket company.

In addition, the official order for tickets should include the following information: (1) the title, author, and dates for each production, (2) the time of performances, (3) the price of tickets, (4) the name of the theatre, (5) the color code desired, and (6) the date by which the tickets are needed. An official purchase order should accompany the order for tickets (see figure 7-15).

It might appear that individual admission tickets are not worth the bother: Why not have some local printers print up some cheap tickets? This question should be easy for business and theatre managers to answer: Well-thought-out and professionally executed individual admission tickets (general admission or reserved seats) enhance a theatre's image at the box office, facilitate bookkeeping and auditing procedures, and help ensure that box office errors and subsequent inconveniences to patrons will be kept at a minimum. This should be worth the extra money, time, and effort. Besides, it's good managerial education for students.

Complimentary Tickets

"Annie Oakleys," "passes," "comps"; these are all ways of saying free tickets. For some reason theatres are expected to give away generous amounts of free tickets for their productions. People don't expect a shoe store to give away shoes, or a department store to give

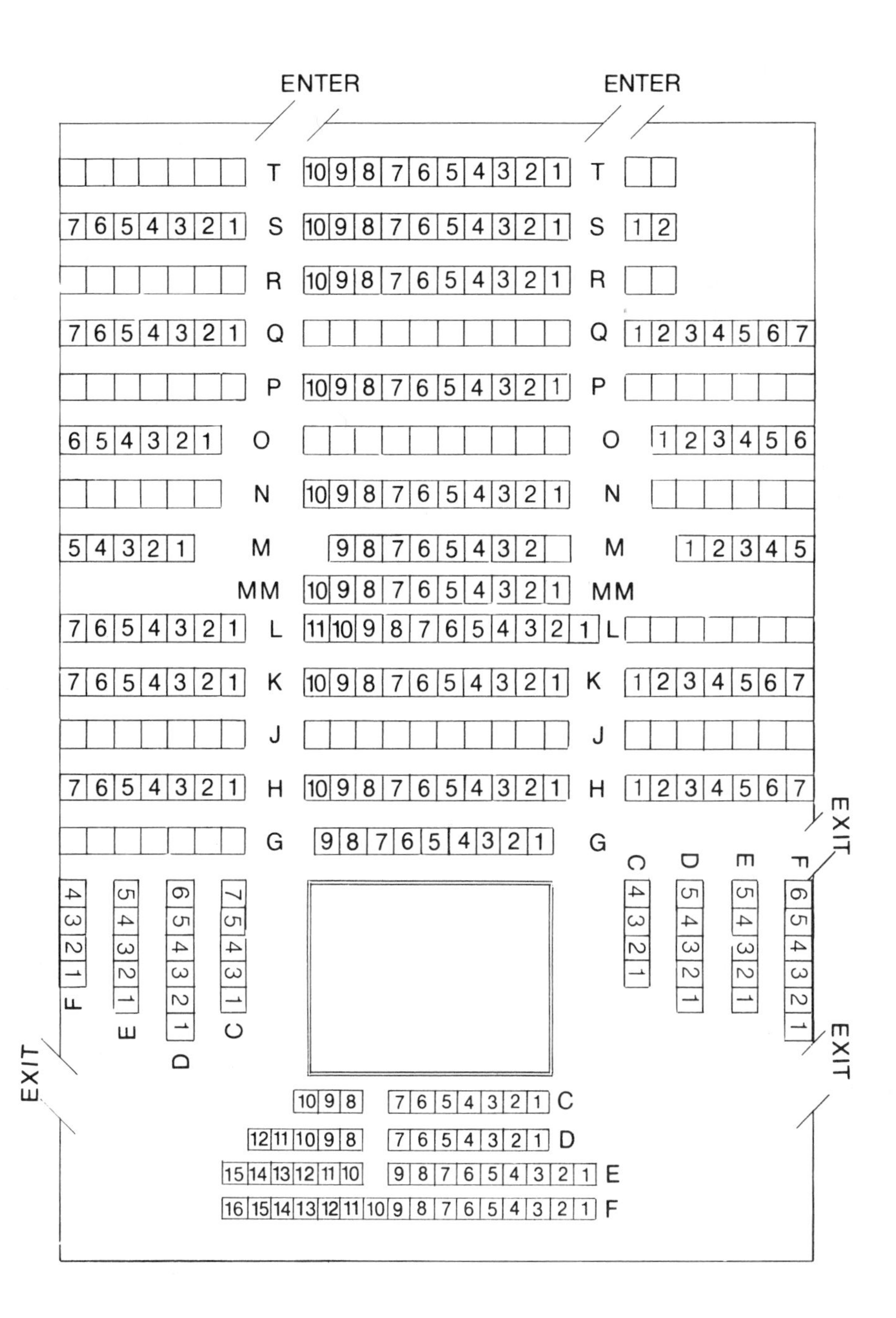

Figure 7-14. A House Plan

July 6, 1970

Weldon, Williams & Lick Co.
Fort Smith, Arkansas 72901

Gentlemen:

We are pleased to give you our order for reserved seat tickets for our 1970-71 season as per your estimate dated June 25. Attached you will find our ticket design, house plan, and school purchase order.

Our season consists of:

"Our Town" by Thornton Wilder
October 7, 8, 9, 10, 1970

"Waiting for Godot" by Samuel Beckett
December 2, 3, 4, 5, 1970

"Everyman" Anonymous
March 3, 4, 5, 6, 1971

"The Mikado" by Gilbert & Sullivan
May 5, 6, 7, 8, 1971

All performances are at 8:00 P.M., Wednesday thru Saturday. Please use red for all Wednesdays, emerald for Thursdays, orange for Fridays, and blue for Saturdays.

We would appreciate delivery by September 1.

Sincerely,

William Jones, Drama Director
Washington High School
Princeton, Ohio

WJ:vs

Figure 7-15. Sample Order to Ticket Printer

away dresses, or a dentist to fill teeth gratis, but they expect a theatre to give away *its* product, a play.

A complimentary ticket list can be a burden, a source of embarrassment, an inconvenience, and a general headache for theatre managers. It can also lead to empty seats, poor public relations, and general confusion if it is not handled according to a definite, reasonable policy.

Policy. An educational theatre manager would do well to urge the theatre staff to adopt a policy of "no comps." This would mean that the theatre has a product which it offers for *sale* to patrons, and that the only manner in which a person can receive the product is to purchase it. After a year or so, people get the idea that theatre tickets must be purchased—that they will not be given away.

It should be made clear, however, that educational theatre always thanks and rewards those who help it—who donate time, services, props, costumes, newspaper space, radio and television time, etc. The only way the theatre can thank and reward its benefactors (and those whom the theatre hopes to obtain as benefactors) is by expressing its feelings in the acknowledgments section of the program and by offering complimentary tickets for a production or for the season. This should be the only exception to the rule. If this policy is well promulgated and is carried out in a consistent manner, the theatre will be much better off. Making further exceptions leads only to problems. Give one "VIP" a comp and the theatre manager must inevitably give away dozens and scores. It's surprising how many "instant VIPs" a theatre attracts.

Procedure. A theatre should never send individual admission tickets to persons on a complimentary ticket list without first ascertaining that they wish to attend, and to attend a particular performance. This helps ensure that the comps will be used. The indiscriminate dissemination of free tickets can mean many unused tickets and empty seats.

A simple card (see figure 7-16), mailed to each person on the comp list a week prior to the opening of the box office and informing him that the theatre wishes to present him with complimentary tickets, is usually sufficient. The card should have a returnable portion for indicating the performance for which the tickets are desired.

The audit procedure for complimentary tickets also is simple: the

```
Bradley University
CAROUSEL PLAYHOUSE

We are pleased to present you with ___ complimentary
tickets to ________________________ on ____________
Please circle the date you wish to attend,and return
this form to the Playhouse no later than __________.
Your tickets will be returned to you.

    ____________________          ____________________
      Managing Director             (please sign here)
```

Figure 7-16. Complimentary Ticket Form

theatre manager merely staples the audit stub to the returned card and audits it as a complimentary ticket on the box office reports. The tickets which are sent out should be punched or otherwise marked and identified so that they cannot be turned in for a refund.

SUMMARY (B)

The box office is in many respects the nerve center of the theatre the week prior to opening night and during a production. Directors, actors, technicians all want to know how the sales are going. "Are we going to have a big opening-night crowd?" the young lead asks. "Is the Dean coming?" asks a nervous director. "Any nights sold out?" asks another.

The public also has interested questions. "Can we still get two seats together for Saturday?" asks a voice over the phone. "What are the best tickets you have for any night?" shouts a patron at the window, competing with the voice on the phone for the attention of the box office worker. "But I want to sit next to Mrs. Watson in the third row. Don't you have tickets for one of the seats next to her?" "What do you mean, you don't have two aisle seats?"

The box office crew, the box office manager, and the business manager answer most of the questions, and provide a certain amount of preshow excitement—at least they are supposed to. This is *their* time to be "on," their time to shine; and it has taken much work and devotion. It's all part of the theatre process. It's not as glamorous as acting—working with papers, figures, letters, stubs, and forms—but it's just as necessary and rewarding.

8 House Management

THE PLAYS FOR the theatre season have been selected; the budget prepared, submitted, and approved; the first play cast and rehearsed; the scenery designed and built; materials ordered and received; the publicity written and disseminated; the tickets racked and sold. And now it is opening night. To the management staff, much of the work of play production may seem to be behind it. The only task which seems to remain is to entertain the audience, which is in the hands of the actors.

Even though there is truth in all this, the business management staff still has many duties and functions to perform in its final task: to see to the comfort and well-being of each member of the audience.

Operating the theatre or auditorium, the lobby area, etc., is a function of the management staff under the direction of the house manager. This area of responsibility includes (1) selecting the house staff, (2) preparing the house, and (3) greeting the audience.

SELECTING THE HOUSE STAFF

It is probably as important to select a capable house staff as it is to select a well-qualified, capable, and impressive cast of actors and actresses. A theatre patron, after all, has only three contacts with theatre personnel: the box office worker who sells him his ticket, the usher who greets and seats him, and the actors who entertain him. Thus it is only reasonable that great care should be exercised in selecting and training each of these groups so that the total impression and the image the audience receives of the theatre, and the experience of attending the theatre, are favorable.

It is the job of the house manager to oversee the ushers, to handle audience problems, and in general to represent the theatre management to the audience. He should therefore be a responsible, reliable student who can handle people effectively, solve problems, and be diplomatic and tactful. Since he must also train and supervise the ushering staff, he should be capable of exercising authority and commanding the respect of other students.

In selecting the ushers and usherettes, the house manager or managing director should select students he knows will make a good impression upon audiences. They should be capable of dealing with such complaints as "I thought these seats were on the aisle; could you give me better seats?" "The lady in front of me has a gigantic hat on, and I can't see"; such questions as "How long is the intermission?" "What's the next play?" "Where are the restrooms?" and such requests as "Could you keep these tickets at the door for our friends, who will be late? One of them will be wearing a blue dress and will be looking for me."

People are strange, and those who attend the theatre are no exception; they expect to be treated as individuals with important and unique problems. It is the job of the house manager and his staff to see that these people are treated as they desire, as important—as well as making them feel at home. This, of course, isn't always easy.

PREPARING THE HOUSE

Working under the direct supervision of the managing director, the house manager is responsible for all performance-night activities—from the front doors of the theatre to the stage curtain, with the exception of the box office. This means that, prior to each performance, the house staff must make certain that the house and lobby areas are clean, well lighted, and in general ready and presentable for the audience. The programs and litter left behind by the preceding audience must be picked up; lights must be checked and burned-out bulbs replaced; heating and ventilating facilities must be checked so that the proper temperature will be maintained during the upcoming performance; washrooms must be spotless.

For most educational theatres, this work is usually the responsibility of the school's maintenance office—an administrative function of the school. Theatre productions are activities of the entire school, as are basketball and football games, lectures, and concerts, and the school should make certain that its facilities are presentable for these activities, to which the public is invited. The managing director should therefore enlist the aid of the proper administrative officer of the school to see that the theatre area is on the schedule of the cleaning staff during performance runs.

Even so, the theatre's house staff should be responsible for checking the theatre area again, just prior to the arrival of an audience. A clean, well-prepared atmosphere should be provided for a theatre audience's optimum enjoyment of the productions. Exit doors that work and are lighted, clean drinking fountains, clean and unobstructed aisles, lighting that is bright enough for patrons with poor vision, and fresh air are important.

The Lobby Display

In addition to the regular housekeeping chores, the staff should improve the theatre atmosphere by setting up lobby displays. These can be art exhibits, arranged in cooperation with the art department; a display of costume designs done by students in a drama class; or a display of set designs by the staff designer or students in a play production class—to name just a few possibilities.

In addition to being decorative—a display helps give the lobby a more pleasant appearance—a display can also be instructive and informative. Most lobby displays feature pictures of the cast (in character or publicity shots) and short sketches about each member's background, academic major, earlier roles, special activities or hobbies, etc. This type of display usually includes information and pictures pertaining to the director, the designer, and various production staff members.

Another possiblity is a display that features pictures of the current production's rehearsals or a model or artist's rendering of the set, or pictures of the play's author and the actors in the original production, or information on the history and background of the play. Such information helps audience members understand and better appreciate the play, and make their stay in the lobby somewhat more pleasurable during intermissions.

An informative display need not involve the current play as such but may exhibit peripheral or "offbeat" aspects of the play production process. For example, a series of drawings can show the progress of a set design from the first meeting between the director and designer to the completed product. Or various types of lighting instruments can be displayed along with diagrams of the purpose and use of each type. Another possibility is a makeup demonstration, showing the various types of makeup used in the theatre, how each is applied, and the special effects that can be achieved.

A creative house manager can think of any number of methods for decorating the lobby so that the audience has a better appreciation of the theatre and the experience of attending the theatre.

GREETING THE AUDIENCE

There is no substitute for treating audience members with respect and courtesy. A theatre exists to serve the public, and the ushers and other theatre personnel should conduct themselves with the idea of polite service uppermost in mind. The following scenario illustrates the proper treatment of theatre patrons by the house staff.

As a couple enters the theatre door the house manager, neat and well dressed, greets them with "Good evening. May I see your tickets, please?" After checking the tickets to make sure that they are for the correct night, he says: "If you will give these to the usherette at aisle B, she will seat you. You may check your coats at the far end of the lobby if you wish."

After checking their coats and perhaps freshening up in a restroom, the couple approaches aisle B and a friendly usherette, who says "Good evening. May I have your tickets, please?" As the patron gives her the tickets she says "Follow me, please," and leads them down the aisle toward their seats, counting out two programs. Stopping just beyond the proper row, the usherette turns to the couple and smiles as she extends her arm toward the row, saying,

"You have seats three and four." As the couple enters the row the usherette gives them their programs and tickets, saying "I hope you enjoy the performance."

How much better this is than having a patron try to find the correct aisle, row, and seat by himself, and in general wander around as though no one cares whether he is there or not. Polite and thoughtful treatment is bound to enhance the overall impression and image which the patron receives of the theatre. If this impression is favorable, attending the theatre is bound to be a pleasurable experience. And that, in short, is what house management is all about.

In addition, the house staff must be prepared for a number of contingencies. Having several hundred people under its roof, a theatre should—indeed, according to law, *must*—reasonably attend to the safety of each member of the audience. However, the educational theatre manager need not concern himself with all the legal aspects of owning a place of public amusement inasmuch as the board of education and various school officials make sure that proper insurance and liability coverage are carried, that building codes and fire regulations are adhered to, etc. But there are other contingencies which the educational theatre should provide for and reasonable precautionary measures it should take to ensure the comfort and safety of patrons.

1. The house manager should have a phone and an outside line available to him at all times.
2. The house manager should have the phone numbers of the police and fire departments and the school's authorized physician and ambulance service in case of emergency.
3. A public phone should be available to theatre patrons, as well as a place to obtain change (the box office).
4. All house personnel should be familiar with the location of normal and emergency exits, washrooms, telephones, and light switches.
5. The house manager should have a list of the physicians who attend each performance and their seat locations. Physicians notify a medical exchange of their off-duty whereabouts, and if the exchange calls the theatre for a particular doctor the house manager can get him quickly if he knows where he is sitting.
6. The house manager must always be available to assist persons

who might become ill. A special room should be prepared nearby for such emergencies.

7. Ushers and usherettes must be instructed by the house manager on the proper procedures in case of a fire or similar emergency. Also, these procedures should be carefully planned in advance. And, of course, it is important that the house staff is always calm and knows what to do, how to do it, and when to do it.

8. Smoking regulations must be strictly enforced, and smoking should not be allowed in the seating area.

9. Exit doors should be lighted and clearly marked.

10. Doors that lead into the lobby from the body of the theatre should be kept open during intermissions to minimize congestion and ease traffic patterns.

11. Patrons should be notified when an intermission is about to end.

12. Patrons should not be encouraged to rush out after the final curtain. Give them time to unwind and talk in the lobby, and visit the actors and the director if they wish.

13. Immediately after all patrons have left the theatre, the house staff should search the house for lost articles.

14. If a coat check is used, it should be adequately staffed, and especially at the end of performances, when business is heaviest.

SUMMARY

As mundane as it might seem, sweeping the house and looking for lost articles is really part of the play production process. It is a part of overall theatre activity, education, and experience. True, house management has none of the built-in glamor of the stage and does not receive plaudits or congratulations in the green room. In this respect it is like most of the commercial management functions and responsibilities discussed in this book—it involves a great deal of detail and unnoticed work, with little or no public recognition. But it is part of the whole play production process, and indispensable.

Theatre consists of a drama performed by actors on a stage before an audience. House management, and indeed all of theatre management, deals with each of those aspects, and in particular the audience. But the management staff also helps ease the burdens of the directors, designers, technical personnel, and actors when their artistic activity comes into contact with the everyday problems of commerce in the production of a play. If these burdens are eased; if the production is better because of management procedures; if the audience is secured and then entertained, management has done its job. Energy, interest, and competence in managing the budget, tickets, publicity, and house is in its own way as important as competence in acting, designing, and directing. And, to a dedicated total-theatre student, it is just as rewarding.

Bibliography

The Nature of Educational Theatre

Anonymous. "The Educational Theatre: Symposium," *Theatre Arts,* XXXIV (April/May, 1950), 50-56.

Anonymous. "School and College Drama," *New York Times Supplement,* April 6, 1950, 260.

Bogard, Travis (ed.). "International Conference of Theatre Education and Development: A Report Sponsored by AETA, June 14-18, 1967," American Educational Theatre Association, August, 1968.

Clark, I. E. "High School Theatre: How to Start a Dramatic Program and Keep It Going," *Players Magazine*, XXVI (February, 1950), 109-110.

Halstead, William P. "Educational Show Business Has No Business: Reply," *Theatre Arts*, XXXVI (July, 1952), 3.

Heffner, Hubert C. "Theatre and Drama in Liberal Education," *Educational Theatre Journal*, XVI (March, 1964), 16-24.

Hobgood, Burnet M. "Theatre in U.S. Higher Education: Emerging Patterns and Problems," *Educational Theatre Journal*, XVI (May, 1964), 142-159.

Hodge, Francis. "A Symposium on the Aims and Objectives in Educational Theatre," *Educational Theatre Journal*, VI (May, 1954), 106-119.

Lowry, W. McNeil. "The University and the Creative Arts," *Educational Theatre Journal*, XIV (May, 1962), 99-112.

Morrison, Jack. "College Play Production Organization," *Quarterly Journal of Speech*, XXXV (April, 1949), 178-181.

———. "Educational Theatre, A Working Myth," *Educational Theatre Journal*, IX (December, 1957), 273-279.

Motter, Charlotte Kay. "A Method of Integrating the High School Drama Program," *Educational Theatre Journal*, XIX (May, 1960), 94-97.

Seymour, Victor. "Theatre Keeps PACE in Secondary Education," *Educational Theatre Journal*, XX (October, 1968), 389-397.

Taylor, Harold. "Education by Theatre," *Educational Theatre Journal*, XV (December, 1963), 299-310.

Theatre Management: Philosophy and Practices

Beckhard, Richard, and Effrat, John. *Blueprint for Summer Theatre*. New York: John Richard Press, 1948.

Bernheim, Alfred L. *The Business of the Theatre*. New York: Actors Equity Association, 1932.

Dodrill, Charles W. "Theatre Management Selected Bibliography," A Report of the Theatre Administration Project of the American Educational Theatre Association, 1966.

Hinsdell, Oliver. *Making Little Theatre Pay*. New York: Samuel French, Inc., 1925.

Plummer, Gail. *The Business of Show Business*. New York: Harper and Row, 1961.

Richey, Robert L. "Theatre Management Practices," *Educational Theatre Journal*, VIII (December, 1956), 311-315.

Smith, Milton. *Play Production for Little Theatre, School and Colleges*. New York: Appleton-Century, Inc., 1948.

Sparks, Melba Day. "High School Theatre Management," *Dramatics Magazine*, January, 1960, 32-33.

Sponseler, Whitney. *A Manual for High School and College Theatrical Administration*. Hollywood: American Legitimate Theatre Service, 1956.

Stanton, Sanford E. *Theatre Management*. New York: Appleton-Century, Inc., 1929.

Sweeting, Elizabeth. *Theatre Administration*. London: Pitman and Sons, Ltd., 1969.

Tompkins, Dorothy Lee. *Handbook for Theatrical Apprentices*. New York: Samuel French, Inc., 1962.

Young, John. *The Community Theatre*. New York: Harper and Row, 1957.

Theatre Organization

Dean, Alexander. *Little Theatre Organization and Management*. New York: Appleton and Company, 1926.

Johnson, Albert. "Organization and Management of An Institutional Theatre," *Quarterly Journal of Speech*, April, 1941, 198-206.

Williams, Dallas. "The Need for Production Organization," *Educational Theatre Journal*, II (May, 1950), 159-162.

Box Office

Anonymous. "Pre-Sales Plan for Selling Blocks of Tickets," American National Theatre and Academy, 1952.

Nelms, Henning. *Building an Amateur Audience*. New York: Samuel French, Inc., 1936.

Pollock, Channing. *The Footlights Fore and Aft*. Boston: R.G. Badger, 1911.

Wiley, Jon. "A System of Box-Office Operation," American National Theatre and Academy.

Advertising and Publicity

Baus, Herbert. *Publicity in Action*. New York: Harper and Brothers, 1954.

Friedlander, Harold. "Billboards and Posters for the Stage," *Theatre Crafts*, IV (March-April, 1970), 22.

Croy, Peter. *Graphic Design and Reproduction Techniques*. New York: Hastings House, Publishers, 1968.

Griffin, A. "Promotion Pays Off," *Theatre Arts*, XXXIX (October, 1955).

Kleppner, Otto. *Advertising Procedure*. Englewood Cliffs, N. J.: Prentice-Hall, Inc., 1966.

Kildahl, Erling E. "Educational Theatre Publicity," *Educational Theatre Journal*, IX (December, 1957), 306-310.

Kobre, Sidney. *Dynamic Force of Public Relations Today*. Dubuque: William C. Brown, Company, 1964.

Martin, David Stone. "Putting a Show on a Poster," *Theatre Crafts*, II (March-April, 1968), 6-10.

Messenger, Carl A. "How to Build an Audience," American National Theatre and Academy, 1955.

Morison, Bradley G., and Fliehr, Kay. *In Search of an Audience: How An Audience Was Found for the Tyrone Guthrie Theatre*. New York: Pitman Publishing Company, 1968.

Morison, Bradley G. "Reaching the Audience," *Theatre Today*, IV (Winter, 1971), 16-18.

Samrock, Carl. "New York Press Agent On and Off Broadway," *Theatre Crafts*, III (March-April, 1969), 36-42.

Simon, Bernard. "Don't Forget Publicity," *Theatre Arts*, XXXIII (March, 1949).

________. "It Pays to Publicize," *Theatre Arts*, XXXVIII (August, 1954).

________. *Simon's Directory of Theatrical Materials, Services and Information*. New York: Package Publicity Service, 1970.

Appendix

Play Publishers and Addresses

American Playwrights Theatre
154 N. Oval Drive
Columbus, Ohio 43210

Anchorage Press
Cloverlot, Kentucky 40223

Baker's Plays
100 Summer
Boston, Mass. 02110

Century Library, Inc.
225 W. 44th Street
New York, N. Y. 10036

Coach House Press
53 West Jackson Blvd.
Chicago, Illinois 60604

Dramatic Publishing Company
86 East Randolph
Chicago, Illinois 60601

Dramatists Play Service
440 Park Avenue South
New York, N. Y. 10016

Metromedia-on-Stage
1700 Broadway
New York, N. Y. 10036

Music Theatre International
119 W. 57th Street
New York, N. Y. 10019

Rogers & Hammerstein Repertory
120 East 56th Street
New York, N. Y. 10022

Tams-Witmark Music Library
757 Third Avenue
New York, N. Y. 10017

Ticket Printing Firms and Addresses

Administrative Ticket Service
131 Mineola Blvd.
Mineola, N. Y. 11501

American Ticket Company
3159 W. 36th Street
Chicago, Illinois 60632

Globe Ticket Company
112 North 12th Street
Philadelphia, Pa. 19107

International Ticket Company
267 Fifth Avenue
New York, N. Y. 10016

National Ticket Company
1564 Broadway
New York, N. Y. 10036

Ticket Reservations Systems
300 North State Street
Chicago, Illinois 60610

Weldon, Williams and Lick, Inc.
P.O. Box 168
Fort Smith, Arkansas 72901